"Moreover the Lord saith,
Because the daughters of
Zion are haughty, and
walk with stretched forth
necks and wanton eyes,
walking and mincing as
they go, and making a
tinkling with their feet:
Therefore the Lord will
smite with a scab the
crown of the head of the
daughters of Zion, and the
Lord will discover their
secret parts."
                Isaiah 3:16–17

Woe to the Women– The Bible Tells Me So

The Bible, Female Sexuality & the Law

A revised edition by Annie Laurie Gaylor
Illustrations by Alma Cuebas

Published by
Freedom From Religion Foundation
www.ffrf.org
P.O. Box 750
Madison, WI 53701

ISBN: 1-877733-12-1

In memory of

RUTH HURMENCE GREEN
(January 12, 1915 – July 7, 1981)

Ruth Green's often expressed "dearest
wish" was to "alert women" about sexism in
religion "before they get to be 66, like me."
A late-blooming feminist and writer, Ruth
Green authored *The Born Again Skeptic's
Guide to the Bible*, published in 1979, which
was inspirational in the conception and
writing of this book.

Dedicated to
my daughter

SABRINA DELATA GAYLOR

Table of Contents

A NEW INTRODUCTION
Genesis of
Woe to the Women

THE GENESIS (so to speak) for this little book about the treatment of women in the bible was an undergraduate class I took at the University of Wisconsin-Madison in the late 1970s. The interdisciplinary women's studies class, taught by a female law professor, was called "Female Sexuality and the Law." We studied the law, current and historical, pertaining to all aspects of women's rights and status. Religion's sway on those laws was scarcely mentioned.

For the required term paper, I decided to explore the ambitious topic of biblical law as it pertains to women. My trouble in finding books detailing precisely what the bible says about women inspired me to read the bible for myself, and, eventually, to write the kind of handy guide I wished had been available to me. Wherever I went for about a month that particular spring, my King James Bible and a large notebook went with me. I read the bible in snatches, between classes, a part-time job and student reporting. My notebook was soon full, just as I was full of amazement — not only at the scurrilous treatment of women in the bible, but that its primitive notions and bloodthirsty morality could continue to command such respect. As a third-generation freethinker, I had been exposed to a bit of bible criticism, but reading the bible made a true unbeliever out of me. Like Ruth Green, a friend whose book, *The Born Again Skeptic's Guide to the Bible*, was published by the Freedom From Religion Foundation in 1979, I felt that I needed to wash my hands in Grandma's Lye Soap every time I opened that vaunted volume.

The most obvious source for information on biblical law

regarding women is the Mosaic code, or Pentateuch (the first five books of the bible). Most religionists are familiar only with the "Ten Commandments," but there are more than 600 such commandments supposedly dictated by Jehovah to Moses, many self-contradictory. As the sinfulness of sex is one of the Mosaic preoccupations, and women are typecast as sin-citing Eves, Delilahs and Jezebels, one need not be a prophet to predict how poorly women fare in the biblical scheme of justice. Using our class topics as a framework, I organized biblical laws and lore into a term paper on the bible's mandates on rape, marriage, and reproductive rights, analyzing its residual hold on U.S. law. (I never have forgiven that professor for giving my 60-page term paper a "B+.")

After graduating from college in 1980, I founded and published a regional monthly feminist newspaper, *The Feminist Connection*, for the next four years. On the theory that feminists should "know thine enemy," I capitalized on my homework by turning my notes and term paper into a regular editorial column about the bible and women, called "The Bible Tells Me So." I kept the tone light-hearted as each month I tackled a different topic, such as the bible's dictates on women's hygiene, motherhood or sexual assault. The short columns added up. The following year, my mother, Anne Gaylor, as president of the Freedom From Religion Foundation, asked me to weave them into book form. That summer, while covering the phones one week when Foundation staff was out of town, I put the book together.

The original title of my term paper: "Woman: What Have I to Do with Thee?" came from the contemptuous remark Jesus makes to his mother. Although very partial to that revealing title, I decided the alliterative "Woe to the Women," from another bible verse, was a more accurate summation. *Woe to the Women: The Bible Tells Me So* was born, its subtitle taken straight from my term paper: "The Bible, Female Sexuality & the Law." It was continuously in print from 1981 until 2002.

The ripple effect has been fun. *Woe to the Women* has been the focus of radio and TV talk shows, as well as newspaper interviews and speech invitations. One memorable outing was a "People Are Talking" TV appearance for myself and my mother in Baltimore in 1983. The noon talk show was co-hosted by a young and openly feminist Oprah Winfrey. During the lively show, viewers and audience members were asked to vote about whether they thought the bible was sexist. As I recall, "our side" got close to 40 percent of the vote — not bad! One of Oprah's producers later told us Oprah used our show as part of her audition tape for a new solo-hosting job with "A.M. Chicago," which eventually became "The Oprah Winfrey Show."

I even met my husband through *Woe to the Women*. After discovering my book through a freethought mail-order service on the West Coast, Dan Barker, a newly "deconverted" minister from California, wrote me in March 1984. Dan still likes to tease me by saying that he sent me a "fan letter," but that I never wrote him back. In his brief, matter-of-fact letter, Dan mentioned, intriguingly, that he had just left religion after years of immersion in a religious career, and asked for more information about joining the Freedom From Religion Foundation. With the best of intentions, I held onto the letter at a particularly busy time of my life, fully intending to make a personal response. Finally, guiltily, after a month or so, I passed Dan's inquiry on to the Foundation office. With her unerring eye for an interesting story, my mother, in replying, asked Dan to write about leaving fundamentalism. His article, "I Just Lost Faith in Faith," which was published in the Foundation's newspaper, *Freethought Today*, later grew into a book, *Losing Faith in Faith: From Preacher to Atheist*, that has become the Foundation's bestseller.

The Oprah Winfrey show happened to invite my mother and me back on as guests that fall in Chicago. They also were interested in inviting a Foundation member who had formerly been very religious to appear with us. My mother thought Dan's dramatic story would suit their purposes. The show agreed. Dan and I consequently met each other for the first time over breakfast just before taping the Oprah Winfrey show in Chicago. Dan did a great job, and the rest, as they say, is history. We were married in May 1987. Before our daughter's birth, Dan and I made a pact not to saddle our child with a biblically-derived name. Our daughter, Sabrina Delata Gaylor, was born in 1989.

Her middle name is Delaware Indian for "thought," which acknowledges Dan's Native American heritage.

What's new in this revision?

This revision largely has retained the original text; asterisks update a few dated references. In addition, there is an index and several new chapters:

• "What Does the Bible Say About Abortion?" (replacing the original chapter on abortion)

• "The Religious War Against Women"

• "Rethinking the Sermon on the Mount"

• A "guest sermon" by Dan debunking that perennial claim that the bible isn't sexist in the original Greek.

• "The Continuing Threat," bringing up to date what has changed (and not changed) for women and religion since *Woe to the Women* was first published in 1981.

• Relevant bible passages about women in full at the end of the book. (After all, many of us feminists don't like to be seen in public with a bible.)

Re-discovering feminist bible criticism

Twenty-three years ago, I had turned for research and rhetoric to Elizabeth Cady Stanton's classic two-volume work, *The Woman's Bible*, published in 1895 and 1898. No modern feminist matches Stanton's eloquence and discernment, but it seemed to me an update and practical reference on women and the bible was in order. In homage to Stanton's work, which got her officially repudiated by the very woman's movement she had started, I began each chapter of *Woe* with one of her pithy quotes.

Only many years later, in researching my anthology of women freethinkers, *Women Without Superstition: No Gods — No Masters*, published in 1997, did I become aware that Elizabeth Cady Stanton was not the first or only woman to write a book repudiating the bible. Several other women had been "inspired" to take on that most orthodox of books.

The Godly Women of the Bible by an Ungodly Woman of

the Nineteenth Century is the smile-inducing title chosen by Ella E. Gibson, whose book was published circa 1878. *Godly Women* appears to be the first feminist, freethinking analysis of the bible. Although Gibson's book was continuously in print for several decades through the Truth Seeker Company, only one college library at the time I was doing my research even listed a circulating volume. Gibson wrote of the bible that "any family which permits such a volume to lie on their parlor-table ought to be ostracized from all respectable society."

The beautifully written *Men, Women and Gods*, by Helen H. Gardener, was published in 1885. A series of well-received lectures given in 1884 was turned into a book of the same name published by The Truth Seeker, with a foreword by Gardener's friend, the "great agnostic" Robert G. Ingersoll. Gardener, who became a close friend of Stanton, later serving on Stanton's *Woman's Bible* committee, quipped that while most feminists found Stanton's *Woman's Bible* too radical, Gardener found it not radical enough. Part I of Gardener's book contains a succinct summary of the treatment of women in the Old and New Testaments (limited to portions that would not "soil my lips nor your ears"). Gardener urged: "Of all human beings a woman should spurn the Bible first."

Matilda Joslyn Gage's *Woman, Church and State* (1893) opened the eyes of Gage's contemporaries to woman-hating abuses stemming from religious doctrines such as celibacy, exposing the barbarism of the Christian witch-hunts. An activist, Gage founded the Woman's National Liberal Union in 1890 to fight the religious right of her era from a freethinking, feminist perspective. The resolutions could have been written today, warning of encroachments by theocrats "composed of both Catholics and Protestants" aiming to unite church and state. Gage cautioned: "in order to help preserve the very life of the Republic, it is imperative that women should unite upon a platform of opposition to the teaching and aim of that ever most unscrupulous enemy of freedom — the Church."

Social reformer Charlotte Perkins Gilman trenchantly rejected the religious right "family values" of her day in *His Religion and Hers: The Faith of Our Fathers and the Work of Our*

Mothers (1923). Gilman pointed out that the major "death-based" religions had all repeated the mistake of making a servant of "the mother of the race."

The first wave of pioneering American feminists was well-acquainted with the bible and its repressive teachings toward women. Elizabeth Cady Stanton, who galvanized the women's movement by calling for woman suffrage, later recalled "how the bible was hurled at us from every side." Among the feminist elite, it was taken as a given that support of women's rights meant opposition to the tyranny of religious views about women. Feminists often spoke of "salvation" of the world, not through worship of a male deity, but through the emancipation of women. Susan B. Anthony wrote: "I am a full and firm believer in the revelation that it is through *woman the race is to be redeemed.*" Many women freethinkers sought to "save" woman — from religion. Margaret Sanger, whose stirring motto was "No Gods — No Masters," wrote in her autobiography that she "wanted each woman to be a rebellious Vashti, not an Esther."

Yet it is still the Esthers, the Mother Teresas of the world, who are socially sanctioned, while the modern-day, freedom-fighting Vashtis, such as Bangladesh's Taslima Nasrin, endure death fatwas. My thrill in (re)discovering the freethought heritage of the feminist movement was tinged by frustration that I and many other women in succeeding generations have had to re-invent the wheel. At least we are in very good company.

It seems like "fate" that my husband, Dan, who first contacted me after reading *Woe to the Women*, helped revise this edition. Dan designed the template (based on the original design by talented graphic artist Jane Rundell of Mazomanie, Wis.), and also proofed this edition — including the chivalrous task of checking all bible citations and texts. Dan also performed the Herculean chore of indexing this edition. He found himself growing increasingly indignant, as I had, when he read and reread the bible's insults toward women. Dan quipped that he was relieved to find nothing demeaning toward women in the Book of Daniel. *Freethought Today* assistant editor Lynn Lau patiently scanned the original text, laid out the book, made countless picayune changes, and had the onerous task of cutting and pasting the new section of bible verses appearing at the conclusion of this book.

I especially thank my mother Anne Gaylor for assigning me the original task of writing *Woe to the Women*, and encouraging (well, gently prodding) me to revise it. Her feminist determination has made the world a kinder place for many women. She has been persevering in her quest for more than a quarter century to restore the constitutional principle of the separation of church and state to an honored position in our society. She is the best role model ever of an unbiblical heroine.

Annie Laurie Gaylor, editor
Freethought Today
August 2004

FOREWORD

Invariably any freethought analysis of the bible is met with the same indignant cry: "But you're taking these passages out of context!"

"Context" indeed! The bible is a literary mishmash with a wavering plotline, contradictions galore, few stories that are cohesive enough to have a beginning and an end, and a string of curses and dire threats woven together in no particular order. It is this confusing collection that some people claim was written by the Lord's finger and that others tell us may not be true but is surely so good, enriching and moral that we must hear it preached at all secular gatherings.

Religionists rarely, if ever, object to bible verses being "taken out of context" by clergypersons. Only when someone begins to take too close a look at bible law and lore, to judge it like any other book, to dare to criticize its teachings does "context" become a consideration.

This book is written as a guide for the reader who is too busy (or too non-masochistic) to study the bible. It is being published with the expectation of inspiring women and men to read and judge the bible for themselves. To this end a listing of bible citations about women has been compiled so that readers may check the "context" for themselves. This listing can be found at the back of the book.

All passages cited and quoted are from the King James Version of the bible.

Annie Laurie Gaylor
Madison, Wisconsin
July 1981

PROLOGUE

*The Bible and the Church have been the
greatest stumbling blocks in the way of
women's emancipation.*
                    —Elizabeth Cady Stanton

The Bible

In the book of John, when Mary points out to her son Jesus that guests at a wedding have no wine to drink, Jesus acknowledges her statement with this response: "Woman, what have I to do with thee?" *John 2:4* What indeed?

This haughty, scornful question attributed to the bible character whom Christians today term their savior perfectly illustrates the contempt the Judeo-Christian tradition shows for women. A reading of the bible reveals that women in it play one of two major roles: they are either superfluous, or diabolical. There lurks no remnant of the worship of woman for her biological usefulness that existed in earlier ages and other cultures.

Although woman's childbearing role is acknowledged, it is cursed: "I will greatly multiply thy sorrow and thy conception; in sorrow thou shalt bring forth children; and thy desire shall be to thy husband, and he shall rule over thee," is the Lord's famous edict appearing by Chapter 3 of Genesis. The New Testament promotes an equally anti-female indifference through the vehicle of Jesus. He pretends not to recognize his worried mother, asking her insolently: "Who is my mother?" *Mark 3:33* As the adult messiah, he refuses to bless his mother. When a woman in a crowd cries out to bless "the womb that bare thee, and the paps which thou hast sucked," he says, "Yea, rather, blessed are they that hear the word of God, and keep it." *Luke: 27–28*

And so we come to the crux of the bible — "the word."

What is this word, and what does it mean for women?

This book is devoted to the biblical words on women. Although only about ten percent of the bible even mentions women, as Elizabeth Cady Stanton documents in her book *The Woman's Bible*, nevertheless it manages to deal with every possible feminine issue. No details about women were apparently too trite or private to escape biblical attention, not even bowel movements or flat chests (see Song of Solomon for both). Women's periods, childbirth confinement, hair styles, housewifely duties, and neighborly ways are all noted in the bible — usually with scorn, over-familiarity, frequently with loathing and fear.

Why is this documentation of the sexism of the bible being made? Nearly 40 percent of the American public, when polled in the late 1970s by Gallup, said they believe the bible is literally true, word for word.* Yet few people actually read the bible, making the public vulnerable to the authority of religious demagogues, who pick and choose among bible passages to promote their causes. And others continue to give obeisance and respect for religious teachings, without bothering themselves to read those teachings. Uppermost among religious goals is the desire to return women to the status of *kinder, kirche, kuche*. The bible and the zeal of fundamentalists are the ideal weapons for fighting women's emancipation, not only because preachers claim exclusive communion with a wrathful deity, but because the bible is infested with misogyny.

Female Sexuality

The bible wastes no time in establishing woman's inferior status, her uncleanliness, her transgressions and her God-ordained master/servant relationship to man (all by Genesis 3). Women in the bible, when they are mentioned, exist as appendages. After all, according to the favored version of creation, woman is merely Adam's spare rib. Biblical women are possessions first and foremost. Fathers own them, sell them into

---

* This finding has remained more or less consistent for the past two decades.

bondage, even sacrifice them. The bible sanctions rape under most circumstances. Women are commanded to be inferior and subservient to their husbands. Wives have a precarious status, subject to Mosaic-law sanctioned bedchecks as brides and later, sanctioned jealousy fits and no-notice divorce. Virgins are "booty," the spoils of war. Many biblical women are characterized as "harlots" or "whores" whose transgressions and powers of allurement are described as no less than satanic. When nations rebel or displease the biblical Lord, the nations are referred to as lewd women, and graphic descriptions of their punishment, frequently sadistic and sexual, are ordered.

Scorn for women's bodies — many times turning to outright loathing — is present in full force in bible lore and teachings. Women's sexuality, reproductive capacity and biological difference from the men who wrote the bible were used against women to justify their poor status and lack of rights. An example of the way bible law employs squeamishness against women's bodies to justify discrimination is illustrated by the divorce rule. This allows a husband to hand a wife a bill of divorcement and boot her out of the house if some "uncleanness in her" is discerned. *Deuteronomy 24:1* Naturally, Old Testament scripture does not accord fastidious wives the same right.

Revilement of female sexuality reaches a particularly intemperate pitch in Proverbs, many of the prophesies and in the epistles of Paul.

The Book of Ruth and the vastly overrated Song of Solomon (all four pages of it) are commonly cited as evidence of the bible's benevolent view of women. Upon closer examination the role models offered the religious woman prove stereotyped, conventional and inadequate. The few bible heroines to be found in it are generally glorified only for their obedience and battle spirit.

An understanding of the bible's attitude toward women will prove invaluable in comprehending why religionists are still in the forefront of opposition to the Equal Rights Amendment, abortion, birth control and programs to aid women. In reading the bible we can begin to understand where the roots of our patriarchal heritage lie. The Mosaic law pertaining to women and gospel teachings about woman's place are truly the bedrock upon which so many of the Western World's present laws rest.

The Law

Our culture is steeped in Judeo-Christian heritage. Although most people never read the entire bible, its impact is pervasive. Biblical characters have become entrenched in our literature mythology: every school child knows about Noah and his ark. In slightly different versions cliché expressions such as "Man does not live by bread alone" and "Eat, drink and be merry" have their origins in the bible. We all understand that a "Jezebel" is a woman who is dishonorable and a temptress, even if we are not really familiar with the particulars of the biblical Jezebel. And, of course, the story of Adam and Eve is most famous of all, perhaps rivaled only by Luke's description of Jesus' nativity.

But the impact of the bible is not confined to a non-legal sphere. When the Western world was a Catholic church-state, the bible was the reputed holy foundation upon which the laws of society were founded, built and interpreted. The bible continued its role as the "living word of God" throughout the holy wars and European Reformation.

The first settlers in the United States brought this book, and their respective religions based upon it, to form religiously-distinguished colonies, where persecutions and even witch-hunting were continued.

In 1787, when the U.S. Constitution was adopted, the Age of Reason, as it is now known, had begun and freethought was in flower. The "founding fathers" were largely deists. The United States became the first nation to ratify and live under a constitution declaring separation of state from church.

Nevertheless, religious revivals surged again, and today the United States is reputed to be one of the most pious (Judeo-Christian) nations in the world.

Religious encroachments on secular life are pervasive, including entanglements as tangible as the posting of the Mosaic law — the Ten Commandments — in public schoolrooms. Historically, "divine law" has been invoked by many of those with an interest in stemming the tide of women's emancipation. Today American women fight for sexual equality, for constitutionally guaranteed equality under the law, for control of their own sexuality: the right to decide for themselves whether to be a mother, for full marital partnership, against rape and images that degrade women's bodies. This fight goes on against a backdrop of the bible, whose ancient, male teachings, for many, still make time stand still. The 1976 Gallup poll claiming that 38 percent of the U.S. public believes the bible is "literally true" revealed that another 45 percent believe it is, if not literally true, the "inspired word of God."

An examination of the Mosaic law and the anecdotal treatment of women in the Old and New Testaments reveals the repressive impact the biblical view of female sexuality continues to hold on civil law through this day.

1 CREATION
Eve was framed

*The bible teaches that woman brought sin and
death into the world, that she precipitated the
fall of the race, that she was arraigned before
the judgment seat of Heaven, tried, condemned
and sentenced. Marriage for her was to be a
condition of bondage, maternity a period of
suffering and anguish, and in silence and
subjection, she was to play the role of a
dependent on man's bounty for all her
material wants, and for all the information
she might desire . . . Here is the Bible position
of woman briefly summed up.*
    —*Elizabeth Cady Stanton*

IN THE BEGINNING . . .

Many Jews and Christians (and their apologists) ironically
claim that each other's religion has oppressed women, while
their own has uplifted women. But Jews and Christians have a
common denominator. She is Eve, whose "transgression" has
been used to keep even her modern daughter in the proper biblical position: prone, with the foot of one of Adam's descendants
resting on her neck.

Through her innocence, the mythical Eve of Genesis, like
the Greek Pandora, causes the downfall of humankind. Because
she handed Adam the "apple," which he willingly accepted, she
becomes the seductress. The knowledge this first couple learns

is sexual in nature, and their ultimate punishment is a physical death. Hence Eve (woman) is equated with sex, which is equated with death. Woman = Sex = Death. This simple equation began with Eve, and culminated in the death of tens of thousands, if not millions, of women who were burnt as witches because the bible says "Thou shalt not suffer a witch to live." *Exodus 22:18*

Because of Eve's role in supposedly destroying innocence, the Old Testament heaps scorn upon the heads of women, clearly obsessed with the so-called uncleanliness of women, and with "harlots" and "whores."

The New Testament reaffirms Eve's scapegoat status. Because Eve showed initiative and an interest in acquiring knowledge (with its subsequent result), church officials used the story to deny women education, the right to teach, free speech and, in general, opportunity.

Contradictory versions of creation

Mainline Judeo-Christian theists have chosen to ignore the original version of creation, which sets up an egalitarian relationship in the very first chapter of Genesis:

"So God created man in his own image, in the image of God created he him; male and female created he them."

Both man and woman are then blessed and told they have dominion together over the earth.

The more famous version of creation, in Chapter 2 of Genesis, better flattered the ego of the male theist, describing the creation of Eve as a mere afterthought, a "help meet" fashioned out of man's spare rib.

The episode for which women have been blamed throughout the ages follows this second version. Interestingly, only Adam was directly warned by the Lord not to eat of the tree of knowledge of good and evil. Eve learns of his caveat only by hearsay for she was merely Adam's extra rib at the time the injunction was decreed. Nevertheless, this story has become the basis of the Evil Eve legend, used to portray women as innately disobedient, sensual-minded seductresses whose charms literally lead to the downfall of the male of the species.

The authors of Genesis believed that motherhood and childbirth must be a sorrow to women, and that women must be ruled over by men. *Genesis 3:16*

By the end. . . .

The myth of Adam and Eve is thrown back into the faces of women countless times by New Testament writers. Timothy epitomizes the way in which the story was exploited in order to oppress and blame women: "Let the woman learn in silence with all subjection. But I suffer not a woman to teach, nor to usurp authority over the man, but to be in silence. For Adam was first formed, then Eve. And Adam was not deceived, but the woman being deceived was in the transgression." *1 Timothy 2:11–14*

2 WOMEN ARE PROPERTY

So I bought her for me . . .

*Whatever the Bible may be made to do in
Hebrew or Greek, in plain English it does not
exalt and dignify women.*
                    —*Elizabeth Cady Stanton*

WOMAN'S FIGHT FOR emancipation has involved the struggle to be recognized as a legally independent, autonomous human being. At the root of the enslaved woman's legal problems is this once-common belief: A woman cannot own property because she is herself property owned by a man. Women's property rights in the United States are not fully won, awaiting the adoption of such reforms as the Equal Rights Amendment guaranteeing equality under the law, and marital property reform, with its assumption that marriage is an economic partnership between equals.

The bible instructs that men own women through a variety of teachings.

Possessions

Women in the bible are without doubt the possessions of men. In the tenth commandment of the Mosaic code (Deuteronomy 5 version) man is given a list of things he should not covet. In the same breath as "his neighbor's ass" is "his neighbor's wife." (In an Exodus version of the Ten Commandments, the wife is listed second to "thy neighbor's house," presumably indicating that inanimate objects take priority over women. *Exodus*

20:17) Even male animals own their female peers; the Noah's ark story refers to animals as "male and his female." *Genesis 7:2*

Leviticus spells out sin offerings discriminating between the sexes of the sacrificial kid. If a ruler sins, he shall offer up a male kid. *Leviticus 4:22–23* If a commoner sins, he shall offer up a female goat. *Leviticus 4:27–28* Meat offerings were accessible to the *male* children of Aaron to eat. *Leviticus 6:14–18* Biblical language even diminishes the role of the mother. Men "beget," women rarely "bear."

Women can be bought

"So I bought her to me for fifteen pieces of silver, and for an homer of barley, and an half homer of barley." *Hosea 3:2* This is one of innumerable instances in which men in the bible buy wives. The story of Ruth, allegedly a romance, ends when Boaz buys her. *Ruth 4:10* Perhaps the most shocking instance is when David buys Michal, daughter of King Saul, with the foreskins of 200 Philistines. *1 Samuel 18:27*

Since women can be bought, they naturally can be sold. Disposition depends upon their male owners, which is not the case for male indentured servants. While God tells Moses that a Hebrew male servant shall serve six years, on the seventh he is to go free. *Exodus 21:2* But if he is married, and his wife was provided by the master, she and the children must remain enslaved. (If he protests this inhumane arrangement and wishes to stay with his wife, the Lord orders the master to "bore his ear through with an awl," to a doorpost, to keep him in bondage forever.) *Exodus 21:4–6*

The bible tells us, "if a man sell his daughter to be a maidservant, she shall not go out as the menservants do." *Exodus 21:7* The master has three options, one of which he must choose by a time limit which he himself apparently specifies. He may resell her, but not to a strange land (meaning non-Israelite land), he may marry her himself, or his son may marry her. If he decides against all three arrangements, she can go free. *Exodus 21:8–11* Theoretically, a bondwoman could be sold and resold, remaining in bondage all of her life. Unisex rules for the treatment of Hebrew bondpersons are apparently provided in contradictory rules in Deuteronomy 15:12–15, but because of the bible's use of masculine pronouns it is difficult to be sure these rules were really meant to encompass women.

Bondwomen were at the mercy of their masters, and could be assigned sexual duties. Because women were male property, however, the bible takes a harder line when a master "lieth carnally" with a bondmaid betrothed to another man. Should a master tamper with her, "she shall be scourged" — but not put to death "because she was not free." The male sinner is merely ordered to present a ram for a trespass offering and is forgiven. *Leviticus 19:20–22*

Women are sacrificed

We've all read about the way in which the Lord "tests" Abraham's faith by ordering him to sacrifice his beloved son Isaac, only to have an angel intervene at the last moment. But who has heard the story of Jephthah and his nameless daughter, whom he really does sacrifice?

A good warrior, Jephthah strikes a deal with the Lord, vowing that if the Lord will allow him to win a battle, whatsoever comes out of his doors to greet him upon his return will be offered up as a burnt offering to the Lord. His only child, a daughter, greets him. Jephthah is remorseful, he even tears his clothes, but the sacrifice, like the show, must go on. Jephthah's daughter is allowed a two-month retreat on the mountains to "bewail my virginity" before the deed is done. *Judges 11:30-40* Although ministers conveniently overlook this passage today, Elizabeth Cady Stanton's remarks in *The Woman's Bible* indicate that the 19th-century religionists knew about — and rationalized — this passage: "We often hear people laud the beautiful submission and the self-sacrifice of this nameless maiden. To me it is pitiful and painful."

Ezekiel describes a typical rampage by the Lord: "And her daughters which are in the field shall be slain by the sword; and they shall know that I am the LORD." *Ezekiel 26:6–8* Even though "daughters of the field" is used metaphorically to describe outlying settlements, the feminine usage is threatening and demeaning to women.

Less fatal sacrifices of daughters were made, as when Caleb offers anyone who slays an enemy his own daughter (presumably to wed). *Judges 1:12–13*

Vowless women

The powerlessness of women is well-illustrated by the rule of the vows. For men, it is uncomplicated. If a man makes a vow to the Lord he must keep it.

But the rules for women's vows teach us that a woman's very existence has to be validated by a man, either her father or her husband. The rules laid down in the Mosaic code are as complicated as a Chinese puzzle for women. The gist of the rules is that her vows shall stand if her husband or father allows them to, but will not if either one "disallows" them. "Every vow, and every binding oath to afflict the soul, her husband may establish it, or her husband may make it void."

If this male family authority disallows the vow, "the Lord shall forgive her," making this set of commandments a kind of protection for the powerlessness of women. Should a husband not invalidate her vow immediately, then it is he who must "bear her iniquity" in breaking the vow. *Numbers 30:1–16*

Yet this is a funny sort of protection when it hinges on woman's inferior spiritual status. When Anne Hutchinson in the 17th century held prayer meetings in her home advising individuals to make a covenant with their god irrespective of gender, she not only broke the gospel edict against women teaching, but clearly ignored this Mosaic law on vows — transgressions for which she was vilified.

Women ain't worth much

Women are worth less than men, literally . . .

In Leviticus 27, the Lord very conveniently lists "estimations" of people's worth, so Israelites will know how much they owe a priest each year. The following chart reveals that women are generally worth half as much as men. (Interestingly, U.S.

labor statistics reveal that women today are indeed worth about half as much as men, typically earning between 56–59 percent as much.)*

Age	Male Worth	Female Worth
1 month to 5 years	5 shekels of silver	3 shekels of silver
5 to 20 years old	20 shekels	10 shekels
20 to 60 years old	50 shekels	30 shekels
60 years & up	15 shekels	10 shekels

In the first chapter of Numbers, there is a poll of the people — the male people that is (ultimately for war use). Clearly, biblical women were not citizens.

Inheritance

Amazingly, biblical women were able to effect a reform of their inheritance laws, when the daughters of Zelophehad pleaded the cause for female inheritance to Moses himself, in the book of Numbers, pointing out that when their father died sonless, his wealth went to his brethren.

The Lord declares, "The daughters of Zelophehad speak right: thou shalt surely give them a possession of an inheritance among their father's brethren." Accordingly, if a man dies and leaves no son, his inheritance goes to his daughter. If there is no daughter, it goes to his brothers, if no brothers then to his kinsman next to them. Note: daughters apparently get nothing if there is a son; wives aren't mentioned at all, and sisters and aunts are also neglected. *Numbers 27:1–11*

This unexpected egalitarianism is explained further on in Numbers. The "daughters of Zelophehad" are commanded to marry "only to the family of the tribe of their father," so the inheritance stays in the family. The daughters of Zelophehad were placeholders, not rightful heirs. The bible relates they docilely did as they were told, so that "the children of Israel may enjoy every man the inheritance of his fathers." *Numbers 36*

---

* A Congressional study released in November 2003 found that women still earn only 79.7 cents for every dollar paid to men.

Smiting servants

A passage in Exodus makes clear how Southern slave-owners were able to buttress the practice of slavery by quoting the bible. The Mosaic code states that if a man "smites" a servant, male or female, and they die, the master must "surely be punished." In a volume where blood is splashed on nearly every page as some fatal punishment is spelled out or exacted, it seems surprising that in this case, the bible does not delineate how the master shall "surely be punished" for killing his slaves.

However, it does make a further concession: If the servant lives for a day or two, then dies, the master shall not be punished at all, for the servant "is his money." In other words, housing an unprofitable invalid servant is punishment enough to the owner. *Exodus 21:20–22* This passage is highlighted to illustrate the only types of equality allowed to women in the bible. Although men and women are not often treated equally, cases of punishment or violence are the exceptions. As Elizabeth Cady Stanton put it, after reading a particularly vindictive threat in Leviticus 26:29 ("And ye shall eat the flesh of your sons, and the flesh of your daughters shall ye eat"), "The 29th verse at last gives us one touch of absolute equality, the right to be eaten."

3 RAPE

To every man a damsel or two

A humane person reading these books for the first time, without any glamour of divine inspiration, would shudder at their cruelty and blush at their obscenity. Those who can make these foul facts illustrate beautiful symbols must have genius of a high order.
—Elizabeth Cady Stanton

THE BIBLE TEACHES that women are male property, buyable, saleable, abductable . . . and rapeable. Innumerable passages deal with women as booty. After the slaughter of a village, the victors are commanded to kill everyone, especially male children and nonvirgins. "But all the women children, that have not known a man by lying with him, keep alive for yourselves." (The victors are also instructed to steal livestock; the total booty is listed in this order of importance: 675,000 sheep, 72,000 beeves, 61,000 asses, 32,000 *virgins.*) *Numbers 31:17–35*

"And this is the thing that ye shall do, Ye shall utterly destroy every male, and every woman that hath lain by man." They found 400 young virgins under these orders and took them back to camp. *Judges 21:11–12*

Women virgins, however, weren't always kept alive, as this passage indicates: "And David smote the land, and left neither man nor woman alive." This time the booty was livestock only, not virgins. *1 Samuel 27:9*

Hast thou a desire?

"And seest," asks the bible, "among the captives a beautiful woman, and hast a desire unto her, that thou wouldest have her to thy wife?"

If so, read on for the instructions: Take her home, pare her nails, shave her head, have her bewail her parents for one month, then "go in unto her, and be her husband." ("Go in unto" is quaint bible jargon for sexual intercourse, in this case, rape.) "(If) thou have no delight in her, then thou shalt let her go whither she will; but thou shalt not sell her at all for money . . ." *Deuteronomy 21:11–14* The last-minute order not to sell a "used" woman into further slavery is the only biblical compunction expressed over using women as the spoils of war.

This is one of many wartime rape orders: "the city shall be taken, and the houses rifled, and the women ravished . . ." *Zechariah 14:2*

Or: "Their children also shall be dashed to pieces before their eyes; their houses shall be spoiled, and their wives ravished." *Isaiah 13:16*

To every man a damsel

Women's status as booty is so pronounced that a mother, worried about her son's delay in returning from battle, accounts for it in this way: "Have they not divided the prey; to every man a damsel or two?" *Judges 5:30*

The bible's cavalier attitude toward abducting women is illustrated when a town short on young virgins takes 400 after battle. This turns out to be an inadequate supply, so the township conspires to "lie in wait in the vineyards" near a feast of the Lord. "And, see, and behold, if the daughters of Shiloh come out to dance in the dances, then come ye out of the vineyards, and catch you every man his wife of the daughters of Shiloh." *Judges 21:19–23*

The Mosaic law

Mosaic law encompasses chapter upon chapter of very specific laws, yet deals with a limited range of possible rape crimes, totally ignoring the possibility that a nonvirgin can be raped, for example. Specifically, the Mosaic law deals with three possibilities: city rape, field rape and rape of the unbetrothed.

City rape. If a virgin woman is engaged "and a man find her in the city, and lie with her" she shall be stoned because, the bible assumes, she "cried not." He shall be stoned to death too, because "he hath humbled his neighbor's wife." *Deuteronomy 22:23–24* Such is the bible's compassion toward rape victims.

Field rape. "But if a man find a betrothed damsel in the field, and the man force her, and lie with her; then the man only that lay with her shall die . . . for he found her in the field and the betrothed damsel cried, and there was none to save her." *Deuteronomy 22:25–27*

Although it's presumably admirable the Lord doesn't order the rape victim killed along with the rapist this time, the disproportionate punishment of the rapist did not aid the cause of ending rape.

Rape of the unbetrothed. Since the bible regards rape as a crime committed by men against other men's property, rape of nonvirgins or unbetrothed women is not considered worthy of much attention.

Therefore Mosaic law makes little distinction between seduction and rape when an unengaged woman is involved.

If a man entices an unbetrothed maid, he must marry her. If the father refuses permission (the daughter has no say, of course) the enticer must pay the father according to the dowry of the virgins. *Exodus 22:16–17*

If a man *rapes* an unbetrothed virgin and "they are found," he must pay the "damsel's father" 50 shekels of silver (no provision for inflation) and he must marry her. Ironically, the only major distinction between rape and seduction is that the rapist-husband may never divorce his wife "because he has humbled her." *Deuteronomy 22:28–29* The bible's charity toward rape victims is to force them to remain married to their rapists.

Do to them as is good

Episodes of rape in the bible consistently are described from the point of view of the avenging male whose honor has been stained. Because Dinah, the daughter of Jacob, has been "defiled" by a Hivite, his fellow villagers are all tricked and slain by her male relatives, and their stock, women and children are taken. *Genesis 34:1–31* With this story the bible makes it explicit that rape is a crime against men and against honor rather than against women.

King David's son rapes his half-sister Tamar. "Then Amnon hated her exceedingly: so that the hatred wherewith he hated her was greater than the love wherewith he had loved her. And Amnon said unto her, Arise, be gone. And she said unto him, 'There is no case: this evil in sending me away is greater than the other that thou didst unto me.' " *2 Samuel 13:1–16* Tamar recognizes that since Amnon has had sex with her, he rightfully owns her, and she expects to marry him, actually protesting when he sends her away. Another of her brothers eventually kills Amnon, in the way of honorable biblical men.

Even if a male relative's honor is besmirched by rape, it's a different story when the relative himself offers up the woman for rape. This happens a couple of times in the bible in an effort to stave off sexual abuse of men by other men.

The famous story of Sodom involves two angels, who descend on Sodom to stay with Lot. The men of the village demand that Lot release the angels for their pleasure. Lot is appalled: "do not so wickedly." Instead he casually offers his two virgin daughters to them: "do ye to them as is good in your eyes: only unto these men do nothing." *Genesis 19:1–8* (Incidentally, the women are spared because the angels smite the mob of men with blindness.)

Another similar case of using women as bait ends on a grislier note. A male traveler and his concubine are invited to stay at the home of an old man. But angry mobs demand that the man be given to them "that we may know him." Instead the host offers them his own virgin daughter and the guest's concubine: "do with them what seemeth good unto you: but unto this man do not so vile a thing."

The crowd grows angrier, so the cowardly male guest pushes his concubine into the street, where "they knew her, and abused her all the night until the morning: and when the day began to spring, they let her go . . . And her lord rose up in the morning, and opened the doors of the house, and went out to go his way: and behold, the woman his concubine was fallen down at the door of the house, and her hands were upon the threshold. And he said unto her, Up, and let us be going. But none answered." *Judges 19:20–28*

He then took her apparent corpse home and divided her with a knife into 12 sections, signifying the 12 tribes of Israel, and sent one to each of the tribes, thereby prompting a huge battle. *Judges 19:29* The moral of this sorry tale is that women can, with impunity, be sacrificed, raped, tortured and killed in order to save men. Although the death of a man's concubine — if caused by "strangers" — must be avenged, no judgment is made of him for sacrificing her in his stead to this mob of assailants. The terse language likewise reveals no sympathy for her, nor does he mourn her death. She becomes merely a piece of propaganda used to continue wars.

Rape to get even with men

As a sort of army maneuver, Absalom "went in unto his father's concubines in the sight of all Israel." *2 Samuel 16:22* David, with typical biblical "justice," consequently imprisons the *concubines* for life. *2 Samuel 20:3* (After all, they had besmirched his honor by being raped, and broken the Mosaic code forbidding father and son to lie with the same woman.)

David's many wives are also raped with impunity, in order to punish David for seducing the married Bathsheba and arranging for the convenient death of her husband. The Lord declares: "Thus saith the Lord, Behold, I will raise up evil against thee out of thine own house, and I will take thy wives before thine eyes, and give them unto thy neighbour, and he shall lie with thy wives in the sight of this sun." *2 Samuel 12:11* The biblical deity obviously views the rape of innocent women as a fine tool to punish his chosen men.

The Lord also views rape as a way in which men can needle *him*. In listing the licentiousness of a fallen nation, the Lord notes, "a man and his father will go in unto the same maid, to profane my holy name." *Amos 2:7* Rape is never, however, regarded as a crime against *women*.

Incest: Genesis' warped family values

Incest is technically forbidden under Mosaic law, although incest and sexual assault were not worthy of being listed among the "Top Ten" Mosaic prohibitions. Leviticus, Chapter 18, is devoted to taboos against marrying near relations, or "uncovering nakedness," in King James parlance. There are instructions against "uncovering the nakedness" of fathers and mothers (Leviticus 18:7–8), sisters or half-sisters (18:9,11), granddaughters (18:10), aunts (18:12–13), uncles and aunts by marriage (18:14), daughters-in-law (18:15–16), and having sex with both a woman and her daughter (18:17). The penalty is to be cut off from people (18:29). There is no distinction between incest by age or consent. A near relation molesting a 4-year-old or raping a 14-year-old rates no special penalty, and would not be punished more severely than a brother-in-law who had an affair with a consenting sister-in-law.

Chapter 20 of Leviticus repeats many of the injunctions found in Chapter 18, and warns that the penalty is childlessness. *Leviticus 20:17, 19–21* The death penalty is spelled out for "lying with" your father's wife or daughter-in-law. *Leviticus 20:11–12* A special curse is directed at one who "lies" with "his father's wife." *Deuteronomy 27:20* Paul says that if you fornicate with your father's wife, you should be "taken away," and delivered to Satan. *1 Corinthians 5:1–2,5*

But biblical stories are replete with unpunished incest. If Eve was "cloned" by the biblical deity — as the second, favored version of creation purports — incest starts with Adam and Eve. The bible never explains who Cain's unnamed wife is and how she arrived in the vicinity, and whom their progeny could marry, other than their closest relations.

The esteemed figure of Abraham, father of Judaism, Christianity and Islam, married his half-sister. *Genesis 20:2* He was aware of the incest taboo, for he used his kinship with his wife to save his life and for personal gain. He passed off his wife as his sister, prostituting her to the Pharaoh. This enraged the biblical deity, who, with typical biblical justice, punished the unwitting *Pharaoh* for his favorite's subterfuge. *Genesis 12:11–19* Abraham repeats this trick with King Abimelech, who is only warned in a dream not to touch Sarah. *Genesis 20:1–14* Abraham excuses his conduct to the king by pointing out, "And yet indeed she is my sister; she is the daughter of my father, but not the daughter of my mother." *Genesis 20:12*

The bible's most scurrilous slander about incest involving daughters is the story of Lot and his two daughters. (These are the same daughters Lot was glad to offer to a mob of rapists in order to save male angels. The daughters were spared only because of the intervention of angels. *Genesis 19:1–11)* The destruction of Sodom and Gomorrah follows. Lot's disobedient wife is conveniently out of the picture, having been turned into a pillar of salt for turning back to look. *Genesis 19:26* The scene is set when Lot inexplicably takes his two daughters to dwell in a cave in a mountain. *Genesis 19:30*

What is next described has undoubtedly suggested, provoked and excused countless incestuous attacks upon helpless young daughters by their fathers or father figures. Perpetuating the ultimate myth about incest, the bible claims that the *daughters* contrive to seduce their father.

"And the firstborn said unto the younger, Our father is old, and there is not a man in the earth to come in unto us. . .

"Come, let us make our father drink wine, and we will lie with him, that we may preserve the seed of our father.

"And they made their father drink wine that night: and the firstborn went in, and lay with her father; and he perceived not when she lay down, nor when she arose."

The firstborn then entices the younger sister to do likewise. The daughters (who are not important enough to be named) both bear sons, naturally, and these sons found the tribes of the Moabites and the Ammonites. *Genesis 19:29–38*

In this ultimate tale of patriarchal reversal, it is the young, virgin *daughters* who desire and seek intercourse with their father. They seem strangely over-zealous in their civic duty to repopulate the earth and find a man who will "come in unto us." They reveal no revulsion, distress or squeamishness. These virgins take charge and know precisely what to do. *They* get their *father* drunk. *He* has no idea what they have done, is therefore the hapless victim of their premeditation, and clearly bears no responsibility. No one in this lecherous incest fantasy is depicted feeling any shame or guilt. In inevitable bible tradition, these young girls are depicted as the seductresses and sexual provocateurs, seeking sex for their own purposes with their ancient father.

By providing fodder and rationale for the incestuous sexual predator, this famous story has surely warped morality and blighted many young lives. After all, is not Lot called righteous? *II Peter 2:4–8*

Potiphar's wife

Probably as damaging as any of the callous biblical rules about rape victims is the tale of the treacherous woman known only as "Potiphar's wife," who "cast her eyes" upon Joseph. When the respectable Joseph spurns her advances, she aggressively grabs hold of his garment. When he flees, the scorned woman claims he raped her, and the long-suffering Joseph is jailed. *Genesis 39* Some translations of the bible describe Potiphar as a eunuch, which might at least help explain his wife's actions.

In this famous story, an insidious stereotype was born: that claims of rape are spurious, making the accused rapists, not the victims, the wronged.

Lord discovering secret parts

The Lord does some of his own avenging handiwork in Isaiah: "Moreover the Lord saith, Because the daughters of Zion are haughty, and walk with stretched forth necks and wanton eyes, walking and mincing as they go, and making a tinkling with their feet: Therefore the Lord will smite with a scab the crown of the head of the daughters of Zion, and the Lord will discover their secret parts." *Isaiah 3:16–17* Interestingly, in the accepted Catholic version of the bible, this passage is not nearly so explicit. Church officials probably feared — and rightly so — that such language would offend even the devout.

Does this passage mean the biblical Lord is a rapist? Apparently. This passage comes from a prophet in whose prophesying rebellious people are represented most commonly as "haughty" women. Even if it is interpreted metaphorically, the ugly and hateful imagery epitomizes the rape mentality of the bible. Clearly, "haughty" women deserve to be sexually abused because of their demeanor and dress, according to the bible.

* * *

Once begun, rape law reform has come swiftly in the United States, but it has been fought at every step by a psychological mindset that thinks (save for exceptional cases) that no woman really can be raped. Rape is occasionally considered male privilege, as in marriage laws that were on the books in most states. Treatment of rape in the bible is consistent with this mindset. Enforcement of rape laws in modern times has been handicapped by statutes calling for disproportionate punishment; that is, the death penalty in many southern states. This, too, we discover, has its origins (or at least won its legal influence) through the bible. Interestingly, the origin of the need for a rape victim to "cry out" in order to secure a conviction, a traditional legal requirement, also originated with the Mosaic law.

In 1977, when Judge Archie Simonson of Madison, Wisconsin, called rape a "normal reaction" after three boys gangraped a high school girl in a school hallway, he defended his remarks on the basis of his religious beliefs. Although he was recalled because of his remarks on the bench, women should not forget that his attitude comes not out of a vacuum, but out of the bible.*

---

* Among the numerous examples of sexual assailants who commit crimes under the guise of religion, or justify sexual abuse by scripture, is the criminal case of Allen Harrod, 56, a self-proclaimed religious prophet from California. Harrod was convicted in February 2004, along with his former wife, of 32 counts of child sexual abuse and transporting minors for illicit purposes. He received the maximum conviction of life plus 62 years. Harrod, originally a Mormon, wrote "scriptural interpretations" justifying the molestation of children, turning to 19th century Mormon theology and its endorsement of bible-based polygamy for inspiration. Under the aegis of his church, he required his own daughter and other teenagers to perform sexual acts at least weekly for years, starting when they were as young as four.

A study released by Rev. Ronald Barton and Rev. Karen Lebaczq (March 1990) for the Center for Ethics and Social Policy of the Graduate Theological Union at Berkeley, found that a quarter of all clergy have engaged in sexual misconduct.

The harm caused by male and clergy prerogative, set up by the bible, is nowhere better demonstrated than in the Roman Catholic priest abuse scandal. A survey by the U.S. Roman Catholic Church released in February 2004 showed that four percent of U.S. priests have been accused of sexually abusing 10,667 children from 1950–2002.

LEVITICUS 19:20–22 *"And whosoever lieth carnally with a woman, that is a bondmaid, betrothed to an husband, and not at all redeemed, nor freedom given her; she shall be scourged . . . and the sin which he hath done shall be forgiven him."*

4 THE PROSTITUTE

Her house is the way to hell

*Although the Mosaic code and customs so
plainly degrade the female sex, and their
position in the church to-day grows out of
these ancient customs, yet many people insist
that our religion dignifies women. But so long
as the Pentateuch is read and accepted as the
Word of God, an undefined influence is felt by
each generation, that destroys a proper respect
for all womankind.*

—*Elizabeth Cady Stanton*

BIBLICAL LAW WAS uncompromising when it came
to "bad" women.

As was true of women ruled under traditional common law,
it was not necessary for biblical women to take remuneration in
order to be considered whores; in fact, references to money
changing hands in the bible are nil.

Priests can't take "whores" or "profane" women to wed,
nor even a divorced woman. *Leviticus 21:7*

If a priest's daughter "profane herself by playing the
whore" she must be *burned. Leviticus 21:9* Biblical harlots (the
favored term) seem mostly guilty of one crime: seducing men
(that is, taking the lead). Whereas males enticing women who
are unbetrothed are let off lightly with a rap on the knuckle and
an order to marry their seducees, women who engage freely in
sex are so terrible a threat that harlot-metaphors comprise the

bulk of biblical warnings against losing faith.

Kill whores

In one biblical episode, the Lord authorizes the grotesque mutilation of two whores (and neatly absolves their male partners of any guilt, a trick emulated to this day by the criminal justice system).

These women were guilty of the following crimes: they "committed whoredoms" in Egypt, where they pressed their breasts and "bruised the teats of their virginity."

God delivers Aholah, the elder harlot, into "the hands of her lovers . . . These discovered her nakedness: they took her sons and her daughters, and slew her with the sword." The bible, with a gleefully macabre pun, adds ". . . she became famous among women; for they had executed judgment upon her." *Ezekiel 23:1–10*

But her surviving sister Aholibah was worse still, "more corrupt in her inordinate love . . . She doted upon the Assyrians her neighbours, captains and rulers clothed most gorgeously, horsemen riding upon horses, and all of them desirable young men." The impropriety of women having sexual urges and judging male desirability is clear. The sin of promiscuity — as committed by women, for it is rarely a sin for men in the bible — is evidently compounded when the men she trifles with are "all of them desirable."

Much angered, the Lord orders her lovers, "all of them desirable young men," it repeats, "captains and rulers, great lords and renowned, all of them riding upon horses," to descend upon her.

"(They) shall deal furiously with thee: they shall take away thy nose and thine ears . . . and shall leave thee naked and bare: and the nakedness of thy whoredoms shall be discovered, both thy lewdness and thy whoredom . . . thou shalt pluck off thine own breasts . . ." *Ezekiel 23:11–47* The passage concludes that this atrocity was necessary in order to teach women "not to do after your lewdness." *Ezekiel 23:48*

Authorization of grotesque sexual mutilation indicates a

pathologically sick hatred for women and their bodies. Is it any wonder that our modern culture, placing such a high value on the book in which such descriptions are found, regularly produces men who "hear voices" telling them to destroy women, religious men who specialize in sexual mutilation? Lawrence Singleton has gained his place in the record books of misogyny for a crime committed in 1978, when he kidnapped and raped a 15-year-old hitchhiker. When she begged to be freed, he not only cut off the ropes that bound her but her arms. His defense? She was, he slanderously claimed, a prostitute.*

The western world is still enthralled with the idea of Jack the Ripper, an English killer in the 19th century who slashed six prostitutes to death. Countless movies revive his crimes, and he even had an imitator — Peter Sutcliffe, arrested in 1981 as the Yorkshire Ripper, who killed 13 women because he heard "what I believed then and believe now to have been the voice of God."

Although five of his victims were not prostitutes, Sutcliffe claimed the murders were a "divine mission" to rid the world of prostitutes.**

Chambers of death

Biblical "harlots" (and there are many mentioned) personify evil. The following passage epitomizes the dire biblical warnings about them especially if they are "strangers."

On a "black and dark night" a youth encounters a woman "subtil of heart" (like the snake). "Now is she without, now in

* Singleton served eight years of a 14–year sentence. After a public outcry over his early release, he spent one year living on the grounds of San Quentin prison until his parole in 1988. He was convicted of the brutal murder of a woman in Florida in 1997, and was sentenced to death. He died of cancer in prison in 2001. The local prostitute whom he savagely murdered did "tricks" to pay for rent and diapers.
** The bible-induced killings of women continue. In 2003, religionist Gary Ridgway, the Green River Killer in Washington State, pleaded guilty to killing 48 women, more than any other confessed serial killer in U.S. history. In his courtroom statement, Ridgway said: "I wanted to kill as many women as I thought were prostitutes that I possibly could." Associated Press reported: "Friends knew him as a friendly, if overbearing, meticulous man who liked to read the Bible at work."

the streets, and lieth in wait at every corner." The imagery is more befitting a panther than a woman.

"So she caught him, and kissed him, and with an impudent face said unto him . . . I have decked my bed with coverings of tapestry . . . I have perfumed my bed with myrrh, aloes, and cinnamon. Come, let us take our fill of love until the morning: let us solace ourselves with loves . . . With her much fair speech she caused him to yield, with the flattering of her lips she forced him. He goeth after her straightway, as an ox goeth to the slaughter, or as a fool to the correction of the stocks . . . For she hath cast down many wounded: yea, many strong men have been slain by her. Her house is the way to hell, going down to the chambers of death." *Proverbs 7:9–27*

Note the author's evident horror that a woman could be sexually aggressive. Note also the release of the man from responsibility for his actions. Although he is labeled a fool, the woman "forced" him — with her lips yet! — to "yield" (the Evil Eve motif).

The influence of such biblical passages leaves little wonder why prostitutes continue to be singled out for legal prosecution while customers largely get off scot-free. It was not uncommon during the 20th century for states or municipalities to adopt far more severe penalties for prostitution than for the solicitation of prostitution. Even where sanctions are similar, police conduct more sweeps for prostitutes than for their clients. The onus falls upon the woman, whose exaggerated, satanic sexuality is blamed for male misconduct.

The language of pornography

The so-called "word of the Lord," in Ezekiel 16, issues a seemingly endless denunciation of straying Jerusalem, comparing it to a beautiful woman whom the Lord (acting as pimp) clothed in silk, and decorated.

"But thou didst trust in thine own beauty, and playedst the harlot because of thy renown, and pouredst out thy fornications on every one that passed by . . ." *Ezekiel 16:15* The Lord says he will "strip thee also of thy clothes. . . . and they shall stone thee with stones, and thrust thee through with their swords. And they shall burn thine houses with fire, and execute judgments upon thee in the sight of many women: and I will cause thee to cease from playing the harlot . . ." *Ezekiel 16:40–41*

This is the *language of pornography*, with its male control of a woman's body, its sex hate, its grotesque sexual humiliation, punishment and violence.

More of the same continues in the book of Hosea, where the Lord orders Hosea, "Go, take unto thee a wife of whoredoms and children of whoredoms: for the land hath committed great whoredom, departing from the Lord." *Hosea 1:2*

Then the Lord proceeds to petty and corporal cruelties of Hosea's wife (a metaphor for the Lord's people currently out of favor): "And now will I discover her lewdness in the sight of her lovers, and none shall deliver her out of mine hand." *Hosea 2:10*

The short book of Nahum is devoted to the destruction of the city of Nineveh. The book attributes to the Lord a speech using revealingly woman-hating language, in which God sputters out his hate for the city in this manner:

"Because of the multitude of the whoredoms of the well-favoured harlot, the mistress of witchcrafts, that selleth nations through her whoredoms, and families through her witchcrafts.

"Behold, I am against thee, saith the Lord of hosts; and I will discover thy skirts upon thy face, and I will shew the nations thy nakedness, and the kingdoms thy shame . . ." *Nahum 3:4–6* And so it continues.

Revilement of the whore reaches its peak toward the end of the Old Testament, not to be repeated until that hallucinatory book, the Revelation. Elizabeth Cady Stanton called its author "victim of a terrible and extravagant imagination and of visions which make the blood curdle." As she pointed out, "Satan and women are the chief characters in all the frightful visions. . . ."

The whore of the Revelation is a terrifying creature, described as "the great whore that sitteth upon many waters." She is seated upon "a scarlet coloured beast, full of names of blasphemy, having seven heads and ten horns." She holds a golden cup "full of abominations and filthiness of her fornication."

Her fate? ". . . the ten horns which thou sawest upon the beast, these shall hate the whore, and shall make her desolate and naked, and shall eat her flesh, and burn her with fire." *Revelation 17:1–16*

"Thou shalt not suffer a witch to live"

From such excessive warnings about the evil sexual endowments and powers of women, it is only a slight distance to the execution of the verse "Thou shalt not suffer a witch to live." *Exodus 22:18* Although the supernatural (sexual) powers of witches are not delineated in Mosaic law as they later were by the Roman Catholic Church, the bible promotes a dark, sick view of female sexuality.

Woman was viewed as a temptress because she was defined through her sexuality by the bible and the Church. As sex was sinful, so did women, by virtue of being women, sin. This idea gradually led to witch-hunting.

The purges began in the 1300s and ended in the 1700s, but their heyday was in the 15th and 16th centuries. The single most influential factor in witch-hunting was the *Malleus Maleficarum*, a handbook on what a witch was, how to detect her, how to torture her, and then how to kill her. It was published in 1486 and was sanctified by Pope Innocent VII who, after reading it, appreciatively wrote his *Bull Summis desiderante*, one of the most influential condemnations of witches and women ever issued by the Catholic Church. The Faculty of Theology at the University of Cologne also gave the handbook their mark of approval, and after that, the purge was on.

This handbook single-handedly was responsible for the death of thousands of women. The authors of this book, two Dominican Inquisitors named Heinrich Kramer and Jacob Sprenger, stated point-blank: "All witchcraft comes from lust which in women is insatiable." Specifically, they catalogued the seven primary crimes witches committed:

1. arousing passion in men
2. causing impotence
3. castrating men

4. changing men into beasts
5. using or doling out birth control
6. performing abortions
7. committing infanticide

All of these crimes are sex or reproduction related. The two authors, speaking more generally, outlined the many inherent and evil characteristics of women, which did not distinguish between the ordinary woman and the witch. To be a woman was one breath away from becoming a witch. To be a woman was nearly tantamount to being evil. This is what the bible taught, and what its believers put into practice.

EXODUS 22:18 *"Thou shalt not suffer a witch to live."*

5 THE 'STRANGE' WOMAN

Keep thee from the evil woman

*This utter contempt for all the decencies of life,
and all the natural personal rights of women
as set forth in these pages, should destroy in
the minds of women at least, all authority to
superhuman origin and stamp the Pentateuch
at least of emanating from the most obscene
minds of a barbarous age.*
                    —Elizabeth Cady Stanton

THE OLD TESTAMENT is a volume of war. The biblical Lord turns upon his chosen people with regularity, so it is simple to guess how often he has his chosen people turn on "strangers," those people from other lands, tribes or races who are not Israelite.

This passage spells out the Lord's philosophy most chillingly:

"When the Lord thy God shall bring thee into the land whither thou goest to possess it and hath cast out many nations before thee. . . .

"Thou shalt smite them, and utterly destroy them; thou shalt make no covenant with them, nor shew mercy unto them. . . .

"But thus shall ye deal with them; ye shall destroy their altars, and break down their images, and cut down their groves, and burn their graven images with fire.

"For thou art an holy people. . . .

"The Lord did not set his love upon you, nor choose you, because ye were more in number than any people; for ye were the fewest of all people;

"But because the Lord loved you, and because he would keep the oath which he had sworn unto your fathers, hath the Lord brought you out with a mighty hand, and redeemed you out of the house of bondmen, from the hand of Pharaoh king of Egypt." *Deuteronomy 7:1–8*

The biblical lord is a bit schizoid on the subject, blowing hot and cold (mostly cold). Three chapters later in the same book containing the above instructions, the Lord says, "Love ye therefore the stranger; for ye were strangers in the land of Egypt." *Deuteronomy 10:19*

But the Lord does not blow hot and cold about "strange women;" strange women are forever and for always out of his favor.

To ward away the evils of the strange woman (whose evil ways have been described in the chapter on prostitution) the Lord orders his men to appear before him three times a year — but not his women. *Exodus 34:23* This is a precaution "lest . . . thou take of their daughters unto thy sons, and their daughters go after their gods, and make thy sons go after their gods." *Exodus 34:16*

In Numbers, Israel is described committing "whoredom with the daughters of Moab," which "kindled" the Lord's anger against Israel. This is when the Lord orders Moses, "Take all the heads of the people, and hang them up before the Lord against the sun." *Numbers 25:1–4*

When an Israelite brought a Midianite princess to a congregation in the sight of Moses, the son of a priest takes a javelin in his hand, "and thrust both of them through, the man of Israel, and the woman through her belly." *Numbers 25:8* The message is that any intermarriage or other peaceful friendship with people of other nations would result in the defilement of the Lord's people. In other words, "strange *women*" defile the tribes of Israel.

The Jezebels

The bible is riddled with "strange women," most unidentified. But some are famous.

Samson's wife, by crying, persuaded Samson to tell her a riddle's answer, which she then broadcast to the Philistines. *Judges 14*

Delilah, whom Samson loves, is offered 1100 pieces of silver if she can entice the secret of his strength from him. She succeeds. Samson is taken and blinded. *Judges 16:4–21*

Even wise King Solomon could not withstand the fatal charms of "strange women." "But King Solomon loved many strange women . . . his wives turned away his heart after other gods." *1 Kings 11:1–4* (Considering the fact that he was married to 700 women, and had 300 additional concubines, it is not so surprising that he could be led astray. Nevertheless, the bible does not use this occasion to condemn polygyny, but only to condemn "strange women.")

Jezebel, that prototypical "strange woman," according to the bible, "stirred up" her husband Ahab's "wickedness" in worshipping another deity. *1 Kings 21* For acting out the proper role of supportive, religious wife to her weak-willed husband — that is, for believing in the "wrong" religion — she is thrown off a wall. The bible notes gruesomely, "some of her blood was sprinkled on the wall, and on the horses . . ." She was then trodden underfoot by the horses. In the meantime, the man who had ordered her violent death drinks and dines. He then orders her burial, but as only bits and pieces of her can be found, her remains are given to the dogs. *2 Kings 9:23–37*

The Revelation authors, not finding this revilement adequate, reinvoke the story, accusing Jezebel of seducing their "servants to commit fornication." *Revelation 2:20–23*

Even women of the proper background, the bible warns us, can lead men astray, such as Job's wife. After God and Satan make a bargain to challenge the faith of Job, his children and servants are killed, his wealth is lost and his body is afflicted with grievous sores. Yet Job's faith survives. Understandably, his long-suffering wife's faith becomes a little worn; she tells him to curse God. Job replies, "Thou speakest as one of the foolish women speaketh." *Job 2:10* This story has been used to show how superior is the religious faith of men, and how inconstant is woman's.

Proverbs' strange women

Not surprisingly, the book of Proverbs displays the most resentment toward "strange women."

"To deliver thee from the strange woman, even from the stranger which flattereth with her words . . . For her house inclineth unto death, and her paths unto the dead." *Proverbs 2:16–18* Proverbs exhibits true paranoia on the subject:

"To keep thee from the evil woman, from the flattery of the tongue of a strange woman. . . .

"For by means of a whorish woman a man is brought to a piece of bread: and the adulteress will hunt for the precious life.

"Can a man take fire in his bosom, and his clothes not be burned?

"So he that goeth in to his neighbour's wife; whosoever toucheth her shall not be innocent . . ." *Proverbs 6:24–29* Here Proverbs seems to define the adulteress as synonymous with the "strange woman," who contaminates others. However, the male adulterer, according to Proverbs, does not contaminate others, merely his own soul.

Again: "A foolish woman is clamorous . . . Stolen waters are sweet, and bread eaten in secret is pleasant. But he knoweth not that the dead are there; and that her guests are in the depths of hell." *Proverbs 9:13–18*

"The mouth of a strange woman is a deep pit: he that is abhorred of the Lord shall fall therein." *Proverbs 22:14* "For a whore is a deep ditch, and a strange woman is a narrow pit. She also lieth in wait as for a prey, and increaseth the transgressors among men." *Proverbs 23:27–28* Could the bible better illustrate its blame-the-woman philosophy than by this passage?

6 THE UNCLEAN SEX

Her filthiness
is in her skirts

*Bible historians claim special inspiration for
the Old and New Testaments containing . . .
customs that degrade the female sex of all
human and animal life, stated in most
questionable language that could not be read
in a promiscuous assembly, and call all this
"The Word of God."*
—Elizabeth Cady Stanton

HAVE YOU MADE your sin atonement this month,
you menstruous woman, you?

According to the word of the Judeo-Christian God, women
are unclean, once-a-month outcasts who are menaces to society
and must do penance for the natural functions of their bodies.
The bible throws a few damning praises at woman's sexual
delights for men in the Song of Solomon, but otherwise treats
the female body as a hygienic horror. Women's physicality is
inextricably linked in the bible with servitude, lewdness, and
what Simone de Beauvoir called "otherness," which becomes an
excuse for the objectification and oppression of women in bible-
influenced law.

The bible contains many grooming and hygiene tips for all
people. For instance, it ordains that if a man (generic meaning,
no doubt) touches the "carcase" of "unclean creeping things," he
shall be both unclean *and* guilty. *Leviticus 5:2* But women, as
the descendants of Eve, bear the brunt of biblical squeamishness, especially as they are linked with sex. The bible reveals a

great horror of sex throughout most of its books (interestingly juxtaposed with casual reference to sexual activity and sexual imagery that are shocking by the standards of any age).

Even before the Mosaic law is handed down with its numerous digs at women's bodies, Moses is advising men in preparation for the Mt. Sinai visitation: "come not at your wives." *Exodus 19:15* (Today's parallel is the football coach who instructs his players not to indulge the night before a big game.) This idea is reiterated in 1 Samuel 21:4–5.

By Leviticus, the Word is out: women are unclean. Both men and women are unclean after sex until evening. *Leviticus 15:16–18* This leads to confusion. If a couple has sex shortly before sundown, are they only unclean a few minutes, whereas a couple that has sex in the morning is unclean all day? We'll never be sure.

A menstruous woman is unclean seven days and must be "put apart." Whoever touches her is unclean, the bed is unclean, the furniture is unclean. *Leviticus 15:19–23* After periods, women must offer not only a sin atonement but a burnt offering. The bible specifies "two turtles or two young pigeons," which must be taken to the priest. The priest then begs "an atonement for her before the Lord for the issue of her uncleanness."

If a man has intercourse with a menstruating woman, and as the bible puts it with unusual delicacy, "her flowers be upon him," he is unclean seven days. *Leviticus 15:24* This sanction is made stronger later, when couples that have intercourse during menstruation are told they will be "cut off" from their people, a scary threat in a nomadic culture. *Leviticus 20:18* Today, couples marrying in Israel are still handed instructions advising them of this sanction.* When Jesus' garb is touched by a "woman with issue," a poor creature who had apparently been menstruating without cease for years, she is cured — but not

---

* In fact, since 1953, only couples marrying in the Orthodox Jewish tradition are considered lawfully wedded. The government of Israel recognizes civil marriages performed *outside* Israel, but not inside Israel. Consequently, one in five couples there travels abroad to be married. Likewise, interfaith marriages are not prohibited, but they are not legally recognized.

before he feels his "virtue" go out. *Mark 5:30*

Even childbirth is unclean (see Chapter 8 on Motherhood).

Woman's uncleanliness is the basis of male divorce rights. "When . . . it come to pass that she finds no favour in his eyes, because he hath found some uncleanness in her: then let him write her a bill of divorcement." *Deuteronomy 24:1* Her former husband cannot remarry her for "she is defiled; for that is an abomination before the Lord." *Deuteronomy 24:4*

Out! damned spot

The book of Ezekiel takes the most exception to woman's so-called uncleanliness.

In order to be considered a lawful and just man, one must not "hath come near to a menstruous woman," an act put on par with lifting "up his eyes to the idols of the house of Israel." *Ezekiel 18:6*

"[T]heir way was before me as the uncleanness of a removed woman," Ezekiel 36:17 charges, in condemning the house of Israel.

The Lord threatens to "discover thy nakedness unto them, that they may see all thy nakedness," because the daughters of Zion's "filthiness was poured out, and thy nakedness discovered through thy whoredoms with thy lovers . . ." *Ezekiel 16:36–37* The thought is clearly stated that women possess "filthiness" which pours out of their bodies.

A long diatribe against Jerusalem is conducted in this manner:

"Jerusalem hath grievously sinned; therefore she is removed: all that honoured her despise her, because they have seen her nakedness: yea, she sigheth, and turneth backward.

"Her filthiness is in her skirts . . . Jerusalem is as a menstruous woman . . ." *Lamentations 1:8–17*

In a blistering condemnation of Israel, it is termed a "bloody city" that "shew all her abominations," committing perversions including not showing a difference "between the unclean and the clean." *Ezekiel 22:2–26*

The New Testament does not dwell on woman's uncleanliness to the extent of the Old Testament. Yet a Greek woman comes to Jesus, saying her young daughter has "an unclean spirit," falling at his feet to beg him to "cast forth the devil" from her daughter. (This is the famous story when Jesus replies, "it is not meet to take the children's bread, and to cast it unto the dogs." Only when she further humbles herself does Jesus condescend to "cure" her daughter. *Mark 7:25–30)*

It may also be noted that Mary Magdalene must have seven devils cast out of her in Mark 16:9 and Luke 8:2, an incident tending to create the impression that women are more prone to inhabitation by devils.

Because of women's innate lewdness, Paul emphasizes the virtues of eunuchs and celibates: "It is good for a man not to touch a woman." *1 Corinthians 7:1* (Also *Matthew 19:12*) Virgin males are described as "not defiled with women" and are praised. *Revelation 14:4*

But perhaps the crowning touch comes when Jesus tells his most faithful disciple Mary Magdalene, who has been weeping for him, to "Touch me not," for he has not yet ascended, and the touch of a woman would apparently make the ascension impossible. Yet Jesus almost immediately asks Thomas to touch him. *John 20:17, 27*

One of the Lord's favorites, David, was a Peeping Tom.

7 MARRIAGE

He shall rule over thee

... The Pentateuch is a long painful record of war, corruption, rapine, and lust. Why Christians who wished to convert the heathen to our religion should send them these books, passes all understanding. It is most demoralizing reading for children and the unthinking masses, giving all alike the lowest possible idea of womanhood, having no hope nor ambition beyond conjugal unions with men they scarcely knew, for whom they could not have had the slightest sentiment of friendship, to say nothing of affection.
—Elizabeth Cady Stanton

THE CIVIL LAWS regarding marriage are traced directly to religion. "By marriage, the husband and wife are one person in law: that is, the very being of legal existence of the woman is suspended during the marriage, or at least incorporated and consolidated into that of the husband, under whose wing and protection she performs everything..." wrote William Blackstone in 1765. Court and case law throughout the United States continued to decree three marriage requirements in keeping with this 17th century interpretation of marriage. Women were mandated to fulfill domestic, sexual and childcare duties in exchange for support by their husbands, who were empowered to choose the couple's domicile. These gender-stereotyped duties jived very well with bible teachings, which can be credited with patenting the "one flesh: *his*" doctrine of marriage.

Woman quickly loses her identity

The favored version of creation illustrates that woman was made expressly to serve as a "help meet." Adam concludes: "This is now bone of my bones, and flesh of my flesh . . . Therefore shall a man leave his father and his mother, and shall cleave unto his wife: and they shall be one flesh." *Genesis 2:23–24* In essence, before the second chapter of the bible is concluded, woman has lost her identity.

After the "fall," God tells Adam's as-yet-unnamed wife: "(Thy) desire shall be to thy husband, and he shall rule over thee." *Genesis 3:16* Following language leaves little doubt about which gender has not only the power, but the favor of the Lord: "Blessed is the man. . ." begins Psalm 1. Man, says Psalm 8:5, is "a little lower than the angels." Woman's place in this hierarchy is evidently unworthy of mention.

Women's subservient role in the church is tied to their wifely status.

". . . the head of every man is Christ; and the head of the woman is the man; and the head of Christ is God." *1 Corinthians 11:3*

"Let your women keep silence in the churches: for it is not permitted unto them to speak; but they are commanded to be under obedience, as also saith the law.

"And if they will learn any thing, let them ask their husbands at home: for it is a shame for women to speak in the church." *1 Corinthians 14:34–35*

Paul's letter to the Ephesians illustrates the New Testament's favorite doctrine of male supremacy, in which woman's relationship is yet again compared to man's relationship (and inferiority) to God. "Wives, submit yourself unto your own husbands, as unto the Lord.

"For the husband is the head of the wife, even as Christ is the head of the Church: and he is the saviour of the body.

"Therefore as the church is subject unto Christ, so let the

wives be to their own husbands in every thing." The husband is never ordered to submit to his wife. Husbands are required to "love their wives as their own bodies." *Ephesians 5:22–28*

Although the epistle of Paul the Apostle to the Colossians is not quite four pages long, it too manages to find room to order women to submit themselves:

"Wives, submit yourselves unto your own husbands, as it is fit in the Lord." As usual, a following text orders men to love their wives, but how can a master truly love a servant — and just as important — why should a servant love her master? (Incidentally, this epistle also orders servants to obey their masters as they fear God, a biblical edict exploited by slave-owners and anti-union employers.) *Colossians 3:18–22*

Peter warns that not only must women learn in subjection, but they must be afraid of conversing with their husbands:

"Likewise, ye wives, be in subjection to your own husbands; that, if any obey not the word, they also may without the word be won by the conversation of the wives;

"While they behold your chaste conversation coupled with fear . . ." This passage invokes the story of an Old Testament wife to scare women into submission. "Even as Sara obeyed Abraham, calling him lord . . ."

Husbands are told to honor these wives "as unto the weaker vessel." *1 Peter 3:1–7*

Similarly, husbands are told "every one of you should know how to possess his vessel in sanctification and honour . . ." *1 Thessalonians 4:4* Here we have the beginning of the Christian skill of placing women on a pedestal of clay.

These and similar passages re-establishing Eve's "transgression" as the basis for woman's subjection and silence, were utilized in our own country to attempt to bar women from public speaking, public professional careers, and from voting and participating in politics.

Marital silly putty

Biblical wives are silly putty in the hands of their husbands. As has already been documented, men frequently bought wives, or could rape an unbetrothed woman to force her to marry him. But there were problems even with the less criminal relationships. Genesis sets the scene for the typical biblical romance:

"That the sons of God saw the daughters of men that they were fair; and they took them wives of all which they chose." *Genesis 6:2*

Or: "And Judah saw there a daughter of a certain Canaanite, whose name was Shuah; and he took her, and went in unto her. And she conceived . . ." *Genesis 38:2–3* It is considered natural that men take all the sexual initiative and that women remain passive. A marriage is described as little more than a man's decision and ability to "go in unto" a woman, as the bible delicately puts it.

A descendant of Cain takes two wives. *Genesis 4:19* Sarai gives her maid Hagar to Abram. *Genesis 16:2* The Lord's favorite, Abram, renamed Abraham, passes off his 70-year-old wife Sarah as his sister in his travels because she is beautiful (70 is young by Genesis standards) and he fears a jealous man will kill him. (Incidentally, Sarah *is* his half-sister.) She goes to live with Pharaoh, who gives Abraham many riches in return. With typical biblical justice, it is Pharaoh who falls into trouble with the Lord for his unwitting adultery. *Genesis 20* Sarah's part in the adultery is looked upon as demonstrating proper marital obedience. Abraham uses his wife twice in this manner; biblical character Isaac later pretends Rebekah, his wife, is an available sister. *Genesis 26:7–9* The moral: Wives should be happy to use their bodies for the economic benefit of shifty husbands, a strange contradiction in a bible which scourges women who play the harlot for their own benefit.

Other biblical hanky-panky includes Jacob being "given" Leah in marriage by her father as a mean trick. Leah's jealous sister Rachel, who also eventually marries Jacob, is barren and gives her handmaid Bilhah to Jacob. Leah also gives him a handmaid. *Genesis 29*

David flees, leaving behind his wife Michal, whom he has purchased with the foreskins of 200 Philistines, taking Abigail and Ahinoam as his other wives. *1 Samuel 25:39–43* In the meantime, Saul gives daughter Michal (David's first wife) away! David takes at least six wives before his 30th birthday, and anxiously works to reacquire Michal.

By 2 Sam 5:13, "David took him more concubines and wives." He eventually gets Michal back, but when she reproves him for "vowing to be vile before maidservants" the Lord makes *her* barren for life. *2 Samuel 6:20–23* Soon he is spying on Bathsheba who is "very beautiful to look upon" *2 Samuel 11:2*, and decides to "lay with her; for she was purified." *2 Samuel 11:4* (He knew this because she had been bathing when he first espied her.) He sets up her husband to be killed in battle in order to be able to marry her. God punishes him by having all his wives raped by neighbors. When David is old and has trouble staying warm, well-wishers summon a fair young virgin to lie on his bosom. But bible language lets us know that David, in modern parlance, could not "get it up." *1 Kings 1:1–4*

In 1 Kings we also learn that King Solomon had 700 wives and 300 concubines. *1 Kings 11:3*

Polygyny is holy

While the Lord orders adulterers both male and female to be killed, men had the upper hand since they could marry as many available women, Mormon-style, as they liked. In addition, they could keep bondwomen and concubines. Other big marriers besides Solomon include King Rehoboam, with 18 wives and 60 concubines, and King Abijah, with 14 wives. *2 Chronicles 11:21, 2 Chronicles 13:21*

The polygyny privilege goes without saying; no bible author even bothers to spell it out. It is merely accomplished. For example, Genesis characters Isaac and Rebekah grieve over their son Esau when he marries two women — not because he marries two women but because they're *Hittites. Genesis 26:34–35* Esau acquired even more wives. *Genesis 36:2–3*

Only three passing references in the form of rules appear pertaining to polygyny. In the Mosaic law, men are advised that if they have two wives, one beloved and one hated, they cannot pass over the firstborn son simply because his mother is hated.

Deuteronomy 21:15 The Mosaic code acknowledges polygyny by decreeing that a bondwoman married to her master does not lose status if he marries another. *Exodus 21:10* In the New Testament, it is declared that if a man wants the office of bishop, one of the conditions is that he have "one wife" (someone ought to tell the pope about this one). *1 Timothy 3:2*

Paul makes an oblique reference to the custom when he tells a wife she is "bound by the law to her husband," and if she has a second husband while the first yet lives, she is an adulteress. No such rule is made for men. *Romans 7:1–3*

Jesus acknowledges polygyny by recounting, without criticism, a parable about ten virgins awaiting the same bridegroom, in Matthew, Chapter 25.

Another bizarre reference to polygyny is found in the threats of Isaiah, who warns of the day when "seven women shall take hold of one man, saying, We will eat our own bread, and wear our own apparel: only let us be called by thy name, to take away our reproach." Here the idea of polygyny is to be eschewed, but only because these women are aggressive, and the marriage will not be one of submission and dependence on their part. *Isaiah 4:1–2*

Virginity test

Women, unlike men, were required to be virgins at marriage. Although fornication was an abomination for both male and female, and was particularly reviled by the New Testament, only biblical women were truly at risk if they were not virgins at the time of marriage. The Mosaic law supplies this interesting rule:

"If any man take a wife, and go in unto her, and hate her, and give occasions of speech against her, and bring up an evil name upon her, and say, I took this woman, and when I came to her, I found her not a maid: Then shall the father of the damsel, and her mother, take and bring forth the tokens of the damsel's virginity unto the elders of the city in the gate . . . And they shall spread the cloth before the elders of the city."

If the "proof" is there, the husband is chastised and fined

100 shekels of silver, payable to the bride's father — whose honor, naturally, has been hurt. The poor humiliated bride has no honor to salve. Instead the man is forbidden to divorce the bride he so willingly smeared and endangered. It never, apparently, crossed biblical minds that she might prefer to be separated from him.

"But if this thing be true . . ." continues the Mosaic code, "Then they shall bring out the damsel to the door of her father's house, and the men of her city shall stone her with stones that she die: because she hath wrought folly in Israel, to play the whore in her father's house: so shalt thou put evil away from you." *Deuteronomy 22:13–21* The status of women's hymens became not only a public concern but evidence of women's loyalty to their fathers and to Israel itself. One wonders how many unfortunate women were stoned to death because they lacked hymens, had in fact lost their virginity earlier (perhaps to their very same husband), or because they had done their laundry too industriously!

The viciousness of this code finds an echo in the Mosaic law's honoring of a husband's jealous nature. "(If) the spirit of jealousy come upon him, and he be jealous of his wife, and she be defiled: or if the spirit of jealousy come upon him, and he be jealous of his wife, and she be not defiled: Then shall the man bring his wife unto the priest . . ."

The priest scatters the dirt and dust from the tabernacle floor — presumably including the residue of the many animal sacrifices and burnt offerings brought to him — in holy water. With incomparable hospitality, he offers this tasty brew to the suspected wife, who must drink it. If she is guilty, her thigh is to rot and "thy belly to swell," and she "shall be a curse among her people." Given the vile drink and the subjectivity of observing whether a belly "swells" (probably judged by whether she had cramps or vomited), the test may very well have been unpassable, just as later tests for witches were a no-win situation. The bible does note that if she passes it, she is freed and, as a reward, "shall conceive" — a son, no doubt. Men are advised to have a priest execute this test anytime they are jealous. "Then shall the man be guiltless from iniquity, and this woman shall bear her iniquity." *Numbers 5:13–31* Thus the bible encouraged men to indulge in their "spirit of jealousy," because, regardless of the outcome, they shall emerge purer. The further irony is that no such test exists for the wife, who had ample cause to feel jealousy when her husband lawfully becomes a bigamist.

Social double standards for men and women over fornication and adultery persist in our society, and may be perpetuated at the discretion of courts.

It is better not to marry

Today fundamentalists tell us marriage is the pinnacle of a woman's life — indeed it is to be her major ambition.

Yet the epistles of Paul say otherwise. A passage in Luke has been interpreted to mean that a person is worthier of heaven if he or she doesn't marry: ". . . they which shall be accounted worthy to obtain that world, and the resurrection from the dead, neither marry, nor are given in marriage . . ." *Luke 20:34–35*

The following requirement set down by Jesus for his disciples is hardly conducive to marriage (at least to marital bliss):

"If any man come to me, and hate not his father, and mother, and wife, and children, and brethren, and sisters, yea, and his own life also, he cannot be my disciple." *Luke 14:26*

In First Corinthians 7, Paul makes it clear that the unmarried woman may better serve her lord because she "careth for the things of the Lord, that she may be holy both in body and spirit." *1 Corinthians 7:34* Interestingly, the unmarried man need only try to please the Lord in an unspecified fashion, but need not be "holy in both body and spirit." *1 Corinthians 7:32*

Marry if you must

Paul has a contradictory, can't-make-up-his-mind attitude toward marriage: "It is good for a man not to touch a woman," he says. "Nevertheless, to avoid fornication let every man have his own wife, and let every woman have her own husband." Paul recommends occasional periods of abstinence (time for fasting and prayer) but not of so long a duration that "Satan tempt you . . . for your incontinency." Paul then sighs, "I would that all men were even as I myself (a celibate)."

Of course, Paul's most famous statement on marriage is "if they cannot contain, let them marry: for it is better to marry than to burn."

Although virginity is recommended for both sexes, Paul makes it clear that it is not only recommended but *de rigueur* for women. He assures men that they do not sin if they marry. The wording he uses to reassure women on this score is slightly different: "if a *virgin* marry, she hath not sinned." *1 Corinthians 7:1–40*

1 KINGS 11:1–4 *King Solomon had 700 wives and 300 concubines.*

8 MOTHERHOOD

In sorrow thou shalt bring forth children

One would think that potential motherhood should make women as a class as sacred as the priesthood. In common parlance we have much fine-spun theorizing on the exalted office of the mother, her immense influence in moulding the character of her sons: "the hand that rocks the cradle moves the world," etc., but in creeds and codes, in constitutions and Scriptures, in prose and verse, we do not see these lofty paeans recorded or verified in living facts.

—Elizabeth Cady Stanton

MOTHERHOOD IS A CURSE. "I will greatly multiply thy sorrow and thy conception: in sorrow thou shalt bring forth children . . ." *Genesis 3:16* This passage was used by clerics in the 1800s to attempt to deny women any anesthesia during childbirth.

Childbirth is unclean. Women who bear sons are only unclean seven days, but must "continue in the blood of her purifying" 33 days. In the meantime, they can touch no hallowed thing nor come to sanctuary. *Leviticus 12:1–4* But after the birth of a daughter, these unclean and purifying days double. *Leviticus 12:5* Even Mary, mother of Jesus, undergoes purification. *Luke 2:22* Despite such diligent cleansings, the bible makes it clear men don't escape unscathed these dirty births: "Man that is born of woman is of few days, and full of trouble . . .

Who can bring a clean thing out of an unclean? not one." (Not even God?) *Job. 14:1–4* Paul says that even though woman was the transgressor, "Notwithstanding she shall be saved in childbearing, if they continue in faith and charity and holiness with sobriety." *1 Timothy 2:15*

Miraculously, it can almost be assured that a biblical mother's firstborn will be a son. The bible is also filled with what one might assume to be a disproportionate number of barren women. The Lord and his angels and the Holy Ghost variously visit women, gleefully shutting and opening up wombs and impregnating women: Genesis 21:1–2, 25:21, and 1 Samuel 2:21 all involve the Lord as impregnator. Angels do the insemination in Judges 13:3 and Genesis 6:2–4. The Holy Ghost makes its visit in Matthew 1:18. (And this is only a partial list!)

The fertility game is used occasionally as punishment: Michal is childless because she reproves her husband David for parading before the maidservants naked, *2 Samuel 6:23*, another case of the bible's peculiar brand of justice.

Women are expected to die fearlessly if they have a son. *Genesis 35:17* The patriarchal authors of the bible even claim: "A woman when she is in travail hath sorrow, because her hour is come: but as soon as she is delivered of the child, she remembereth no more the anguish, for joy that a man is born into the world." *John 16:21* Luke 2:23 reads, "As it is written in the law of the Lord, Every male that openeth the womb shall be called holy to the Lord."

This school of thought proclaiming that the birth of a male baby will redeem a woman antedates Freud by some time.

Bible mothers are in no way venerated. Probably the most positive language to be found in the bible about motherhood comes when a displaced tribe that is being lamented is described as a mother, first as a lioness, finally as an abandoned vine. But the praise and the lamentation, of course, refer to loss of their national power in war. *Ezekiel 19*

More typically, you'll find scornful language, as when King Solomon is described as being approached by "two harlots" who both claim one baby as their own. *1 Kings 3:16*

The progeny of an unmarried mother is reviled: "A bastard

shall not enter into the congregation of the Lord; even to his tenth generation . . ." *Deuteronomy 23:2* That's 250 years! God has a long memory.

Jesus reflected this view of motherhood. "Who is my mother?" he asks. *Matthew 12:48* "Woman, what have I to do with thee?" he asks her yet another time. *John 2:4* When a woman hearing him speak praises his mother: "Blessed is the womb that bare thee, and the paps which thou hast sucked," Jesus replies with the disdainful words, "Yea, rather, blessed are they that hear the word of God, and keep it." *Luke 11:27–28*

Then there is the bible's vengeful side. "Rejoice, thou barren that bearest not; break forth and cry, thou that travailest not . . ." *Galatians 4:27* "(Woe) unto them that are with child, and to them that give suck in those days!" *Matthew 24:19* "For, behold, the days are coming, in which they shall say, Blessed are the barren, and the wombs that never bare, and the paps which never gave suck." *Luke 23:29*

9 DIVORCE & ADULTERY

She eateth and wipeth her mouth

As long as our religion teaches woman's
subjection and man's right of domination, we
shall have chaos in the world of morals.
Women are never referred to as persons,
merely as property, and to see why, you must
read the Bible . . . see how many other
opportunities for the exercise of sex were given
to men . . . (while) the single one of marriage
to one husband was allowed to women.
                    —Elizabeth Cady Stanton

THE OLD TESTAMENT favored no-fault divorce —
but only for men. The Mosaic law allows a man merely to hand
his wife a "bill of divorcement," and out she goes. *Deuteronomy
24:1* A woman is not accorded the same right. No discussion is
ever made of child custody or support, much less alimony. The
bible actually provides incentive to divorce and remarriage. In
the passage spelling out male divorce rights it is noted that a
newly married man is excused from war and business for one
year "to cheer up his wife." *Deuteronomy 24:5*

Jesus, depending on which book in the New Testament you
use as your guide, forbids or allows divorce. He forbids it, if you
read Mark (10:2–9). If you read Matthew, he allows no divorce
unless the wife is a fornicator (5:32), hearkening back to the idea
that women *must* be virgins at the time of their marriage,
whereas men have sexual license. In both books we find those
hallowed, androcentric words: "What therefore God hath joined

together, let not man put asunder." *Matthew 19:6* and *Mark 10:9*

Adultery is painted as a vile act for a woman in the Old Testament: "Such is the way of an adulterous woman; she eateth, and wipeth her mouth, and saith, I have done no wickedness." *Proverbs 30:20*

". . . but thou hast played the harlot with many lovers; yet return again to me." *Jeremiah 3:1*

"Surely as a wife treacherously departeth from her husband, so have ye dealt treacherously with me . . . saith the Lord." *Jeremiah 3:20*

The New Testament makes adultery a sin to be feared by man and woman alike, but somehow, the blame still seems to lie with women.

Jesus magnifies the sin of adultery with his edict — made newly famous by former President Jimmy Carter — that "whosoever looketh on a woman to lust after her hath committed adultery with her already in his heart." The following verse is apparently his advice on what the sinner who lusted ought to do: "And if thy right eye offend thee, pluck it out, and cast it from thee: for it is profitable for thee that one of thy members should perish, and not that thy whole body should be cast into hell." *Matthew 5:28–29* Self-mutilation, based on this advice, still occurs in American society.

If a man "put away" his wife, except for committing fornication, he causes her to commit adultery when she remarries, as does the man who marries her. *Matthew 5:32* However, it seems that the divorced man does not commit adultery in such a case. In another version, if either a man or woman divorce and remarry, they both commit adultery. *Mark 10:11–12*

DEUTERONOMY 24:1 *"When a man hath taken a wife, and married her, and it come to pass that she find no favour in his eyes, because he hath found some uncleanness in her: then let him write her a bill of divorcement, and give it in her hand, and send her out of his house."*

10 MEN, BE MACHO

Thine eye shall not pity her

(Circumcision's) prominence as a religious observance means a disparagement of all female life, unfit for offerings, unfit to take part in religious services, incapable of consecration.

—Elizabeth Cady Stanton

MEN: ARE YOU circumcised? These days most men are; it's hospital routine. This "sanitation procedure," today considered by many to be an unnecessary barbarism, has its roots in Chapter 17 of Genesis — the first indication of the biblical Lord's ongoing preoccupation with penises and their issue.

The Lord "appeared" before 90-year-old Abram, promising him he will become "exceeding fruitful" and that his "seed" will become nations and kings. The catch? "Every man child among you shall be circumcised." *Genesis 17:10* Abram's heirs and subjects must be "marked." This is the famous covenant.

Mercifully, the African/Muslim custom of female circumcision, that is, mutilation or removal of the clitoris and other female genitalia, was not part of the covenant. Nevertheless, as the circumcision was the Lord's "mark" of a chosen people, women's status was zilch.

The Lord laid down his rules: Every man child that is eight tender days old must be circumcised, including any baby guest in the house or baby slave ("he that is bought with thy money").

But woe unto the uncircumcised! ". . . the uncircumcised man child whose flesh of his foreskin is not circumcised, that soul shall be cut off from his people . . ." (Pun unintended.)

God meant what he said. When his favorite Moses had not seen to it that his son by a Midianite woman was circumcised, that Lord tries to kill Moses. His wife Zipporah, whose good sense rebelled at this heathen custom, impatiently solved the problem with a sharp (ouch!) stone. *Exodus 4:24–26*

Any lord that could work up such concern about the tips of penises could easily meddle in other quite personal items. Onan's brother, with the unlikely name of Er, displeases the Lord, who slays him. The Lord orders Onan to replace Er as his wife's husband. Onan "knew it was wrong" and conscientiously "spilled his seed on the ground." (As Ruth Green put it in *The Born Again Skeptic's Guide to the Bible*, Onan made quite a splash.) The biblical Lord finding this a waste of good sperm, also slays Onan. *Genesis 38:7–10*

This Law of Onan, as it came to be called, was later invoked in Deuteronomy's Mosaic code, where the Lord orders that if a brother dies, leaving a childless wife, his brother must "go in unto her," and their firstborn must be named for the dead brother (the assumption being that women only bear sons). Should the brother refuse to do this, the woman is entitled to spit upon him and "loose his shoe" publicly before the elders. *Deuteronomy 25:5–10*

Male drawbacks

But, naturally, being male in the bible means more than possessing a circumcised penis, or being willing to fill in as proxy on quick notice for a brother. The real criteria of machismo are revealed in Leviticus, when the Lord lists his standards for becoming a priest. Number One requirement is that the applicant be male. The other standards are similarly physical: "Whosoever he be of thy seed in their generations that hath any blemish, let him not approach to offer the bread of his God." *Leviticus 21:17*

Blemishes include being blind, lame, having a flat nose, or "anything superfluous," being brokenfooted, brokenhanded, or "crookbackt," or a dwarf, or one who "hath a blemish in his eye, or be scurvy, or scabbed, or hath his stones broken . . ."

Despite the Old and New Testament praise for eunuchs, a man had better have intact "stones" to serve his lord. *Leviticus 21:18–21* The Lord later expands on this theme, saying, "He that is wounded in the stones, or hath his privy member cut off, shall not enter into the congregation of the Lord." *Deuteronomy 23:1*

Although these passages might make many less-than-perfect men feel unworthy, the fact that males must conform to these regulations in order to become priests just reaffirms the Lord's favoritism with men. One passage in the bible, however, really *does* pick on men:

"Thou shalt not delay to offer the first of thy ripe fruits, and of thy liquors: the firstborn of thy sons shalt thou give unto me." *Exodus 22:29* Not surprisingly, this order to sacrifice firstborn sons has become one of the forgotten passages of the bible.

Men can be unclean too!

Although women bear the brunt of the blame for bringing "uncleanness" into the world, the Lord is not overfond of any "issue" from male or female genitalia.

If any man's "seed of copulation" goes out from him, he shall wash and be unclean until "the even." His garment is also unclean. *Leviticus 15:16–17* In fact, the wording in this set of codes seems to indicate that it is male "issue" which defiles women during sex: "The woman also with whom man shall lie with seed of copulation, they shall both bathe themselves in water, and be unclean until the even." *Leviticus 15:18*

Lots of biblical loins

There are many miscellaneous biblical passages dealing with male genitalia: David was ordered to kill 100 Philistine men in order to win the hand of Michal; in his ardor he killed 200 and brought their foreskins home with him. *1 Samuel 18:25–27* David plays with himself before the Lord and displays his nakedness; the Lord approves (and, as we know, strikes Michal barren for reproving David). *2 Samuel 6:20–23*

In Kings we get this sort of classy dialogue: "My little finger shall be thicker than my father's loins," says one macho. *1 Kings 12:10* "Pissing" is everyday biblical jargon and the Lord is very concerned with where men direct theirs: In 1 Kings, Elijah says the Lord says, "I will cut off from Ahab him that pisseth against the wall . . ." *1 Kings 21:21*

Ezekiel reads like the gruesomest sadistic pornography: In Chapter 29:7–8 the Lord "madest all their loins to be at a stand. Therefore thus saith the Lord God; Behold, I will bring a sword upon thee, and cut off man and beast out of thee" — a bloody castration which could not more clearly show the bible's unwholesome attitude toward sex.

(Most of the sex hatred is directed toward women. But the bible's attitude toward sex in general is negative; sex is unclean, frequently brutal, usually without tenderness or affection. The most positive directives by the Lord to men about sex are when he orders rape.)

In Ezekiel 8:2 we even have a special appearance by the Lord's loins. Ezekiel describes the guest appearance thus: "Then I beheld, and lo a likeness as the appearance of fire: from the appearance of his loins even downward, fire; and from his loins even upward, as the appearance of brightness, as the color of amber . . ." (Of course, the Lord has already "mooned" Moses on Mt. Sinai: "And I will take away mine hand, and thou shalt see my back parts . . ." *Exodus 33:23*)

Lord of war

It is impossible to analyze the bible's standards of masculinity without taking into account war. After all, "The Lord is a man of war: the Lord is his name," as Exodus 15:3 reminds us. Women's part in wars, besides serving as booty, was to sing and dance in praise of battles, to cheerlead, as when they sing out for David, "Saul hath slain his thousands, and David his ten thousands." *1 Samuel 18:6–8*

Two war anecdotes illustrate the bible's machismo standards. In Deuteronomy, the Mosaic code makes provisions for what would seem to be an unlikely situation: "When men strive together one with another, and the wife of the one draweth near for to deliver her husband out of the hand of him that smiteth him, and putteth forth her hand, and taketh him by the secrets: Then thou shalt cut off her hand, thine eye shall not pity her." *Deuteronomy 25:11–12* Imagine living in a society where the penis was so sacrosanct that a loyal wife would suffer amputation just for touching one!

In Judges, a tale is told about "a certain woman" who throws a piece of millstone at Abimelech's head "to brake his skull." Abimelech "called hastily unto the young man his armourbearer, and said unto him, Draw thy sword, and slay me, that men say not of me, A woman slew him. And his young man thrust him through, and he died." *Judges 9:53–54*

Clearly, women were worth so little, and men so much, that the worst that could be said of a man was, "A woman slew him."

We can contrast this with the most vile curse the Lord could make of a nation: "Behold, thy people in the midst of thee are women." *Nahum 3:13* Or "Jerusalem is as a menstruous woman." *Lamentations 1:17*

The Lord's favoritism toward men is even apparent in his curses, when he alternately threatens horrible fates and "a land of milk and honey" — depending upon whether or not his people are obedient. A particularly blood-curdling list in Deuteronomy, after vile curses such as forcing delicate women to eat children (*Deuteronomy 28:53–56*), then enumerates all of the good things to come to Israel if they obey the Lord. But the blessings promise nothing good for the women.

The male preoccupation of the bible writers was so pronounced that, in the New Testament, they even cite the 52 "generations of Jesus" from the side of Mary's *husband* Joseph, despite their claim that the birth resulted from a virgin birth! *Matthew 1:16*

Even when men in the bible are criticized, it is frequently because of their association with women. As we know, Job laments, "how can he be clean that is born of a woman?" *Job 25:4*

Conversely, women derive vicarious status from men, as when St. John notes that a travailing woman forgets her anguish as soon as "a man is born into the world." *John 16:21*

Sometimes men are criticized for their association with men: "Know ye not that the unrighteous shall not inherit the kingdom of God? Be not deceived: neither fornicators, nor idolaters, nor adulterers, nor *effeminate, nor abusers of themselves with mankind. . ."* [emphasis added] *1 Corinthians 6:9*

Repeated put-downs of women, caveats not to "come at" wives at crucial times, and abhorrence of women's periods and childbearing underlie the bible's firm sex stereotyping. There is to be no blurred line between the sexes. Deuteronomy emphasized the sex role/status distinctions by warning, "The woman shall not wear which pertaineth unto a man, neither shall a man put on a woman's garment: for all that do so are abomination unto the Lord thy God." *Deuteronomy 22:5* The New Testament gives insulting rationale for the fact that women's long hair is a "glory" for women but a "shame" for men. *1 Corinthians 11:14–15*

The great equalizer in the bible, as always, remains the Lord's wrath. Isaiah warns that he has no mercy, "they shall eat every man the flesh of his own arm." *Isaiah 9:20* In Ezekiel 5:10, fathers eat sons and sons eat fathers. Men are ordered to "let not thy soul spare for his (son's) crying" during punishment (*Proverbs 19:18*), "for if thou beatest him with the rod, he shall not die." *Proverbs 23:13–14*

Yet, finally, it all comes back to genitals: "Slay utterly old and young, both maids and little children, and women: but come not near any man upon whom is the mark . . ." *Ezekiel 9:6*

With this crude measuring stick of a human being's worth, can there really be any doubt that man made god in his own image?

11 GROOMING

Adorn yourself with subjection

It appears very trifling for men,
commissioned to do so great a work on earth,
to give so much thought to the toilets of
women. . . .
                        —Elizabeth Cady Stanton

W OMEN, ACCORDING TO the bible, must have long hair, "it is a glory to her: for her hair is given her for a covering." Long hair for men, the bible teaches, is a shame.

"Doth not even nature itself teach you, that, if a man have long hair, it is a shame unto him?"

Because man is "the image and glory of God," he does not need to cover his head while praying; women must humble themselves, however, and cover their heads. *1 Corinthians 11:4–15*

The bible doesn't mince words on grooming. Women who call themselves Christians had better understand what it says:

1) Don't braid your hair.

2) Don't wear any gold.

3) Don't wear any pearls.

4) Don't wear any costly array.

Women are to "adorn themselves in modest apparel, with shamefacedness and sobriety." *1 Timothy 2:9*

Interestingly, men throughout the bible are able to adorn themselves with gold, from David, crowned, even clothed in gold, and the prophets, to Jesus, brought gold at his birth. Solomon used acres of gold building a temple. In one case, Rebekah in Genesis is brought gold earrings. *Genesis 24:22, 53* Yet by Revelations "a woman arrayed and decked with gold is a whore." *Revelation 17:1–4*

How's that for double standards?

Peter teaches that there shall be no outward adorning of plaited hair, wearing of gold, or putting on of fine apparel. "But let it be the hidden man of the heart, in that which is not corruptible, even the ornament of a meek and quiet spirit, which is in the sight of God of great price." The idea is to adorn oneself with subjection. *1 Peter 3:3–5*

Deuteronomy 22:5 warns men and women not to wear each other's garments, else they shall be "abominations."

Naturally, these various portions of the Mosaic code have been quoted to condemn the 19th century "bloomers" costume, young men who grow out their hair, and women who wear slacks to court, work or school. Moral Majority President Ronald Reagan made one of his first official proclamations a ban on women at the White House wearing slacks.* Biblical notions have staying power.

---

* Women's pantsuits literally did not come back into fashion until the Clinton Administration (1993–2000).

PROVERBS 31:10 *"Who can find a virtuous woman?"*

12 WOMEN'S NATURE

Woe to the women

*Do our sons in their law schools, who read the
old common law of England and its
commentators, rise from their studies with
higher respect for women? Do our sons in their
theological seminaries rise from their studies
of the Mosaic laws and Paul's epistles with
higher respect for their mothers? Alas! in both
cases they may have learned their first lessons
of disrespect and contempt.*
—Elizabeth Cady Stanton

LESSONS OF DISRESPECT and contempt for women
proliferate in the bible. Perhaps modern woman's greatest
stumbling blocks in the way of her legal fight to overcome discrimination are not the grosser prejudices about women, such as
the view that a woman wants to be raped. The greatest stumbling block may be the lack of respect, the petty scorn, with
which society holds women. Our culture also mandates a set
reaction to women as actors in their various roles of daughters,
wives, mothers, grandmothers, widows. These reactions come
from a view of women's "nature." The bible is full of petty put-
downs, stereotypes and advice about the nature of woman.

The New Testament specializes in encouraging women to
be passive, self-effacing, masochistic, long-suffering. The Old
Testament specializes in vilifying woman for her "nature."

Insults come first

"As for my people," says Isaiah 3:12, "children are their oppressors, and women rule over them . . ."

"In that day shall Egypt be like unto women: and it shall be afraid and fear because of the shaking of the hand of the Lord of hosts . . ." is another of Isaiah's contemptuous views on the nature of women. *Isaiah 19:16*

"Tremble, ye women that are at ease . . ." warns Isaiah 32:11–13.

"Can a maid forget her ornaments, or a bride her attire? yet my people have forgotten me days without number," the Lord whineth. *Jeremiah 2:32*

". . . call for the mourning women . . . and send for cunning women. . . . And let them make haste, and take up a wailing for us, that our eyes may run down with tears . . . and teach your daughters wailing . . ." *Jeremiah 9:17–20*

"Thou art thy mother's daughter, that loatheth her husband and her children; and thou art the sister of thy sisters . . ." goes a long denunciation of Jerusalem. *Ezekiel 16:45*

Consider this curse of woman (surely a mistranslation?):

"And say, Thus saith the Lord God; Woe to the women that sew pillows to all armholes, and make kerchiefs upon the head of every stature to hunt souls! . . . thus saith the Lord God; Behold, I am against your pillows . . ." *Ezekiel 13:18–20* So much for the industrious seamstress.

Of course, the authors of Proverbs had to get their licks in:

"Who can find a virtuous woman? for her price is far above rubies." The perfect wife is described as an uncomplaining workhorse. "She riseth also while it is yet night, and giveth meat to her household and a portion to her maidens . . . ," maketh purchases, candles, tapestry, and above all, "feareth the Lord." *Proverbs 31:10–31* So much for the goodly woman.

"As a jewel of gold in a swine's snout, so is a fair woman which is without discretion." *Proverbs 11:22*

"It is better to dwell in the corner of the housetop, than with a brawling woman and in a wide house." *Proverbs 25:24* "A continual dropping in a very rainy day and a contentious woman are alike." *Proverbs 27:15* "An odious woman when she is married; and an handmaid that is heir to her mistress" are two of the three phenomena which make the earth "disquieted." *Proverbs 30:21–23*

Wives are scapegoats: "A wise son maketh a glad father: but a foolish son is the heaviness of his mother." *Proverbs 10:1*

"The mouth of strange women is a deep pit; he that is abhorred of the Lord shall fall therein . . ." *Proverbs 22:14*

"Give not thy strength unto women," warns Proverbs 31:3.

"And I find more bitter than death the woman, whose heart is snares and nets, and her hands as bands: whoso pleaseth God shall escape from her; but the sinner shall be taken by her." *Ecclesiastes 7:26*

The Old Testament, however, was glad to make use of women. As Elizabeth Cady Stanton observed, "Women were always considered sufficiently clean to beg, work and give generously for the building and decoration of churches, and the support of the priesthood. They might always serve as inferiors, but never receive as equals." Women were ordered to spin, give embroidery, looking-glasses, etc., for the building of a tabernacle which they themselves could not enter. *Exodus 36:6, 38:8*

The New Testament matches the insults of the Old Testament in a passage in Timothy, which describes a "good widow" as one who is desolate, trusts in God, and continually prays and supplicates night and day. She brings up children, lodges strangers, washes saints' feet, and relieves the afflicted — and she doesn't remarry. But, the passage continues, younger widows wax wanton against Christ by remarrying. "And withal they learn to be idle, wandering about from house to house; and not only idle, but tattlers also and busybodies, speaking things which they ought not." *1 Timothy 5:5–13*

Behavior code

Paul writes that women should adorn themselves with good works "which becometh women professing godliness." *1 Timothy 2:10*

Paul also warns against old wives' tales: "refuse profane

and old wives' fables." *1 Timothy 4:7* Some would argue most of the bible qualifies as "old males' tales."

Titus 2 teaches that the aged man should be sober, grave, temperate, sound in faith, in charity, in patience. The advice for aged women's conduct is more explicit. She should be "in behaviour as becometh holiness," not be a false accuser, or given to much wine. She should be a teacher of good things, and teach women to be sober, to love their husbands and children, and to be discreet, chaste, keepers at home, good, obedient to their own husbands in order "that the word of God be not blasphemed." *Titus 2:2–5*

The ultimate gesture by an obedient woman is made in Luke, when a woman "sinner" sees Jesus eating, and kneels to wash his feet with her tears and wipe them with her hair, kissing his feet and putting an ointment on him. *Luke 7:37–48* "Thy sins are forgiven," he tells her. Such abject, servile, sycophantic behavior would be eschewed by any woman with self-esteem, yet such is the Christian woman's role model.

13 ABORTION

In sin did my mother conceive me

It is the contempt that the canon and civil law
alike express for women that has multiplied
their hardships and intensified man's desire to
hold them in subjection.
                    —*Elizabeth Cady Stanton*

WHAT DOES THE bible say about abortion?

Absolutely nothing! The word "abortion" does not appear in any translation of the bible.

Out of more than 600 laws of Moses, *none* comments on abortion. One Mosaic law about miscarriage specifically contradicts the claim that the bible is antiabortion, clearly stating that miscarriage does not involve the death of a human being. If a woman has a miscarriage as the result of a fight, the man who caused it should be *fined*. If the woman dies, the culprit must be killed:

"If men strive, and hurt a woman with child, so that her fruit depart from her, and yet no mischief follow: he shall be surely punished according as the woman's husband will lay upon him; and he shall pay as the judges determine.*

"And if any mischief follow, then thou shalt give life for life, Eye for eye, tooth for tooth . . ." *Exodus 21:22–25*

The bible orders the death penalty for murder of a *human*

---

* The King James version uses the English expression, "with child," but the original Hebrew word, "harah," is simply "conception." Thus, in the original, there is no suggestion that an embryo or fetus is comparable to a "child," further weakening antiabortion arguments.

being, but not for the expulsion of a fetus.

When does life begin?

According to the bible, life begins at birth — when a baby draws its first breath. The bible defines life as "breath" in several significant passages, including the story of Adam's creation in Genesis 2:7, when God *"breathed into his nostrils the breath of life; and man became a living soul."* Jewish law traditionally considers that personhood begins at birth.

Desperate for a biblical basis for their beliefs, some antiabortionists cite obscure passages, usually metaphors or poetic phrasing, such as: "Behold, I was shapen in iniquity; and in sin did my mother conceive me." *Psalm 51:5* This is sexist, but does nothing other than to invoke original sin. It says nothing about abortion.

Moses, Jesus, and Paul ignored every chance to condemn abortion. If abortion is so important, why doesn't the bible say so?

Thou shalt not kill?

Many antiabortionists quote the sixth commandment, "Thou shalt not kill" (*Exodus 20:13*), as evidence that the bible is antiabortion. They fail to investigate the bible's definition of life (breath) or its deafening silence on abortion. Significantly, the Mosaic law in Exodus 21:22-25, directly following the Ten Commandments, makes it clear that an embryo or fetus is *not* a human being.

An honest reader must admit that the bible contradicts itself. "Thou shalt not kill" did not apply to many living, breathing human beings, including children, who were routinely massacred in the bible. The Mosaic law orders "Thou *shalt* kill" people for committing such "crimes" as cursing one's father or mother (*Exodus 21:17*), for being a "stubborn son" (*Deuteronomy 21:18-21*), for being a homosexual (*Leviticus 20:13*), or even for picking up sticks on the Sabbath (*Numbers 15:32-35*)! Far from protecting the sanctity of life, the bible promotes capital punishment for conduct which no civilized person or nation would regard as criminal.

Mass killings were routinely ordered, committed or approved by the God of the bible. One typical example is Numbers 25:4–9, when the Lord casually orders Moses to massacre 24,000 of his own people: "Take all the heads of the people, and hang them up before the Lord against the sun." Clearly, the bible is not pro-life!

Most scholars and translators agree that the injunction against killing forbade only the murder of (already born) Israelites. It was open season on everyone else, including children, pregnant women and newborn babies.

Does God kill babies?

"Happy shall he be, that taketh and dasheth thy little ones against the stones." *Psalm 137:9*

The bible is not pro-child. Why did God set a bear upon 42 children just for teasing a prophet? *2 Kings 2:23–24* Far from demonstrating a "pro-life" attitude, the bible decimates innocent babies and pregnant women in passage after gory passage, starting with the flood and the wanton destruction of Sodom and Gomorrah, progressing to the murder of the firstborn child of every household in Egypt (*Exodus 12:29*), and the New Testament threats of annihilation.

Space permits only a small sampling of biblical commandments or threats to kill children:

Numbers 31:17: "Now therefore kill every male among the little ones." *Deuteronomy 2:34:* "utterly destroyed the men and the women and the little ones." *Deuteronomy 28:53:* "And thou shalt eat the fruit of thine own body, the flesh of thy sons and of thy daughters." *1 Samuel 15:3:* "slay both man and woman, infant and suckling." *2 Kings 8:12:* "dash their children, and rip up their women with child." *2 Kings 15:16:* "all the women therein that were with child he ripped up." *Isaiah 13:16:* "Their children also shall be dashed to pieces before their eyes; their houses shall be spoiled and their wives ravished." *Isaiah 13:18:* "They shall have no pity on the fruit of the womb; their eye shall not spare children." *Lamentations 2:20:* "Shall the women eat their fruit, and children." *Ezekiel 9:6:* "Slay utterly old and young, both maids and little children." *Hosea 9:14:* "give them a miscarrying womb and dry breasts." *Hosea 13:16:* "their infants shall be dashed in pieces, and their women with child shall be ripped up."

Then there are the dire warnings of Jesus: "For, behold, the days are coming, in which they shall say, Blessed are the barren, and the womb that never bare, and the paps which never gave suck." *Luke 23:29*

The teachings and contradictions of the bible show that antiabortionists do not have a "scriptural base" for their claim that their deity is "pro-life."

Spontaneous abortions occur far more often than medical abortions. Gynecology textbooks conservatively cite a 15 percent miscarriage rate, with one medical study finding a spontaneous abortion rate of almost 90 percent in very early pregnancy. It has been pointed out that this would make a deity in charge of nature the greatest abortionist in history!

Are bible teachings kind to women?

The bible is neither antiabortion nor pro-life, but does provide a biblical basis for the real motivation behind the antiabortion religious crusade: hatred of women. The bible is antiwoman, blaming women for sin, demanding subservience, mandating a slave/master relationship to men, and demonstrating contempt and lack of compassion: "I will greatly multiply thy sorrow and thy conception; in sorrow thou shalt bring forth children; and thy desire shall be to thy husband, and he shall rule over thee." *Genesis 3:16* What self-respecting woman today would submit willingly to such tyranny?

The antiabortion position does not demonstrate love for humanity, or compassion for real human beings. World Health Organization estimates maternal deaths at 500,000 a year, with at least one in five stemming from unsafe, illegal abortions. Thousands more are hurt and maimed from illegal or self-induced abortions. Unwanted pregnancies and complications from multiple pregnancies are a leading killer of women. Why do antiabortionists want North American women to join these ghastly mortality statistics? Every day around the world more than 40,000 people, mostly children, die from starvation or malnutrition. We must protect and cherish the right to life of the already-born.

Do churches support abortion rights?

Numerous Christian denominations and religious groups agree that the bible does *not* condemn abortion and that abortion should continue to be legal. These include: American Baptist Churches-USA, American Ethical Union, American Friends (Quaker) Service Committee, American Jewish Congress, Catholics For a Free Choice, Christian Church (Disciples of Christ), Episcopal Church, Jewish Reconstructionist Federation, Lutheran Women's Caucus, Moravian Church in America – Northern Province, Presbyterian Church (USA), Reform Judaism, Union of American Hebrew Congregations, Unitarian Universalist Association, United Church of Christ, United Methodist Church, United Synagogue of Conservative Judaism, Women's Caucus Church of the Brethren, YWCA, and Religious Coalition for Reproductive Choice.

Is America governed by religious faith?

Belief that "a human being exists at conception" is a matter of *faith, not fact*. Legislating antiabortion *faith* would be as immoral and unAmerican as passing a law that all citizens must attend Catholic mass!

The bible does not condemn abortion; but even if it did, we live under a secular constitution, not in a theocracy. The separation of church and state, the right to privacy, and women's rights all demand freedom of choice.

14 HOMOSEXUALITY
Their blood shall be upon them

All other institutions may change, opinions on
all other subjects may be modified and
improved, but the old theologies are a finality
that have reached the ultimatum of spiritual
thought. We imagine our religion with its
dogmas and absurdities must remain like the
rock of ages, forever.

—Elizabeth Cady Stanton

JUST AS THERE are many feminist apologists for the bible, so do there exist gay apologists who remain within the folds of churches conforming to a bible that condemns homosexuality in vicious terms.

After a list of "unclean" acts, including, "Thou shalt not lie with mankind, as with womankind: it is abomination" (Leviticus 18:22), the bible warns that the biblical Lord will "visit the iniquity" upon such persons so that "the land itself vomiteth out her inhabitants." *Leviticus 18:25*

This pleasant imagery is followed by the edict: "If a man also lie with mankind, as he lieth with a woman, both of them have committed an abomination: they shall surely be put to death; their blood shall be upon them." *Leviticus 20:13*

Sexist and homophobic

Typically male-oriented, the Mosaic law does not even consider the possibility of lesbianism (although it dwells in detail upon the possibility of female acts of bestiality, such as in Leviticus 20:16). Nevertheless, you can be pretty sure the writers of the bible expected their masculine nouns and pronouns to be interpreted generically where punishment is concerned.

The New Testament, in any case, makes up for the oversight in Romans, where Paul gripes: ". . . for even their women did change the natural use into that which is against nature:

"And likewise also the men, leaving the natural use of the woman, burned in their lust one toward another . . ." (Note that it is only the woman who is considered to have a "natural use.")

Paul blithely reiterates that people with these sexual preferences have committed acts "worthy of death." But his real gripe seems to be that they "have pleasure in them that do them." *Romans 1:26-32*

The only other major references to homosexuality in the bible are two unsavory incidents wherein mobs of men attempted to molest "male angels" and other men. In the fabled tale of Sodom, the reaction to such a proposition is absolute horror: "do not so wickedly." Instead two virgin daughters are gladly offered in proxy, but the problem is solved when the angels smite the mob with blindness. *Genesis 19:1-11*

In Judges 19:22-29, a similar tale unfolds when a mob demands "to know" a male visitor. Women are again offered; the visitor's concubine is raped all night and found dead the next morning.

These homophobic tales work to engender in the bible reader an impression of maniacal and inhuman male homosexuals.

Although the passages in the bible dealing with the issue of homosexuality would, put side-by-side, scarcely fill a bible page, this has not tempered their messages of bigotry, disgust and vengeance.

Gay men and women, and civil rights advocates in general, learned the literal-mindedness of the new Christian right when

Anita Bryant emerged on the political scene. Now that Bryant is mellowing, new fanatics are taking her place.*

The threat the bible still poses for gay men and lesbians could not be more dramatically illustrated than by the formation in February 1981 of a coalition, some of whose leaders vow to reinvoke the biblical punishment — death — for homosexuals.

Dean Wycoff, with the Santa Clara Moral Majority, said: "I agree with capital punishment, and I believe homosexuality is one of those that could be coupled with murder and other sins."

He called San Francisco "the Sodom and Gomorrah of the United States and the armpit of this perverted movement."

The Santa Clara Moral Majority is part of a coalition of west coast fundamentalists vowing to spend $3 million on a media campaign attacking homosexuality.**

Not surprisingly, homosexuals in San Francisco reported an increase in violence against them. In Madison, Wisconsin, the United, an advocacy group, also called attention to an increase of violence there, including attacks against men and women

---

* Singer Anita Bryant, a former Miss America run-up, was the high-profile spokesperson for Florida Orange Juice. In 1977, Bryant launched a pious "Save Our Children" crusade in response to an ordinance passed by the Miami-Dade County Commission barring discrimination on the basis of sexual orientation. Bryant's battle cry was that children were unsafe from "homosexual recruitment." Bryant's crusade, which dominated news for months, galvanized the homophobic rightwing. A referendum overturned the ordinance. Gay rights activists responded by organizing an orange juice boycott, which cost Bryant her position with Florida Orange Juice. It took until 1998 for a new gay rights measure to pass the Miami-Dade County Commission.

A devout Southern Baptist, Bryant once called the Vietnam conflict "a war between atheism and God," according to the *St. Petersburg Times*. Ironically, after holding her marriage up as an exemplar of male/female romance, Bryant was divorced by her first husband in 1980. The "scandal" hurt Bryant's standing among her conservative Christian audience.

** A loose cabal of Mormon, Roman Catholic and fundamentalist Protestant denominations and religious organizations has spent millions to amend state constitutions to bar gay marriage, succeeding so far in Alaska, Hawaii, California, Missouri and Nevada. The Roman Catholic Church has taken the lead in lobbying and organizing against the November 2003 decision of the Massachusetts State Court ordering that state to recognize gay marriages.

leaving what are considered gay bars.

Although Moral Majority president Jerry Falwell kept his comments noncommittal about his west coast chapter's anti-gay drive, the national organization has issued similar edicts in the past. Moral Majority vice president Greg Dixon gave a sermon on August 8, 1977, about homosexuality:

"When they say homosexuals should have their civil rights, I ask one question: Do you give criminals rights like honest citizens? Absolutely not! Criminals do not have their civil rights," he intoned.

"I say either fry 'em or put them in the pen," he continued. "Don't unleash them on the human race."

Most chilling, Dixon told church-goers, "I don't know how in the world you can get a society that won't even put these murderers to death. I don't know how you can ever get them to put these homosexuals to death. But God's Word would uphold that. They which commit such things are worthy of death."

Anyone who reads the Old and New Testaments knows that Dixon's use of the bible to defend his murderous impulses is absolutely warranted; there is no other way to interpret the bible's words on homosexuality.

With close to 40 percent of our nation's people reporting a literal acceptance of the teachings of the bible, it is clear a campaign calculated to ignite "closet" homophobia is going to present a grave threat to the well-being of lesbians and gay men.*

---

* One of the nation's most appalling hate crimes involved gay college student Matthew Shepard, 21. Shepard was brutally pistol-whipped, and left to die hanging on a fence in rural Wyoming on October 6, 1998. Critically wounded, he was discovered 18 hours later, and died on October 12. His youthful murderers, Aaron McKinney and Russell A. Henderson, are both serving life sentences. (Incidentally, Henderson is an Eagle Scout with Boy Scouts of America, a religious organization that requires members to believe in God, and which successfully took its quest to bar "undesirables," such as gays and atheists, to the U.S. Supreme Court in 2000.)

Rev. Fred Phelps, a religious fanatic and founder of the notorious Westboro Baptist Church of Topeka, Kansas, picketed Shepard's funeral with signs saying Shepard deserved to die. The publicity-hungry fundamentalist hate-monger has carried his celebration of Shepard's death to grotesque extremes.

15

So much for
Christian apologia

*He that is without sin among you, let him first
cast a stone at her.*
—John 8:7

*There is neither Jew nor Greek, there is
neither bond nor free, there is neither male nor
female: for ye are all one in Christ Jesus.*
—Galatians 3:28

FOR FEMINIST FREETHINKERS the above verses
may be more provoking than any of the other passages about
women previously cited in this book. Why? Because these are
the verses repeatedly exhumed by bible apologists to counter
accusations that the bible is sexist. No matter that you may
have just listed a string of biblical denunciations of the female
sex, or citations of Mosaic law relegating women to the status of
slaves. To the religionist who is supposedly interested in
women's rights, these passages, they say, make up for all the un-
fairness, barbarisms and inequities which have preceded.

Should they, in fact, make up for the sexism of the bible?

Jesus' advice about casting stones comes about under
some duress, as Elizabeth Cady Stanton pointed out in *The
Woman's Bible*. The Scribes and Pharisees, enemies of Jesus,
approach him for advice about how to punish a woman accused
of adultery, which Stanton called "a plan to draw Jesus into a
snare."

As she pointed out, had Jesus said the woman should

either be killed or set free, he would have been assuming the power of the state. Had he refused to offer an opinion his credibility as the "son of God" would have been ruined. Hence, his response can be interpreted as politically astute hedging — to save his own skin.

Jesus can be given brownie points for acumen (if he really said those words), but can he really be given credit for feminism? Even if one rejects Stanton's commonsensical interpretation of this passage, one may still find Jesus' philosophy to be sorely flawed.

He put a woman's life at risk when he qualified, "He that is without sin among you . . ." Suppose the crowd had contained smug males who believed they had never "sinned" and would have been happy to harm a "sinner" with impunity.

Why didn't Jesus simply point out it's not nice to throw stones?

Why didn't he take this opportunity to amend "the law" which forbade all adultery regardless of circumstances, and which punished its commission with death? This was Jesus' chance to install a new order, a more tolerant law which did not invade the privacy of his people or condemn adulterers to death, and, after that, to hell.

Why didn't Jesus condemn the double standard, which resulted in punishing adulteresses, but not adulterers?

We must remember the words attributed to Jesus:

"Think not that I am come to destroy the law, or the prophets: I am not come to destroy, but to fulfill.

"For verily I say unto you, Till heaven and earth pass, one jot or one tittle shall in no wise pass from the law, till all be fulfilled." *Matthew 5:17–18*

Jesus may have occasionally placed a different emphasis on the Mosaic code but he never denounced it. This passage obviously shows more tolerance and compassion toward women than most bible passages. But it is difficult to view it as anything more significant than a clever way to avoid denouncing the Mosaic code, a code which Jesus supposedly wrote himself if one believes the "trinity" concept.

And yet, for this oblique kindness, women are expected to

figuratively kneel before Jesus and kiss his feet, as we are told one "sinning" woman did.

The other oft-cited passage of the bible is praised because it says "there is neither male nor female: for ye are all one in Jesus Christ."

Why are we expected to applaud this passage? Because it shows that women may be "saved"? The Judeo-Christian religion would be barbaric indeed if it said otherwise. Or because it says Jesus will not hold it against anyone for being Greek, enslaved or female? Why should he?

In fact, this passage tacitly condones the artificially set standards and divisions between people. Jesus called the Greeks (non-Jews) "dogs," in another passage. *Mark 7:25–30* Here Paul is indicating that even "dogs" may be saved provided they adopt his tenets. Instead of condemning servitude and slavery, Paul is merely ensuring a slave that he or she may also enter into his kingdom, providing. . . .

Religionists who cite this passage for its wonderful implications deserve a dose of their own medicine, for it is necessary to point out that the quotation should be read in its context. The entire chapter is a rationalization explaining somewhat tortuously why it is suddenly possible for those who are not the seed of Abraham to become chosen people. Its meaning is clearly that even women may become Christians, as the verses which precede and follow it make clear: "For as many of you as have been baptized into Christ have put on Christ . . . And if you be Christ's, then are ye Abraham's seed, and heirs according to the promise." *Galatians 3:27–29*

Frankly, its reassurance that even women may be accepted into the flock is insulting. Religionists who expect women to get down on their hands and knees to "thank the Lord" for this dubious privilege are kidding themselves. At most, this passage may give consolation to devoutly religious women who obey the otherwise stifling and scornful tenets of the bible. If it can fuel the cause of female religionists fighting for equal status in their male-dominated religion, so be it. But what self-respecting women would wish to become party to one of the most effective tools ever created for woman's subjection — the Judeo-

Christian religion?

Feminist "salvation"

This section originally appeared in The Humanist Magazine, July/August 1988.

Freethought and feminism, to borrow the words of a song, ought to go together like a horse and carriage: you can't have one without the other. How can you be a freethinker if you are content that half of the human race is subjugated? And how can you be a feminist if you refuse to defer to men on Earth but submit to a divine authority? Very often, one heresy will give birth to the other. On one side of the continuum is a feminist taking his or her first wobbly steps away from religion; on the other end is a nontheist taking his or her first baby steps toward feminism.

Yet, "feminist theology" is a burgeoning field which, at its most radical, makes strong contributions to feminism but ultimately leads feminists astray. Its strongest seduction is the popular belief (or consolation) that "Jesus was a feminist." This is an assertion keeping many Christian women in their places.

It is a mark of the depths of biblical misogyny and women's internalization of it that women still find succor in the scanty references to Jesus and women in the New Testament. We are expected to delight in the fact that the bible says Jesus talked to women! Jesus befriended a prostitute! Jesus even touched an "unclean" woman! (The mystery is not that he should have reportedly done these things but that he didn't do more.)

But the crowning glory, we are told, is found in two New Testament passages. The first reads: "There is neither Jew nor Greek, there is neither bond nor free, there is neither male nor female; for we are all one in Jesus Christ." *Galatians 3:28* The context is a contrived rationalization about why people who are not of the "seed of Abraham" can become chosen people. Its meaning: that women and slaves can also be baptized and go to heaven.

Jesus offered "pie in the sky" egalitarianism for souls in heaven but not on earth, never condemning servitude or slavery.

The second oft-quoted verse is John 8:7: "He that is without sin among you, let him first cast a first stone at her." A woman has been taken in adultery (the adulterer being conspicuous by his absence). The mob convenes to stone her, in accordance with Mosaic law. Jesus, our hero, intercedes, and his supposed wisdom saves the day as the woman's would-be executioners depart. On first glance, a woman's life has been spared and the old code amended. However, from a moral standpoint, the actions of Jesus gambled with a woman's life. Why not point out that it is barbaric to throw stones? If the biblical Jesus were such a great reformer, why did he not take this opportunity to condemn such laws, the death penalty, and the threat of hellfire thereafter?

An interpolation

It might dampen feminist enthusiasm further to know that the passage is a widely-acknowledged interpolation. *The Catholic Encyclopedia*, according to Joseph Wheless in *Forgery in Christianity* (1930), admits that John 8:7 was long considered "spurious" until the Council of Trent declared it "divine truth" in 1546. Danish scholar Georg Brandes wrote in *Jesus: A Myth* (1926 translation):

> It does not appear in the oldest and most reliable manuscripts, and the awkward manner of its insertion breaks the continuity of the story. And the outcome of the incident, with the escape of the woman, is highly improbable. Her executioners would undoubtedly have regarded themselves as sufficiently free from sin and would not have let their victim go merely because a man without any authority urged them to break the Law by letting mercy take precedence of justice.

Nor can this passage be reconciled with Matthew 5:17–18

in which Jesus declares that he came to uphold every jot and tittle of "the law." That law, the Mosaic code, was male supremacist, patriarchal, and based upon blind obedience to a male god. Not only that but, according to the doctrine of the trinity, Jesus wrote that dastardly law himself. He had to uphold it!

As for anecdotal references to women, Jesus' cold question to his own mother, "Woman, what have I to do with thee?" (*John 2:4*) could well be the motto of Christianity. Jesus clearly denounced fertility and goddess worship when he refused to bless his mother. A woman in the crowd had cried out for him to bless "the womb that bare thee, and the paps which thou hast sucked.'" He replied, "Yea, rather, blessed are they who hear the word of God and keep it." *Luke 11:27–28* That word, in a nutshell, is patriarchy.

Regardless of one's interpretation, how could two "feminist" verses possibly erase, excuse, or supercede the misogyny and sexism in the rest of the bible?

But the real issue is not how to interpret John or Galatians or how much evidence one can stack up for or against a feminist reading of Jesus. Either feminism is valid on its own merits or it isn't. Since when do feminists look for male approval before taking a stand? Since when do they defer to male authority? That is like the kid who says, "I'm running away from home, but I'm not allowed to cross the street."

Feminism cannot be argued by authority — much less by male, supernatural authority. Argument by authority is the opposite of feminism. If Jesus had existed and if he had been a feminist, he would have eschewed such arguments himself.

Ultimately, the reason church women are so hung up on the question is because they know that women's voices count for little within the church. They hope that, by invoking a male authority on their side, they can persuade the church fathers to change. But by playing patriarchy's game, they lose. The church depends upon women worshipping "Jesus" and working within the church for its survival.

Let's forget about the mythical Jesus and look for encouragement, solace, and inspiration from real women, people such as Elizabeth Cady Stanton, our own mothers, reformers, rebels, and thinkers who have left behind historic records, good deeds, and literature. Two thousand years of disastrous patriarchal rule under the shadow of the cross ought to be enough to turn women toward the feminist "salvation" of this world.

16 AN OPEN LETTER

Rethinking the Sermon on the Mount

METHODIST HILLARY RODHAM CLINTON, as the wife of President William Clinton, was interviewed by Newsweek's religious religion editor Ken Woodward about her "spiritual life." After keeping him at bay for three months, Rodham Clinton succumbed and consented to an interview (Oct. 31, 1994).

She spoke sympathetically of the religious views of the right, saying they are unfairly stereotyped. She endorsed intercessory prayer, saying a group of friends prayed for her and the president. When asked about her favorite bible passages, she had the grace to sidestep the question, but said at the moment she was thinking about the Sermon on the Mount. To her credit she found Matthew 5, 6 and 7 "filled with challenge," and "very hard to read . . . and fully understand."

In response, I sent her the following letter.

Dear Ms. Clinton:

I re-examined the bible passages you singled out as of special interest in your Newsweek interview. I never had much patience for the Beatitudes, which open chapter 5, because the only pay-off for the meek is in heaven, which is too little, too late. This kind of pie-in-the-sky promise kept the enslaved African-Americans in line, and has tantalized the oppressed with empty promises. While I can see, given the persecution you have endured, how you might find comfort in the beatitude blessing "they which are persecuted," isn't it ironic that your persecutors are almost all "righteous" Christians?

The Jesus of the New Testament next says he came to fulfill "the law" of Moses, which I find especially troubling, given the many unsavory injunctions, such as to kill stubborn sons (*Deuteronomy 21:18–21*), homosexuals (*Leviticus 20:13*), blasphemers (*Leviticus 24:16*) and those of other faiths (*Deuteronomy 7:1–8*) — all of which have been obeyed in the past by muscular Christians.

Surely you do not agree that getting angry with a brother is nearly as bad as killing him? Or that you should go to hell for calling somebody a fool (which, incidentally, Jesus himself does, see Matthew 23:17)?

Do you agree that "lusting in one's heart" is the same as committing adultery?

If Newsweek had asked my opinion, I would have said that Matthew 5 contains one of my *least* favorite bible passages:

"And if thy right eye offend thee, pluck it out, and cast it from thee: for it is profitable for thee that one of thy members should perish, and not that thy whole body should be cast into hell.

"And if thy right hand offend thee, cut it off," etc. *Matthew 5:29–30*

Methodists probably find nonliteral ways to deal with this grisly passage, but the fact is that it continues to inspire chilling mutilations and self-mutilations. Like you, I find this passage "very hard to read."

The next piece of advice is mischief-making and unegalitarian — the proviso against divorce unless a fornicating wife is to blame, of course.

Jesus advises us not to resist evil. Isn't that evil advice? Should we not rescue an abused child or resist a murderous dictator? If someone hit your cheek, would you turn the other? Isn't that masochistic? If someone made you walk a mile under duress, would you go an extra with your kidnapper? Is that what you teach your daughter? Do you think we should always give or lend *whatever* is asked? If we lose a civil lawsuit, should we pay twice as much as we are fined?!

Perhaps the counsel to "love your enemies," if followed, could help prevent wars, but wouldn't it be more practical to end the enmity rather than to pretend a phony "love"? Consider the way Christians can interpret this verse, such as Roy McMillan, the man who directs Christian Action Group and has threatened the life of the President and Supreme Court justices. He regards physicians who perform abortions as his enemy and recently told NBC that when you murder doctors, "you should do it in love." Nor is this helpful advice to the religious battered woman. One is loathe to think of your husband following such advice too closely in his dealings with the opposition! Do we really want our president "doing good" to opposition leader Newt Gingrich, who would subvert our secular democracy? Wouldn't that be at the expense of the country?

One Christian teaching we freethinkers can heartily endorse leads off Chapter 6, in which Jesus rebukes hypocrites who pray in public:

"And when thou prayest, thou shalt not be as the hypocrites are: for they love to pray standing in the synagogues and in the corners of the streets, that they may be seen of men. . . .

"But thou, when thou prayest, enter into thy closet, and when thou hast shut thy door, pray to thy Father which is in secret; and thy Father which seeth in secret shall reward thee openly."

We hope Mr. Clinton and other politicians will re-read this verse before making further comments on the proposed school prayer amendment!

The following verses I also find "filled with challenge." After the Lord's Prayer and some gobbledy-gook about light and darkness, Jesus resumes his impractical instructions for life: take no thought for tomorrow, your life, your next meal and drink, your clothing, "for the morrow shall take thought for the things of itself." Handy if you are a lily of the field but a good way to starve if you're an ordinary human who can't change water into wine and bread into a banquet!

Chapter 7 brings us the famous injunction, much appreciated by black collar criminals, "Judge not, that ye be not judged." We don't need a god to tell us it is best not to be hypercritical of other people's harmless habits, or that it is hypocritical to criticize others for things we do ourselves. But this sweeping generality strikes me as corrupting and cowardly. Should we turn off our powers of critical thought out of fear of others turning the same scrutiny toward us? Isn't this self-serving? If we followed this advice, our jury system of criminal justice would fall!

Not pretty is Jesus' injunction, "Give not that which is holy unto the dogs" (dogs being a slur for Gentiles).

I admit to rather fancying the saying, "neither cast ye your pearls before swine," however unfair to pigs, just as the warning about false prophets, (wolves in sheep's clothing) is enduring imagery. But the warning hasn't hurt Pat Robertson's credibility any.

Matthew 7:9 reads: "Or what man is there of you, whom if his son ask bread, will he give him a stone?" Feminist Sonia Johnson pointed out that a stone was all the Mormon church offered women seeking equal rights. It could well serve as a metaphor for the treatment of women by Christianity as a whole, don't you think?

The parlor trick, "seek and ye shall find," I could do without. It inspired that awful campfire song. Of course, its promise of salvation for all is contradicted later in 7:14, with its odious predestination: "Because strait is the gate, and narrow is the way, which leadeth unto life, and few there be that find it."

If we judge Christianity by Matthew 7:16–20, "by their fruits ye shall know them," wouldn't we have to admit that it doesn't pass muster?

Consider the Dark Ages, the Inquisition, witch-hunting, the eradication of heretics, the schisms and doctrinal disputes. Hasn't the church stood in the way of nearly every humanistic reform and endeavor, past and present? Mainstream Christianity opposed abolition of slavery, equality for women, free inquiry and scientific pursuits. Today's fanatics oppose a secular constitution, reproductive rights and many civil rights.

As James Madison wrote in the 1785 *Memorial & Remonstrance:* "During almost fifteen centuries has the legal establishment of Christianity been on trial. What has been its fruits? More or less, in all places, pride and indolence in the clergy; ignorance and servility in the laity; in both, superstition, bigotry and persecution." It is as vital today that we keep religion out of government as it was in Madison's era.

The Sermon on the Mount ends with more veiled threats about what will happen to those of us who do not "do the will of my Father." When this nation was founded, we threw off the tyrant. Why then is it still acceptable to *worship* a tyrant seeking converts through threats that reach beyond the grave?

Sincere Christians certainly have their work cut out for them in separating the biblical wheat from the chaff. Any good is spoiled by the spectre of a vindictive god paranoically insisting that anyone who does not submit to his will and confusing decrees "is in danger of hell fire."

You are a praiseworthy person, but unfortunately the same cannot be said of your god. You ask your religion for substance. It gives you a stone, and its most ardent supporters *throw* them.

Annie Laurie Gaylor, editor
Freethought Today

Hillary Rodham Clinton needs freedom from religion!

The following news item originally ran in Freethought Today, May 1994. It is a reminder of the religious-right hysteria that greeted the nominally liberal Clinton Administration, and the continuing pathological hatred by some religionists of a strong and successful woman.

For many news columnists, it's been time to "Pillory Hillary" since 1992, but the most libelous, vituperative, and hateful attacks on the First Lady, naturally, come from the religious press, who regard Hillary Rodham Clinton as a 20th-century Jezebel. A smart, independent, successful, competent and attractive First Lady who has a genuine partnership with her husband has brought out the worst of the paranoid religious misogynists. The February issue of Newswatch Magazine, "A magazine making clear todays [sic] news in the light of Bible Prophecy," contains a deranged 17-page diatribe based on a polemical book, *Big Sister Is Watching You: Hillary Clinton and The White House Feminists Who Now Control America — And Tell the President What To Do* by Texe Marrs. The gist is that Hillary Clinton fulfills the dire biblical prophecy in Isaiah 3:12, where "women rule over them."

This rag out of Texas spouts: ". . . Hillary Clinton is not just a case of a strong and masculine woman nagging and controlling an effeminate, wimp of a man who just happens to be her husband. Hillary has her own secret agenda, and she has recruited and empowered a loyalist clique of radical lesbian and feminist women to assist her in carrying out that covert agenda."

"Hillary's Hellcats," we are informed, are "psychopaths" conspiring to "set up a New World Order — an order in which feminist ideals shall reign supreme." (This is quite flattering to the reputed influence of feminists!)

You can get the drift just by scanning the subtitles: "Hillary: On the Killing of Babies" (this is where a fundamentalist swears Hillary told her "It is God's law to kill babies"), "Hillary: On Lesbianism and Homosexuality" ("It is Hillary that is pushing the White House's homosexual agenda"); "Hillary the Marxist/Communist," et cetera, ad nauseum. She is even accused of being "at the vanguard of devilish practices."

Next, we have the charge that Hillary Clinton "Speaks with the Ghost of Eleanor Roosevelt," and therefore is engaged in necromancy, an "abomination." *Deuteronomy 18:11* This, because she once joked to a reporter from *USA Today* that she had "imaginary conversations" with Eleanor Roosevelt to help her through the traumatic campaign. Her affinity with Eleanor Roosevelt is more grist for the mill, since Eleanor Roosevelt is dismissed as a "Communist, Lesbian, Radical Feminist."

Worst of all, it seems, is that Hillary Clinton is not a Southern Baptist! No, this uppity woman goes to the uppity United Methodist Church. Clear evidence, we are informed, that "a New Age goddess sits in the White House." (This must be news to the Methodist Church.) There isn't space to summarize the vile references to Roberta Achtenberg, Assistant Secretary of HUD ("Promoting the Pedophile Agenda"), but suffice it to say this is propaganda on par with the anti-Semitic Nazi tracts.

Most creepy is a section filled with libel that ends up comparing Hillary Clinton to Jezebel. Given Jezebel's gruesome fate in the bible, this is chilling. Why should loose cannons be permitted to indulge in this extreme of hate-mongering and libel under the tax-exempt aegis of religion?

17 RELIGIOUS TERRORISM
The religious war against women

*In the early days of woman-suffrage agitation,
I saw that the greatest obstacle we had to
overcome was the bible. It was hurled at us on
every side.*

> —*Elizabeth Cady Stanton*
> *An interview with the Chicago Record*
> *June 29, 1897*

The following speech was delivered on March 14, 1998, from the pulpit of the historic Sixteenth Avenue Baptist Church in Birmingham, Alabama. The occasion was the "week of remembrance and renewal" hosted by the Emergency Coalition for Choice, responding to the January 29 bombing of a Birmingham abortion clinic, which killed guard Robert Sanderson and brutally maimed nurse Emily Lyons. Other speakers on the occasion included Gloria Steinem; Frances Kissling, president, Catholics for a Free Choice; Vicki Saporta, executive director, National Abortion Federation; David Gunn Jr., son of Dr. David Gunn, murdered March 10, 1993, in Pensacola; and the Rev. Carlton Veazy, executive director, Religious Coalition for Choice.

THE GROUP I represent, the Freedom From Religion Foundation, came into existence in part because of the abortion movement, because of the organized religious opposition to abortion rights. My mother, Anne Gaylor, in working for the repeal of antiabortion laws in Wisconsin in the late sixties soon realized that the true enemy of abortion rights and all women's rights was organized religion.

Virtually every vocal opponent of contraception and abortion for the past 30 years argues against these rights on the basis of God and the bible. There were many fine organizations working for women's rights, but none, we felt, getting at the root cause of women's oppression — patriarchal religion and its incursions upon our secular laws. So that's why I'm here today.

The primary organized opposition to reproductive rights in this country always has been religion. In fact, we are in the midst of a religious war not just against abortion rights, but women's rights in general, not just in our country, but worldwide.

In this country, the religious terrorism is directed at birth control and abortion clinics, their patients, medical providers and staff. In Alabama, it is the Army of God bombing abortion clinics. In Algeria, it is terrorists from similarly named groups who are shooting schoolgirls on the streets for not wearing veils.

In America, the foot soldiers of the religious right are engaged in their campaigns of terrorism, harassment, stalking, arsons, bombing, murder, trying to close down legal abortion clinics by force. They do all these things in the name of God. In Afghanistan, the radical Islamic Taliban that has taken over that country is literally halting all medical care for women — the hospitals in the capital city are already closed to women. They've done this, and worse, in the name of Allah.

Islamic fundamentalist theocrats openly talk of jihad, a holy war. So does Patrick Buchanan, who has called for a Christian jihad in this country.

Whether declared or undeclared, there is nothing new in this religious war against women. After the organized women's movement was officially launched 150 years ago this year, Elizabeth Cady Stanton said the "bible was hurled at us on every side." Every freedom won for women in this country, small or large — from wearing bloomers to riding bicycles to not wearing bonnets in church, to being permitted to speak in public, to attend universities, to enter professions, to vote and own property — was opposed by the churches. In the 1970s and '80s, it was the churches — Roman Catholic, fundamentalist Protestant and Mormon — which marshalled political forces to defeat the Equal Rights Amendment.

And the most important right women have strived to obtain is the right to decide if and when to become mothers. Foes of women's freedom know that controlling women's reproduction is the ultimate way to control women. That is why when it comes to abortion, religious opponents are not just hurling bibles. They are hurtling bombs.

This is a *religious* war against women because it relies on threats, force, violence, harassment, terrorism. Pascal said: "Men never do evil so completely and cheerfully as when they do it from religious conviction." And Voltaire reportedly observed that people who believe in absurdities will commit atrocities.

What happened on January 29 was an atrocity. It painfully reopens wounds of all the other atrocities here in Birmingham and elsewhere, also directed against civil rights, especially what happened to four young girls bombed in this church 35 years ago. Violent extremists who oppose equality such as the Army of God and the KKK, are always convinced they are acting in the name of God.

Let me acknowledge the great historic work of the Southern Christian Leadership Coalition, that was headquartered here, and say a grateful word for the work of Religious Coalition for Abortion Rights, Fran Kissling of Catholics for a Free Choice, and anyone of any belief who does not let dogma get in the way of humanity. It is vital in the abortion debate that the mainstreamers and liberal religionists do not yield the moral high ground or let the crazies and fanatics speak for them.

But neither should we let the political debate deteriorate into a contest between believers who say God supports a woman's right, versus the implacable orthodox who scream that abortion is a sin.

Because that's a battle that has no place in our capitol buildings, should not be fought, and can never be won. No two denominations, no two clergy, no two biblical interpretations, seemingly can agree. Where there is one religious authority, there will always be a contrary religious authority. In our secular country, we are all free to believe what we like, but our government must remain above the religious fray.

And that's women's salvation — our precious, uniquely American principle of the separation of church and state.

Our constitution says you cannot legislate your religion. Belief that a "human being exists at conception" is a matter of faith, not *fact*.

You cannot shut down an abortion clinic because *your* church or your pastor or your holy book opposes abortion.

Our government cannot issue a divine fiat saying *when* a soul exists, or *that* a soul exists.

Despite what the Ten Commandments and Judge Roy Moore and Alabama Gov. James and State Attorney General Pryor and the Christian Coalition and the Christian Family Alliance say, in America, we can have as many gods as we like, or none at all.

Women and the men who support women's rights must make it our business to protect our First Amendment, because it protects us. We must fortify the wall of separation between church and state, because it is the only barrier, I repeat, *it is the only barrier*, standing between women's rights and a holy war.

Let's take a cue from the great civil rights movement of the sixties, and keep our eyes on the prize — freedom. As Margaret Sanger said: "No woman can call herself free who does not own and control her own body. No woman can call herself free until she can choose consciously whether she will or will not be a mother."

As we renew our support, we pay homage to the remarkable courage and commitment of Emily Lyons. We renew our support in memory of Robert Sanderson, in memory of Dr. Gunn of Pensacola, in memory of all the women who have died from illegal abortions, the 200,000 women who die every year worldwide because abortion remains illegal or inaccessible. We renew our support in defense of women's lives.

Adlai Stevenson once wrote:

> It is a common heresy and its graves are to be found all over the earth. It is the heresy that says you can kill an idea by killing a man, defeat a principle by defeating a person, bury truth by burying its vehicle.

> Man may burn his brother at the stake, but he cannot reduce truth to ashes; he may murder his fellow man with a shot in the back, but he does not murder justice.

18 GUEST "SERMON"

The rising of the women . . .

This article by Dan Barker was first published in Freethought Today, June/July 1997.

IN APRIL, Annie Laurie Gaylor and I were guests on the Richard Randell radio show in Colorado Springs, primarily to discuss her new book, *Women Without Superstition: "No Gods – No Masters."* Quoting such verses as, "Let the woman learn in silence with all subjection," Annie Laurie showed how scripture has been used to keep women subservient to men.

One of the women who called into the show claimed that she feels blessed to be under the loving authority of her Christian husband, and that the actual Greek words used in the bible imply more of a partnership than a master-slave relationship. After Annie Laurie gave numerous historical and biblical examples of religion's harm to women, an impatient male caller asked, "What are the qualifications of this lady in spewing her venom against the bible?"

"I think it's the other way around," Annie Laurie countered. "The bible is pornographic when it comes to descriptions of women. It talks about 'God' raping women. It talks about . . ."

"But I want to know what your qualifications are."

"I am a feminist and a human being who has a right to judge this book," she responded.

"Have you read the Greek? Do you know the Greek?" he pressed, in a paternalistic tone. "There is nowhere it says 'be subservient.' I don't know where you all got that wording."

"Well, 'subjection' is the word," Annie Laurie continued, "and it means the same thing."

"Oh, no, no, no," he insisted. "See, you need to go find your Greek, my dear. Go find the Greek word, and then you will know what that word is."

"What is that Greek word?" I asked, jumping in.

"I don't have the Greek word in front of me," he said, unfazed, "but if you want to be that critical, before you attackle [sic] the enemy, first learn what the enemy knows."

"I think before you talk about the bible," Annie Laurie suggested, "you'd better read *Women Without Superstition* and read the writings of 50 women who have analyzed religion from the woman's point of view, or otherwise you do not have the authority to talk about it."

"I wouldn't read your trash," he snorted.

His message was clear: how dare a mere woman judge the bible for herself, disagreeing with millennia of male scholarship! Women should be thankful to find their rank in society, happy to learn where they fit into the "Father's" plan, fulfilled in their role as supporters of men who, as "heads" of women, have more responsibility.

I didn't have my Greek text with me, so I wasn't able to look up those verses on the air, but when I got home I did a little research. I had taken two years of New Testament Greek in preparation for the ministry.

The main New Testament word that shows the relationship between women and men is *hypotasso*, which means "submit" and "obey." Judge for yourself whether the bible's use of *hypotasso* (identified by the boldfaced words below) indicates woman's subservience:

"Let your women keep silent in the churches: for it is not permitted unto them to speak; but they are commanded to be under **obedience,** as also saith the law. And if they will learn anything, let them ask their husbands at home: for it is a shame for women to speak in the church." *1 Corinthians 14:34–35*

"Let the woman learn in silence with all **subjection.** But I suffer not a woman to teach, nor to usurp authority over the man, but to be in silence." *1 Timothy 2:11–12*

"Wives, **submit** yourselves unto your own husbands, as unto the Lord. For the husband is the head of the wife, even as Christ is the head of the church . . . Therefore as the church is **subject** unto Christ, so let the wives be to their own husbands in every thing." *Ephesians 5:22–24*

"Wives, **submit** yourselves unto your own husbands, as it is fit in the Lord." *Colossians 3:18*

"Likewise, ye wives, be in **subjection** to your own husbands." *1 Peter 3:1*

"That they [aged women] may teach the young women to be sober, to love their husbands, to love their children, To be discreet, chaste, keepers at home, **obedient** to their own husbands, that the word of God be not blasphemed." *Titus 2:4–5*

W.E. Vine, in *An Expository Dictionary of New Testament Words*, writes: "HYPOTASSO, primarily a military term, to rank under (*hypo*, under, *tasso*, to arrange), denotes (a) to put in subjection, to subject . . . 'subdue' . . . (b) in the Middle or Passive voice, to subject oneself, to obey, be subject to . . . See OBEDIENT, SUBMIT."

The *American Heritage Dictionary* defines "obey" as: "1. To carry out or fulfill the command, order, or instruction of." It defines "submit" as: "1. To yield or surrender (oneself) to the will or authority of another."

This hardly suggests partnership! Nowhere in the bible are men told to "hypotasso" to women.

We don't need to look outside the New Testament to see that *hypotasso* means total subservience:

"Exhort servants [slaves] to be **obedient** unto their own masters, and to please them well in all things; not answering again." *Titus 2:9*

"Servants, be **subject** to your masters with all fear; not only to the good and gentle, but also to the froward. For this is thankworthy, if a man for conscience toward God endure grief, suffering wrongfully." *1 Peter 2:18–19* ("Froward" means "stubbornly contrary and disobedient; obstinate." *AHD*)

"A bishop must . . . rule well his own house, having his children in **subjection** with all gravity; (For if a man know not how to rule his own house, how shall he take care of the church of

God?)" *1 Timothy 3:2–5*

"**Submit** yourselves to every ordinance of man for the Lord's sake: whether it be to the king, as supreme, Or unto governors, as unto them that are sent by him for the punishment of evildoers." *1 Peter 2:13–14*

"Let every soul be **subject** unto the higher powers. . . . Whosoever therefore resisteth the power, resisteth the ordinance of God: and they that resist shall receive to themselves damnation." *Romans 13:1*

"Put them in mind to be **subject** to principalities and powers, to obey magistrates." *Titus 3:1*

"Likewise, ye younger, **submit** yourselves unto the elder." *1 Peter 5:5*

"The Lord Jesus Christ . . . is able even to **subdue** all things unto himself." *Philippians 3:20–21*

"For unto the angels hath he [Lord] put in **subjection** the world to come." *Hebrews 2:5*

"And the seventy returned again with joy, saying, Lord, even the devils are **subject** unto us through thy name." *Luke 10:17*

These verses all use *hypotasso:* to put "under." Women are told to submit to men with the same Greek word used to direct slaves under masters, youth under elders, subjects under kings, criminals under the law. What could be worse? Could there be any stronger evidence that Christian women are meant to be subservient?

The New Testament gives a vivid example of how women should submit:

"For after this manner in the old time the holy women also, who trusted in God, adorned themselves, being in **subjection** [*hypotasso*] unto their own husbands. Even as Sara obeyed [*hypakouo*] Abraham, calling him lord." *1 Peter 3:5–6* How exactly did Sara obey Abraham? Without objecting, she allowed herself to be pimped to King Abimelech, passed off as Abraham's "sister." *Genesis 20:1–11*

That word "obey" (*hypakouo*) is used in many other New Testament verses, such as "Children, **obey** your parents in the Lord" (*Ephesians 6:1*) and "Servants, **obey** in all things your masters" (*Colossians 3:22*). Are these examples of a "part-nership"?

Not all of the callers to that radio show were hostile. Foundation member Jan Brazill phoned in to say, "I've been one of the lucky ones to have already started reading Annie Laurie's book, and it is great. I'm struck by the fact that these women, way back, were fighting against the servitude, and everything that the bible commands of women, speaking out in public and all that. Now we have a group such as the Promise Keepers who are advocating the very same thing.

"What worries me," Jan continued, "is that women are not suitably worried about this. They seem to just go along and take everything for granted. I do think that reading the book that Annie Laurie Gaylor has edited — reading all these writings of women in ages past and the battles that they had to fight — should inspire us, that we need to be vigilant."

19 CONCLUSION

The only feminist

IT WOULD BE blasphemy indeed to write about the bible's treatment of women without putting in a kind word for Queen Vashti. In a book wherein most women are nameless, and which presents models such as "Potiphar's wife" who falsely cries rape and gets the kindly Joseph imprisoned, Queen Vashti is refreshing. She is "the first feminist," but her fate is not so pleasant as her presence.

Religious little girls are taught to admire the likes of Esther. Yet Vashti remains an obscure figure even though she is also described in the Book of Esther.

Persian King Ahasuerus, after a seven-day fete of drinking, orders that Vashti "shew the people and the princes her beauty." Vashti demonstrates her self-respect by refusing to do so, and so starts the great male panic of the bible.

Not only does Ahasuerus "burn with anger," but his advisors quake in their biblical equivalent of boots at the thought of the uprising which her disobedience will inspire.

"For this deed of the queen shall come abroad unto all women, so that they shall despise their husbands in their eyes, when it shall be reported, The King Ahasuerus commanded Vashti the queen to be brought in before him, but she came not."

Therefore the king is advised to issue a public decree dethroning Vashti, also ordering "all the wives shall give to their husbands honor, both to great and small." So diligent are they in averting a mass rebellion before it happens that they considerately translate a decree ordering every man to "bear rule in his own house" in every language spoken in the kingdom.

The king announces a "virgin contest," in which officers gather all the "fair young virgins" to the palace, where they undergo stringent purification. One by one he tries them out, selecting Esther, not knowing she is an Israelite. By this route did one of the bible's greatest heroines attain her power. What did she do with it? She was able to rescue her people from a plot to slaughter them, but became herself the cause of the slaughter of tens of thousands of people including "both little ones and women."

While the story does not end with a feminist uprising or personal victory for courageous Vashti (for all we know she is not only dethroned but beheaded) it is still comforting to feminists today to know that not all biblical women behaved as doormats. The story also demonstrates the way in which bible patriarchs deliberately oppressed women (accounting for their paranoia about a female uprising). The subjection of woman was not *natural* — as some biological historians theorize. It did not come about because women were, by virtue of their fertile bodies, innately domestic, home-loving "frail vessels" in need of protection. Female subjection came about deliberately, with forethought and malice, and the rules of the Old and New Testaments were written, interpreted and twisted to maintain that subjection.

* * *

Reading the bible can be a grueling, tiresome, unpleasant task for a freethinker, as heart-breaking as it is eye-opening about the Judeo-Christian doctrines which have caused much calamity and which fundamentalists seek to entangle with our secular government.

The teachings of the bible are grist for the mill for those interested in keeping women in a subordinate position. It is important for feminists to recognize the heavy role the bible has played in oppressing women, in perpetuating stereotypes and misogyny. The laws we live under today did not spring from a void, but reflect our patriarchal heritage. Understanding the insidious way in which many laws still reflect the mindset of the bible era may not provide direct practical aid in eradicating those laws. But it should help women to examine current laws for residual biblical problems and influence, and should serve as a warning to feminists to beware of further encroachments by religions upon civil law. Unfortunately, it is still true today that women must continue to rebel against unfair treatment just as Queen Vashti — the bible's only feminist — allegedly rebelled ages ago.

20 EPILOGUE
The Continuing Threat

*I have endeavoured to dissipate these
religious superstitions from the minds of
women, and base their faith on science and
reason, where I found for myself at last that
peace and comfort I could never find in the
Bible and the church. . . . The less they believe,
the better for their own happiness and
development. . .*

*For fifty years the women of this nation
have tried to dam up this deadly stream that
poisons all their lives, but thus far they have
lacked the insight or courage to follow it back
to its source and there strike the blow at the
fountain of all tyranny, religious
superstition, priestly power, and the canon
law.*

— *Elizabeth Cady Stanton*
"The Degraded Status of
Woman in the Bible," 1896

IT IS AMAZING how little the religious stranglehold on
women's rights has altered since 1981, when *Woe to the Women*
was first published. It is daunting to consider the continuing
power of patriarchal religion over the lives of women in the
twenty-first century.

We see depressing images in the news of women's thralldom to dogma, such as when thousands of otherwise meek Muslim women demonstrated in the streets of Paris in late 2003, demanding to wear veils, shouting without an ounce of conscious irony: "My veil, my choice." These Muslim Myrmidons parade a symbol of religious submission as slaves might kiss their shackles.

The very origin of the word religion, *religare*, means "to bind," which in turn means "to hold, to make prisoner, to restrain." Patriarchal religion worldwide has, over the course of human history, been largely successful in making women prisoner to such doctrines as original sin. The most blatant modern example is the dehumanizing burqa imposed by the Afghan Taliban, narrowing women's world to one obscured eye-hole. Has there ever been a more overt metaphor for the power of religion to enslave women?

Religion's most insidious success has not been to confine women's bodies but to imprison women's minds. Women such as the Parisian Muslims become their own prison wardens, policing themselves, their own thoughts and actions, and conforming them to religious stricture. Think of the benefit to religion to have such devoted handmaidens do its work for it, whether it is militant women in purdah, or militant religious right spokeswomen, such as Roman Catholic Phyllis Schlafly, the fabled foe of the Equal Rights Amendment.

Status of women and gays in the church

Although Protestant women ministers, who were pioneers back in the late 1970s, are at least one in every eight clergy today, women attracted to the ministry still don't have that choice in most fundamentalist and evangelical sects. (U.S. federal labor statistics, 1996)

Predicated on a literal belief in the bible, such Christian denominations cannot yield on the matter of women's ordination. The notorious Lutheran Church Missouri Synod still excludes women from voting on church business, more than 150 years after Elizabeth Cady Stanton first called for woman suffrage in 1848, and more than 80 years after the 19th Amendment granting women the vote was adopted as part of the U.S. Constitution in 1920!

Although ordained women were always discouraged by the nation's largest Protestant denomination, the Southern Baptist Convention, some women in recent years served various ministerial roles in it. In a stupendously insulting and contemptuous act, the Convention banned women from the ministry in the year 2000, stating: "While both men and women are gifted for service in the church, the office of pastor is limited to men as qualified by Scripture." The denomination predictably turned to 1 Timothy 2:9–14: "I suffer not a woman to teach, nor to usurp authority over the man, but to be in silence." A statement released by the Baptist Faith and Message Study Committee asserted that they "were driven by biblical authority, a sense of urgency, and the near unanimous verdict of our churches. . . . There is no biblical precedent for a woman in the pastorate, and the Bible teaches that women should not teach in authority over men. . . Far less than one percent of churches cooperating with the Southern Baptist Convention have [sic] ever called a woman as pastor." Laudably, former President Jimmy Carter, who once served as a deacon and Sunday school teacher, and his wife Rosalyn, quit the Southern Baptist Convention following this edict.

The exclusion of women ministers logically followed the Southern Baptist Convention's approval of a notorious resolution in 1998 requiring women to "submit graciously" to men, as required by the New Testament: "A wife is to submit graciously to the servant leadership of her husband, even as the church willingly submits to the headship of Christ." It seems that, for Southern Baptists, scripture still stands supreme.

Other Protestant denominations that refuse to ordain women include some Pentecostal, all Eastern Orthodox, and Seventh-Day Adventist.

Needless to say, there are no female imams in Islam, or Orthodox Jewish female rabbis.

The liberal branches of Judaism are similar to the more liberal Christian denominations in their policies on women clergy.

Reform Judaism, the largest and most liberal branch of U.S. Judaism, ordained its first woman rabbi in 1972. By 2004, equal numbers of women and men were studying to become rabbis at the (Reform) Hebrew Union College – Jewish Institute on Religion. The Reconstructionist Rabbinical College ordained its first woman in 1974. The second largest Jewish branch, Conservative, ordained its first woman in 1985. The Jewish Theological Seminary voted to admit women in 1983, with more than 100 female Conservative rabbis ordained to date.

Short-sighted or conventional women pin their hopes in modifying patriarchal religion on the full integration of women into religion as ministers, stewards and scholars. Will the church change women more than they can change the church? The real power women could wield over religion is to reject it. Sonia Johnson liked to say, after her excommunication by the Mormon church in 1979: "One of my favorite fantasies is that one Sunday not one single woman, in any country of the world, will go to church. If women simply stop giving our time and energy to the institutions that oppress, they would have to cease to do so."

Mainstream Protestant churches are still hotly debating the rights of gays and lesbians to be ordained. It is revealing of how slowly change comes to even liberal churches that the ordination of an openly gay bishop by the U.S. Episcopal Church in 2003 is threatening to create a worldwide schism within the Anglican denomination. Yet it is a mark of the achievements of the gay rights movement that the topic of same-sex marriage is taking center stage in theological and legislative debates. Society averts its eyes and refuses to notice that the only organized opponents of gay rights and gay marriage are religious spokespersons and religious lobbies, and the only arguments they can muster come from religious authority.

Fundamentalist ascendancy

In a disturbing backlash to the gains of the women's movement, the evangelical and fundamentalist churches are the fastest-growing Christian denominations in the country, far outstripping their more liberal brethren. The once-a-decade study sponsored by the Association of Statisticians of American Religious Bodies reported that the Assemblies of God boasted a membership increase of 18.5 percent, Southern Baptists grew by 5 percent, while American Baptist Churches USA, a liberal body, declined by 5.7 percent, the Presbyterian Church (U.S.A.) dropped by 11.6 percent, and United Churches of Christ fell by 14.8 percent (Religious Congregations and Membership: 2000).

Fundamentalist Jerry Falwell, in full sway when *Woe to the Women* debuted, has dropped his "Moral Majority" badge in name only, but is still thumping away on his bible on behalf of his rightwing agenda. Feminists, among others, were blamed by Falwell for the terrorist attacks on the United States on Sept. 11, 2001. "I really believe that the pagans, and the abortionists, and the feminists, and the gays and the lesbians, who are actively trying to make that an alternative lifestyle, the ACLU, People For the American Way, all of them who tried to secularize America, I point the finger in their face and say you helped this happen." (Said to agreeing interviewer Rev. Pat Robertson on the "700 Club," Sept. 13, 2001)

Rev. Robertson's own most absurd attack against feminists came in his equally infamous fundraising letter of 1992: "The feminist agenda is not about equal rights for women. It is about a socialist, anti-family political movement that encourages women to leave their husbands, kill their children, practice witchcraft, destroy capitalism, and become lesbians."

Even the liberal YWCA recently succumbed to feminist- and lesbian-bashing. The YWCA dismissed Patricia Ireland, formerly president of the National Organization for Women, as its chief executive officer in October 2003, after a six-month campaign waged against her by ultraconservative groups. Maybe modern feminists should not be so forgiving of the YMCA's past connections with religious zealot Anthony Comstock, the 19th-century postal crusader whose anti-obscenity laws reached far into the latter-half of the twentieth century to ban "indecent articles" (i.e., contraception). Wisconsin became the last state in the nation, in 1974, to finally permit unmarried people to purchase contraception — and only because a federal court decreed it.

Are the Islamic fundamentalist theocrats who openly talk of jihad, or holy war, and who seek to impose *sharia*, repressive fundamentalist religious law, on women, so very different from their Christian cousins? One-time presidential candidate Patrick Buchanan, known for his antiabortion and anti-gay views, called for a "holy war" against secularism in this nation during his primetime-televised speech at the 1992 national convention of the Republican Party in Houston: "There is a religious war going on in our country for the souls of America. It is a cultural war, as critical to the kind of nation we will one day be as was the Cold War itself." As I write this, the highest-ranking law enforcer in the country is Attorney General John Ashcroft, a zealous antiabortionist, who, as a U.S. senator, in accepting an honorary degree in May 8, 1999, told segregationist Bob Jones University: "We have no King but Jesus" in America. (Ashcroft has apparently never read the Declaration of Independence, or he would know that we threw kings out in 1776.)

When the uncovered bosom of the Spirit of Justice, a prominent art deco statue in the reception room of the Justice Building in Washington, D.C., offended him, Ashcroft covered "Justice" up, at the cost of $8,000 in tax dollars, with what looked eerily like a blue burqa. Talk about symbolism!

Roman Catholic dominance

The Roman Catholic Church, the nation's largest denomination, remains the arch-enemy of women's rights. Regular papal decrees against ordaining women as priests, calling for global bans on birth control, abortion, and the use of condoms even to prevent the spread of AIDS, routinely make page-one headlines, as if the pope had actually said something newsworthy. In the face of a pedophilia cover-up scandal that just won't quit, the Catholic Church, displaying no sense of irony, has stepped up its "moral" campaigns. U.S. bishops as I write are on the verge of announcing official "punishment" to be meted out to U.S. Catholic politicians who vote out of Vatican lockstep on abortion, gay rights, and death with dignity.

The Roman Catholic hierarchy's appalling inhumanity to

woman was never made clearer than by its vicious opposition to an abortion for a nine-year-old rape victim in Nicaragua in March 2003. In compliance with Church teachings, abortion is illegal in Nicaragua, as it is in much of the developing world, barring exceptional circumstances such as life endangerment. Even the plight of this nine-year-old child was not considered exceptional enough for the Roman Catholic Church, which values its irrational dogma in inverse proportion to the welfare of girls and women. This little girl thankfully received an abortion, owing to the diligence of her parents and the intervention of the Nicaraguan Attorney General. During the controversy, the country's bishops even wrote a letter comparing abortion to terrorist suicide bombings.

Let this be a cautionary tale: If the Church had its way, contraception and abortion would be illegal around the globe, with no exceptions, and we would return to those dark ages.

The combined efforts of the Roman Catholic and fundamentalist Protestant churches have been successful in keeping feminists in a constantly defensive posture. In the 31 years since the U.S. Supreme Court's *Roe v. Wade* decision, legalizing abortion, much legal ground has been lost, with courts approving parental notification and consent laws, 24-hour waiting periods and other onerous requirements. Currently, about two-thirds of states deny most abortion coverage to needy women eligible for public medical assistance. *Roe v. Wade* itself hangs by a swing vote of the U.S. Supreme Court. Identified abortion providers are found in only 13 percent of counties nationwide. Threats and violence against abortion clinics have increased greatly in the last two decades, with seven homicides to date: three abortion physicians and four clinic volunteers or employees have been murdered in the United States since 1993. Five other doctors or clinic staff in North America have been shot at by religiously-motivated fanatics. Among the religious terrorists was Paul Hill, a Presbyterian minister, sentenced to death for killing Dr. John Britton and clinic escort John Barrett "in the name of God" outside the Ladies' Center abortion clinic in Pensacola, Fla., in 1994. At his last press conference before his 2003 execution, Hill told reporters: "I expect a great reward in heaven." Fugitive

Eric Rudolph, a member of the Army of God, was taken into custody in 2003, for the 1999 bombing of an abortion clinic in Birmingham, Alabama, which killed an undercover officer and grievously wounded nurse Emily Lyons.

The United States consistently sides with the Vatican and the most theocratic Islamist governments in United Nations debates over population control, reproductive rights, women and children. The global gag rule first imposed at the behest of the Vatican by President Ronald Reagan in 1984, cutting off international family planning funds for any health clinic even mentioning abortion, was finally lifted under the Clinton Presidency in 1993. Reimposing it was the first official act of President George W. Bush, on January 22, 2001, devastating healthcare and reproductive choices for millions of women worldwide.

The battle for contraceptive access formally launched by Margaret Sanger in 1914 is far from won. Viagra, a drug to treat male impotence, was almost immediately adopted for coverage by most insurance plans when it was first introduced in 1998. Contrast this with the fact that a majority of states still do not require insurance companies offering prescription coverage to include contraception. Recent attempts to pass federal legislation to that effect have stalled. The refusal to stock the "morning-after pill" by Wal-Mart corporation, started by a religious-right family, affects women nationwide. Wal-Mart is the world's largest corporation, the nation's largest employer and one of the nation's largest pharmaceutical dispensers. The religious war against reproductive rights continues unabated. At this writing, the Bush Administration has stalled attempts to make emergency contraception available over-the-counter nationwide.

Still no Equal Rights Amendment

The first edition of *Woe to the Women* noted the biblical underpinnings of the economic devaluation of women. In the early 1980s, U.S. women were paid an average of 56–65 cents for every dollar paid to men. Today women earn only 79.7 cents for every dollar paid to men, even in professions dominated by women, according to a congressional study released in November 2003. While women are now a majority on college campuses, women in the workplace are still encountering that "glass ceiling." The answer, according to observers of the wage gap, is to pass the Equal Rights Amendment, which has been literally dead since it was officially defeated by forces of the religious right in 1982.

How long must we wait to see passage of this amendment first proposed in 1923? As a student and young woman, I participated, as millions of others did, in the final efforts to pass the Equal Rights Amendment. Feminist groups mobilized desperately to no avail. It was a bitter, helpless experience to come so close to adopting this necessary and just clause to our U.S. Constitution.

The body of the amendment reads: "Equality of rights under the law shall not be denied or abridged by the United States or by any state on account of sex." Such simple justice. Who could object? Many religious denominations, that's who! The Roman Catholic, fundamentalist, and Mormon churches and their proponents steadfastly opposed the ERA.

Also unratified by the United States is the Convention for the Elimination of All Forms of Discrimination Against Women (CEDAW) adopted by the U.N. General Assembly in 1979, a quarter of a century ago, and since ratified by more than 165 countries. The stonewalling over CEDAW places the United States in the company of such misogynist governments as Iran. After three terms by rightwing presidents passed with no action on CEDAW, President Bill Clinton approved the treaty in 1994, sending it to the Senate. One religiously-motivated man, U.S. Sen. Jesse Helms of North Carolina, as chair of the Senate Foreign Relations Committee from 1994 to 2001, single-handedly prevented CEDAW from being voted on. In a highly symbolic contretemps, Sen. Helms used force to physically evict ten female members of Congress from a committee meeting on Oct. 28, 2000. The protest, during which women held placards urging Helms to schedule a hearing date for CEDAW, was staged after Helms had refused to meet with them about it for months. For the record, these brave women were: U.S. Reps. Lynn Woolsey (D-Calif.), Nancy Pelosi (D-Calif.), Corinne Brown (D-Fla.),

Tammy Baldwin (D-Wis.), Patsy Mink (D-Ha.), Donna Christensen (D-Virgin Islands), Eddie Bernice Johnson (D-Texas), Nita Lowey (D-N.Y.), Janice Schakowsky (D-Ill.), and Barbara Lee (D-Calif.). Helms chided these female representatives publicly, telling them to "Please act like ladies."

Women in the United States, which is still considered to be one of the most religious nations in the world, continue to lag behind our secular sisters in Europe when it comes to participation in politics. The United States has never elected a woman president, while currently there are 17 female heads of state worldwide. As of January 2004, only 13 percent of the U.S. Senate is female, and only 14 percent of the House of Representatives. Women fill about 22 percent of state legislative seats. The U.S. ranks 59th out of 181 nations in which women are elected to national legislatures. The national trait of female piety, first recorded by nineteenth-century observers such as de Tocqueville and Harriet Martineau, is still handicapping American women's achievements.

Who can find a virtuous woman?

The small but disproportionately powerful Mormon Church (Church of Jesus Christ of Latter-day Saints), which is less than two percent of the U.S. population, doggedly helped to quash the ERA. Since then, it has spearheaded and subsidized referenda against gay rights and gay marriage. While the church modified its racist policy barring "worthy" black men from its governing priesthood in 1978, it has not moved on questions concerning abortion, women's rights or gay rights. As recently as 1995, Mormon president Gordon B. Hinckley decreed apocalyptically (and apoplectically) in his "Proclamation to the World":

"By divine design, fathers are to preside over their families in love and righteousness and are responsible to provide the necessities of life and protection for their families. Mothers are primarily responsible for the nurture of their children. . . . Further, we warn that the disintegration of the family will bring upon individuals, communities, and nations the calamities foretold by ancient and modern prophets."

The kidnapping of 14-year-old Mormon Elizabeth Smart in 2002 in Salt Lake City, ending in her dramatic recovery and the arrest of a polygamous renegade prophet in 2003, has focused attention on the continuing harm of the early Mormon church's hallowed teachings. Although the Mormon church today officially disowns polygamists, polygamous doctrines straight out of the Old Testament were central to Mormon founding and growth. Keeping alive the polygamous tenets is the Church's little-publicized but intact doctrine of "celestial marriage," which permits Mormon men, through a Temple ceremony, to sign up additional wives to take possession of in Mormondom's polygamous afterlife. (The Mormon wife's destiny as an eternal breeder of "spirit" babies surely makes the Mormon Church's vision of heaven closer to a hell for women!) Dignifying polygamy is the Church's revered treatment of its polygamous founder Joseph Smith and such leaders as Brigham Young. The Mormon Church's major university is named in honor of a church leader "sealed" to some 56 wives over his lifetime.

News sources currently estimate that there are tens of thousands of members of the breakaway (back-to-its-roots) Fundamentalist Church of Jesus Christ of Latter-day Saints and other renegade cults practicing the "celestial law" of polygamy. Girls and women living in isolated, polygamous pockets of North America — often sustained by public welfare, and rife with incest and sexual abuse — might as well be living in third-world theocracies. Often even denied high school education as well as careers, they are indoctrinated into their religious destiny to become male property as plural teen wives and breeders of babies.

The continuing harm of traditional Christian attitudes about marriage and motherhood is exemplified by the tragic case of Andrea Yates. In June 2001, this Texas mother, who had had five children in eight years, systematically drowned her baby and her four other children, ages 7, 5, 3, and 2, in the family bathtub. Yates was found to be suffering from an extreme case of postpartum depression either triggering or coinciding with schizophrenia and psychosis. Her husband Russell Yates, a

NASA engineer, had encouraged her to have "enough boys for a basketball team" and to homeschool their children, despite her repeated hospitalizations for severe mental illness and suicide attempts. In their ultra-traditional marriage, Russell Yates had never changed a diaper, and seemed oblivious to Andrea's downward spiral in carrying out her Proverbial duties. Compounding her problems was the tutelage of a notorious street preacher, Michael Peter Woroniecki, the family's "spiritual adviser." The preacher sent letters to Andrea telling her "all women are descendants of Eve, and Eve was a witch," calling women who worked outside the home "wicked," according to press accounts of the trial. Woroniecki's newsletter, "The Perilous Times," in which he lamented worldly mothers and asked, "What becomes of the children of such a Jezebel?," was submitted as court evidence. Yates built her delusions around these religious ideas. A psychiatrist testified that Andrea told him she believed she had been marked by Satan, and that killing her children while they were young was the only way to save them from hell.

Another major news story has shed light on the continuing legacy of Christian enslavement upon African-American women. When vociferous segregationist Strom Thurmond, a Southern Christian fixture in the U.S. Senate, died at age 100 in 2003, it freed his mixed-race daughter, Essie Mae Washington-Williams, to finally come forward. At age 78, she admitted publicly that Thurmond was her father. Thurmond, at age 22, had impregnated and abandoned her African-American mother, then a 16–year-old housemaid in his parents' house. Used and then discarded, the penniless mother, who lost her job, was forced to give up her baby to the care of relatives. The situation could be straight out of Genesis, with its sordid tales of the permissible sexual use of "bondwomen." It has been pointed out the real reason for anti-miscegenation laws was not to protect "white womanhood" from the black man, but to protect white male predators from having to marry or be responsible toward the black women they preyed upon.

Koranic views

When *Woe to the Women*, which deals with the "holy" book of the world's largest religion, was originally written, Americans were not preoccupied with Islam or Koranic teachings. Interest in the world's second-largest religion has surged since the terror attacks of Sept. 11, 2001. Despite many differences, it is important to remember that Jewish, Muslim and Christian faiths intersect, with parts of the Hebrew bible accepted by all three faiths. Each traces its beginning to Abraham, that hoary old biblical patriarch so willing to sacrifice his son and prostitute his wife. Muslims share another common denominator, Eve, whose "sin" continues to be invoked to put modern women in our proper place, subordinate to men.

The Koran, compiled some 700 years after Christianity began, embroidered on biblical themes such as polygamy, advising: "Marry as many women as you like, two, three, or four" (Koran, Sura 4:3). Today men in many Islamic cultures and nations are permitted up to four wives at a time. Muslim women, known as "submitters," since Islam means "submission," are retold the biblical story of Noah and Lot to teach women what happens to disobedient wives. (They go to hell, Sura 66:10.) Hebrew Testament verses sanctifying a double standard and mandating death for fornication and adultery are followed religiously in some of the Muslim world, taking the form of "honor killings" by male family members against transgressing or unchaste-appearing female relatives. Statistics on honor killing for Jordan, considered the most credible, reveal they account for one in four homicides a year, with only the lightest of sentences meted out to rarely prosecuted male relatives. Until 1999, Egyptian law promised a pardon to any rapist who married his victim, which is straight out of Mosaic law. *Zina*, forbidding sexual activity outside marriage, is routinely invoked to prosecute women rape victims. Stoning women to death for adultery, a biblical injunction, became routine in Islamic Iran following the Islamic revolution of 1979.

Although the New Testament decrees that women must

cover their hair during prayer, and dress in modesty and "shamefacedness," the veiling of women is not explicitly part of biblical tradition. Purdah, the chador and the Taliban's claustrophobic, all-consuming burqa developed from one short Koranic passage, 24:24–31: "And say to the believing women, that they should cast down their eyes and guard their private parts, and reveal not their adornment save such as is outward; and let them cast their veils over their bosoms, and not reveal their adornment save to their husbands. . . ." While many Muslim women worldwide are permitted to satisfy this requirement with light veiling or modest dress, this veiled reference still circumscribes the lives of millions of women. They are hidden not just behind the veil but live in virtual house arrest in several Islamist countries, where women dare not show their faces in public, may not drive cars (Saudi Arabia), leave their house or country without male family consent (Jordan), and where schoolgirls or young women defying Islamic dress codes have been harassed, threatened, mutilated with acid, murdered, or permitted to die rather than expose unveiled faces.

One of the most shocking religious crimes of the new century involved the deaths of schoolgirls in Mecca, Saudi Arabia, who were restrained from fleeing a fire on school grounds by religious police because they were not veiled. Fifteen schoolgirls died and 50 others were injured in March 2002. Witnesses accused the mutaween, also known as the Commission for the Promotion of Virtue and Prevention of Vice, of beating back girls who tried to escape because they were not wearing headscarves and abayas (black robes). Saudi Arabian law requires all women, even foreigners, to cover themselves from head to toe in public. The greatly-feared religious police were absolved of wrongdoing, although for public relations purposes, they were later advised to "smile more." Such is the power of religion, which values religious conventions and control of women above women's lives. Christianity was no different when it was part of a church-state.

Since social inequality breeds violence, it is no surprise domestic violence plagues Muslim as well as "Christian" countries. Divine justification for beatings of women is found in the

Koran (4:34), which encourages men to guard, admonish, and finally beat disobedient women. *The Muslim's Handbook* published in Turkey in 2000, advised its readers to hit a woman "gently," but not to strike her face. The Imam Mohamed Kamal Mostafa, a Koranic scholar in Spain, outraged many women there when his book, *Women in Islam* (2000), included tips on wife-beating. In January 2004, the imam received a suspended sentence of 15 months in jail for inciting violence against women — a small blow against Muslim misogyny.

Bible comes to life with Jewish fundamentalism

Current Israeli law stands as an example of what happens when biblical law comes to life. The power of Orthodox rabbis over the lives of Jewish women in Israel is "vast and malignant," according to feminist author Andrea Dworkin ("Israel: Whose Country Is It Anyway," *Ms. Magazine*, September/October 1990).

"In Israel," Dworkin pointed out, "Jewish women are basically — in reality, in every day life — governed by Old Testament law." The Orthodox rabbis, Dworkin noted, "decide questions of marriage, adultery, divorce, birth, death, legitimacy; what rape is; and whether abortion, battery, and rape in marriage are legal or illegal."

She added, "Under Jewish law, the husband is the master: the woman belongs to him."

This situation began in 1953, when Israel passed a law placing all family and personal matters at the mercy of religious courts: Orthodox Jewish, Christian, Muslim and Druze. In Orthodox Jewish courts, women — classed with children, convicted criminals, and the mentally incompetent — may not testify, be a witness, a judge, or even sign a document. An Orthodox monopoly on marriage, divorce, even burial, gives the rabbinate dominion over civil life. This law turned the clock back a century for women in Israel.

Hebrew law reigns over marriage and divorce. Only Orthodox Jewish marriages are recognized (with the exception that couples who have civil marriages outside Israel are recognized as legally married). As the Old Testament mandates in Deuteronomy 24:1, only a husband may divorce, and then he need only use a "get," or bill of divorcement, and out the door his former wife goes.

Women have no right to divorce, no matter their circumstances. If a wife leaves her husband, the religious courts can officially rule her a "rebellious wife." Such a woman loses custody of her children and any right to financial support. As of 1990, there were an estimated 10,000 such women, known as "chained women" or "agunot," who existed in legal limbo because their Israeli husbands refused to grant them a divorce. These bible-based inequities create the perfect culture for abuse to flourish. Dworkin cited parliament hearings estimating that 100,000 Israeli women are beaten every year by husbands, yet have no right to divorce.

In accordance with Genesis 38:7–10, a childless widow must obtain a ritual release from her deceased husband's brother in order to remarry.

Devout women within Israel are battling for their full freedom to worship. Prayer sections are segregated at the famous Wailing Wall. Although women are allowed to pray, Orthodox law forbids them to read from the Torah at the Wall, as men do. In 2000, the Israeli Supreme Court ruled that women had that religious freedom, but in April 2003, in a 5–4 decision, the Supreme Court reversed itself. The court ordered the government to assign a nearby site at which women may read from the Torah.

Women protesting the ban for the last two decades have been subject to abuse, heckling, egging, tear-gassing, and even stoning by Orthodox male bullies. The Orthodox have even proposed legislation to imprison women who pray in the male tradition for up to seven years. On occasion, women showing bare arms on Israeli streets have been harassed or stoned by Orthodox males.

As Dworkin quipped, "you remember the Old Testament. You've read the Book. You've seen the movie. What you haven't done is live it. In Israel, Jewish women do."

Cast not pearls before swine

Whether in the name of God, Allah, or Yahweh, the surge of fundamentalism and its attempts to destroy or encroach on secular life remains the greatest threat to women's freedom. Scan the globe. We find that dress reform, equal rights, access to education and the means to control their own bodies remain unrealized dreams for all too many women. Why is this?

Elizabeth Cady Stanton answered this question, in a very powerful address to the Woman's Suffrage Association in 1885:

"You may go the world over and you will find that every form of religion which has breathed upon this earth has degraded woman. There is not one which has not made her subject to man. Men may rejoice in them because they make man the head of the woman. I have been traveling this old world during the last few years and have found new food for thought. What power is it that makes the Hindoo woman burn herself on the funeral pyre of her husband? Her religion.

"What holds the Turkish woman in the harem? Her religion. By what power do the Mormons perpetuate their system of polygamy? By their religion.

"Man, of himself, could not do this; but when he declares, 'Thus saith the Lord,' of course he can do it. So long as ministers stand up and tell us that as Christ is the head of the church, so is man the head of the woman, how are we to break the chains that have held women down through the ages? You Christian women can look at the Hindoo, the Turkish, the Mormon women, and wonder how they can be held in such bondage. Observe to-day the work women are doing for the churches. *The church rests on the shoulders of women. . . .*

"Now I ask you if our religion teaches the dignity of women? It teaches us that abominable idea of the sixth century — Augustine's idea — that motherhood is a curse; that woman is the author of sin, and is most corrupt. . . . We want to help roll off from the soul of woman the terrible superstitions that have so long repressed and crushed her."

Progressive activists remain chary of striking Stanton's recommended blow at "the fountain of all tyranny." Religion is still that 800-pound gorilla in our living room and legislature everybody pretends is not there. Feminists, gays and secular groups are fighting hard to salvage the rights they have won at such cost, often going two steps back for every step forward. The combined forces of the Roman Catholic and fundamentalist churches are working, not always together but in concert, to attack secular gains, attain public aid for religiously-segregated education, repeal abortion rights, put prayer and the Ten Commandments in public schools, fight gay rights and gay marriage, unite church and state, and otherwise legislate dogma. While the bible remains revered and above criticism, many of its nearly forgotten biblical passages pertaining to women are "lying in wait" (to use King James Version lingo), to be rediscovered and invoked as the will of God.

The United States of America is a republic governed by a secular constitution barring any religious test for public office. Yet an arresting political poll (Reuters/Zogby 2000) found that when voters were given a hypothetical list of Jewish, black, female, Arab American, gay or atheist vice presidential candidates, the atheist candidate was the most unpopular. In fact, the notion that an openly atheist politician even could or would be nominated as a vice president in the current political climate beggars belief.

Secularists were treated to a distressing lesson in their worth to politicians in the aftermath of the ruling by the Ninth Circuit U.S. Court of Appeals declaring "under God" in the Pledge of Allegiance unconstitutional on June 26, 2002. In a pandering frenzy, members of the U.S. House raced that day to the steps of the Capitol to recite for the benefit of the media the Pledge of Allegiance, shouting out the words "under God." Less than four hours after the ruling, U.S. Senators adjourned important business in order to pass a resolution denouncing the decision, by a 99–0 vote (Jesse Helms was absent). When the ruling was upheld by the body of the Ninth Circuit Court the following year, only seven members of the U.S. House had the guts to oppose a similar resolution condemning the appeals court. The perception that a political candidate or official must pay public homage to religion to be electable grants religion tremendous power. If the choice is standing up to religion or being electable — if the choice is between alienating the church lobby or alienating feminists — it is obvious where the loyalties of many politicians will fall.

"Good news" that you won't find in the "good book" is that secularism is growing visibly in the United States. The definitive American Religious Identification Survey conducted by the City College of New York (2001) reveals that the fastest growing segment of the population is the nonreligious, which grew from 8 percent in 1990 to 14.3 percent in 2001. That's 29 million freethinking Americans! The number of Americans who identified with religion dropped from 90 percent in 1990, to 81 percent in 2001, and self-identified Christians dropped from 86 percent to 76 percent. Secularists have muscle to flex, and now is the time to do it.

* * *

I have to confess, there is one bible verse I sometimes find comforting, particularly when debating a dense "faith head" (to borrow Richard Dawkins' term) on some talkshow or other. It's the admonition in the Sermon on the Mount not to "cast ye your pearls before swine." Eschewing its context, this is one bible verse feminists might take to heart. Women, and humanity, can do so much better than the bible. We can "transcend" religion, and start fresh. We can place value in humanity, this world, the natural world, and work on improving it, instead of wasting our time, money, energy and psyches kowtowing to some unseen, unknown, unprovable supernatural world and its mythical misogynist maker.

As always, after a closer look at the bible, I, like Ruth Green and Nietzsche before me, feel the need to wash my hands of religion. The primitive teachings of this "holy book" should not be part of our laws.

The only true shield standing between women and the bible, that handbook for the subjugation of women, is a secular government. U.S. citizens must wake up to the threat of an encroaching theocracy and shore up Thomas Jefferson's "wall of separation between church and state."

Annie Laurie Gaylor, editor
Freethought Today
August 2004

HANDY GUIDE TO BIBLE SEXISM
Old Testament

To read the bible verses in full, turn to page 165.

GENESIS

1:27–28	Male and female created in image of God; both have dominion
2:7	God creates man first in this second version
2:20	Adam can't find bestial "help meet"
2:22	Woman created from Adam's rib
2:23–24	Married couple "shall be of one flesh" — *his*
3:12–13	Eve was framed
3:16	"In sorrow thou shalt bring forth children . . . and he shall rule over thee"
4:19	Polygyny starts already
Chapter 5	Men beget (as opposed to women bearing)
6:2	Angels are "sons of God" — there are no "daughters of God"
7:2	Male Ark animals own their female peers
12:11–19	Abram prostitutes his wife to Pharoah
16:2	Sarai gives husband her maid: "go in unto my maid"
17:9–14	Circumcision is "mark" that *men* are God's chosen
17:15–19; 21:1–2	Tabloid headline: Sarah pregnant at 90!
19:1–11	Do to virgins "as is good," only don't harm male angels
19:30–38	Sordid tale of daughters allegedly seducing Lot
20:1–13	Abraham tries to prostitute his wife again
20:12	Abraham marries his half-sister
25:21–24	Lord impregnates Rebekah with twins

EXODUS

LEVITICUS

4:22–23	Sinning rulers offer *male* kid sacrifices
4:27–28	Sinning commoners offer *female goat* as sacrifice
6:14–18	*Male* children of Aaron can eat meat offerings
12:1–4	Women who have sons are unclean 7 days
12:5	Women who have daughters are unclean 14 days (double)
15:16	Man's sperm is unclean
15:18	Intercourse is unclean
15:19–33	Menstrual periods are unclean, menstrual sex is unclean; menstruating woman must be "put apart" for 7 days
18:7–17,29	Incest prohibitions (ignored by Genesis protagonists)
18:22,25	Homosexuality is an "abomination"
19:20–22	If a master has sex with his betrothed maid, *she* shall be scourged
20:11–12	Death penalty for sex with dad's wife or daughter-in-law
20:13	Kill homosexuals
20:17,19–21	More incest prohibitions
20:18	Couple having menstrual sex must be "cut off" from people
21:9	If priest's daughter is a whore, she must be burned
21:17	Unblemished males only need apply for position as priest
21:18–21	Priest must have intact "stones" (testicles)
26:29	Absolute equality: the right to be eaten; eat sons and daughters
27:3–7	Women literally worth less than men

NUMBERS

1:2	Census only includes men
5:13–31	Adulteress test encourages jealousy and cruelty
25:1–8	Israel's "whoredoms" result in Lord-ordered

DEUTERONOMY

24:1	Men can divorce women on-the-spot because of some "uncleanness" in her, but not vice-versa
24:4	Divorced woman is an abomination if she remarries her first husband
24:5	Men are rewarded for divorcing, then remarrying
25:5–10	Brother must marry dead brother's wife
25:11–12	If a woman touches the penis of her husband's foe, her hand must be amputated, "thine eye shall not pity her"
28:53	"Eat the fruit of thine own body"
28:56–57	Delicate women will be forced to eat their children

JUDGES

1:12–13	A daughter is the "reward" for a murder
5:24–26	Jael "blessed above women" for hammering Sisera
5:30	To every man a damsel or two
8:30–31	Gideon's "many wives" and one concubine
9:53–54	"Slay me, that men say not of me, A woman slew him"
11:30–40	Jephthah's nameless daughter is sacrificed
13:3	Angel of Lord impregnates barren wife of Manoah
14:20	Samson's wife betrays him and is given to a friend!
16:4–21	Delilah betrays Samson too (he never learns)
19:20–29	Concubine is thrown to murderous mob to save master; her corpse is later cut up by master
21:11–12	Four hundred virgins are stolen
21:19–23	". . . catch you every man his wife . . ."

RUTH

4:10	Boaz buys Ruth to be his wife (how romantic)

1 SAMUEL

2:21	"The Lord visited Hannah," who conceives five times (divine sperm bank)
15:3	Slay all, even suckling
18:6–7	Women cheerlead for war
18:27	David buys Michal with 200 foreskins
21:4–5	Men are holy if they stay away from women
25:39-43	David takes additional wives
27:9	"Neither man nor woman (was left) alive"

2 SAMUEL

5:13	"David took him more concubines and wives"
6:20–23	Michal is barren for life because she scolded David for being vile
11:2–4	David spies on Bathsheba (another great bible romance)
12:11–12	David's wives are raped under God's orders for *his* sins
13:1–29	Incest-rape is eventually avenged by male honor code
16:22	Absalom "went in unto" his father's concubines in the sight of all Israel
20:3	David's concubines are imprisoned because they were raped by his son

1 KINGS

1:1–4	A young virgin is brought to "warm-up" elderly David
3:16–28	Two "harlots" fight over baby

| 11:1–4 | "Strange" wives turn away King Solomon's faith; he had 700 wives and 300 concubines |
| Chapter 21 | Jezebel "stirs up" husband's "wickedness" |

2 KINGS

| 9:32–37 | Jezebel is mutilated and brutally killed as the man who orders her death dines and drinks |
| 15:16 | Rip up women with child |

2 CHRONICLES

| 11:21 | King Rehoboam had 18 wives and 60 concubines |
| 13:21 | King Abijah had 14 wives |

ESTHER

| 1:7–22 | The inspiring tale of Vashti, the bible's first (and only) feminist; and the sordid tale of Esther |
| 2:1–17 | Her replacement, Esther, purified for a year |

JOB

2:9–10	Job's wife is "foolish" for cursing Lord who plagues her family because of a barter with Satan
14:1–4	"Who can bring a clean thing out of an unclean? not one"
15:14	"What is man, that he should be clean? and he which is born of a woman, that he should be righteous?"
25:4	"How can he be clean that is born of woman?"

PSALMS

| 1:1 | "Blessed is the man . . ." |

8:5	Man is "a little lower than the angels"
51:5	"in sin did my mother conceive me"
137:9	dash thy little ones against the stones

PROVERBS

2:16–18	"Deliver thee from the strange woman . . . her house inclineth unto death"
6:24–29	An adulteress is synonymous with "strange women"
7:9–27	Men go to strange women like an ox to slaughter; her house is the way to hell — a long, dire, melodramatic warning making women's powers Satanic
9:13–18	"A foolish woman is clamorous"
10:1	A foolish son is product of mother; wise son product of father
11:22	As a jewel of gold in a swine's snout, so a fair woman is without discretion
19:18	Don't spare for your son's crying
22:14	"The mouth of a strange woman is a deep pit"
23:13–14	If you beat your son, he won't die
23:27–28	Whores and strange women increase transgressions among men
25:24	"It is better to dwell in the corner of the housetop, than with a brawling woman and in a wide house"
27:15	A rainy day and women are compared
30:20	"Such is the way of an adulterous woman; she eateth and wipeth her mouth and saith, I have done no wickedness"
30:21–23	"Odious" women are discussed
31:3	"Give not thy strength unto women"
31:10–31	"Who can find a virtuous woman . . ." and a "goodly woman" is a drudge

ECCLESIASTES

7:26	". . . more bitter than death the woman . . ."

SONG OF SOLOMON

5:4	"My beloved put in his hand by the hole of the door, and my bowels were moved for him."
8:8	"We have a little sister, and she hath no breasts"

ISAIAH

3:12	Women shall rule over Israel — a threat
3:16–17	". . . and the Lord will discover their secret parts"
4:1	Aggressive women are viewed as terrors
9:20	"They shall eat every man the flesh of his own arm" (yum)
13:16	"their wives (shall be) ravished"
13:18	There shall be no pity for the "fruit of the womb"
19:16	Egypt shall be like a woman and shake with fear
32:11–13	"Tremble, ye women that are at ease . . ."
54:1	Barren women rejoice

JEREMIAH

2:32	Women stereotyped
3:1	Compares nation (Judah) to harlot (again)
3:20	Treacherous wife/nation metaphor
9:17–20	". . . send for cunning women . . ."

LAMENTATIONS

1:8–17	"her filthiness is in her skirts . . . Jerusalem is as a menstruous woman"
2:20	"Shall the women eat their fruit, and children"

EZEKIEL

5:10	Fathers shall eat sons and sons shall eat fathers
8:2	Lord's loins make special guest appearance
9:6	"Slay utterly" all but circumcised men
13:18–20	"Woe to the women that sew pillows to all armholes" (no kidding)
Chapter 16	Lord acts as vengeful pimp to his country
16:15	Fornications pour out
16:36–45	Their "filthiness was poured out . . ." Denunciation comparing Jerusalem to filthy women
18:6	Coming near menstruous woman is equivalent of abandoning the Lord
Chapter 19	Motherhood metaphor — decent for a change
22:2–6	Israel is a "bloody city"
23:1–10	Aholah, a whore, is slain by mob under God's orders
23:11–49	Aholibah, a whore, is likewise slain, and sexually mutilated
23:48	"Whores" had to be killed in order to teach other women not to be "lewd"
26:6–8	Slay "daughters in the field" (metaphor) to prove that "I AM *the Lord*"
29:7–8	God performs bloody castration via a sword
36:17	"(Their) way was before me as the uncleanness of a removed woman"

HOSEA

1:2	"land commiteth great whoredom"
2:10	Lord: "I will discover her lewdness in the sight of her lovers"
3:2	A woman is bought for silver and barley
9:14	"Give them a miscarrying womb and dry breasts"
13:16	"Their infants shall be dashed in pieces and their women with child shall be ripped up"

NAHUM

3:4–6	Lord: "I will discover thy skirts upon thy face"
3:13	"Thy people in the midst of thee are women"

ZECHARIAH

14:2	"The city shall be taken and the women ravished"

New Testament

MATTHEW

1:16–17	52 Generations of Jesus cited from *Joseph's* side
1:18	Holy Ghost knocks up Mary
5:17–18	J.C. came to uphold Mosaic law
5:28–29	Mutilate yourself if you "lust in your heart," says Jesus
5:32	Jesus orders no divorce unless a wife is a "fornicator;" if she remarries she is an adulteress but the divorced husband does not commit adultery
12:48	"Who is my mother?" asks Jesus
15:22–26	"It is not meet to take the children's bread, and cast it to dogs"
19:6	"What therefore God hath joined together, let not man put asunder"
19:12	It is good to be a eunuch
24:19	"(woe) unto them that are with child . . ."
25:1–13	Jesus tells polygyny parable without censure

MARK

3:33	Jesus: "Who is my mother?"
5:25–30	Jesus feels his "virtue" go out when touches menstruating woman
7:25–30	Woman and ill child castigated as "dogs" by Jesus
10:2–9	Jesus forbids all divorce in *this* passage
10:11–12	Unisex rule on divorce: both men and women who divorce and remarry are adulterers
16:9	Mary Magdalene had seven devils cast out of her

LUKE

2:22	Mary is unclean after birth of Jesus
2:23	"Every male that openeth the womb shall be called holy to the Lord"
7:37–48	Woman "sinner" bathes J.C.'s feet with tears and dries them with her hair — and he loves it
8:2	More devils cast out of Mary Magdalene
11:27–28	Jesus refuses to bless his mother
14:26	You cannot be Jesus' disciple unless you hate mother, etc.
20:34–35	Better chance to get in heaven if you don't marry
23:29	Blessed are the barren . . .

JOHN

2:1–4	Jesus, in answer to request from his mother: "Woman, what have I to do with thee?"
8:3–11	Jesus risks adulteress' life in this much vaunted verse
16:21	Woman will forget childbirth pain as soon as "a man is born into the world" — hallelujah
20:17	"Touch me not," says Jesus to Mary Magdalene
20:27	Thomas allowed to touch J.C.

ROMANS

1:26–32	Reiterates death penalty for homosexuals
7:1–3	Unfair adultery rule

1 CORINTHIANS

5:1–2,5	Deliver to Satan those who fornicate with father's wife
6:9	Effeminate or homosexual men cannot go to heaven
7:1	"It is good for a man not to touch a woman"
7:2–40	It is better to marry than to burn; but the unmarried serve the Lord better; unmarried women must be more holy than unmarried men
11:3–15	Man is the "head" of woman; long hair is a "glory" for women but a "shame" for men; praying women must cover their heads because only man is in image and glory of God
14:34–35	Women, keep silence; they may only learn from husbands

GALATIANS

3:27–29	". . . neither male nor female; for ye are all one in Jesus Christ"
4:27	"Rejoice, thou barren . . ."

EPHESIANS

5:22–33	"Wives, submit . . ."
6:5	Servants, obey your masters

COLOSSIANS

3:18   More wives, submit yourselves . . .

1 THESSALONIANS

4:4   Women are described as "vessels"

1 TIMOTHY

2:9   Women should adorn themselves in modest apparel, shamefacedness and sobriety

2:10   Women should adorn themselves with "good works"

2:11–14   Women should learn in silence in all subjection; proclaims that Eve was sinful, Adam blameless

2:15   Women will not die in childbirth providing they "continue in faith and charity and holiness with sobriety"

3:2–5   Bishops should have one wife only and keep his children in subjection (Pope should know about this one)

4:7   Warns against "old wives' fables" but not old husbands' tales

5:5-13   Widows should wash saints' feet, not "wax wanton" or be busybodies

5:14–15   Housewife instructions on avoiding Satan

TITUS

2:2–5   Instructions for elderly women's behavior

HEBREWS

11:11   Sara's faith rewarded by son

1 PETER

3:1–2	Women should talk to husbands in fear
3:3–5	Women can't wear braids, gold or fine apparel
3:6	Sara role model of obedient wife
3:7	Wife "a weaker vessel"

2 PETER

2:4–8	Incestuous Lot called "righteous"

REVELATION

2:20–23	Jezebel's "crime" is changed from religious treason to "fornication"
14:4	Virgin males are "not defiled by women"
17:1–16	A whore is stripped, eaten and burned

BIBLE PASSAGES IN FULL

Old Testament

GENESIS

Egalitarian creation story

1:27: So God created man in his own image, in the image of God created he him; male and female created he them.

28: And God blessed them, and God said unto them, Be fruitful, and multiply, and replenish the earth, and subdue it: and have dominion over the fish of the sea, and over the fowl of the air, and over every living thing that moveth upon the earth.

Sexist creation story begins

Gen. 2:7: And the LORD God formed man of the dust of the ground, and breathed into his nostrils the breath of life; and man became a living soul. . . .

Adam can't find "bestial" helpmeet

Gen. 2:20: And Adam gave names to all cattle, and to the fowl of the air, and to every beast of the field; but for Adam there was not found an help meet for him. . . .

Woman created from Adam's rib

Gen. 2:22: And the rib, which the LORD God had taken from man, made he a woman, and brought her unto the man.

Married couple one flesh — his

Gen. 2:23: And Adam said, This is now bone of my bones, and flesh of my flesh: she shall be called Woman, because she was taken out of Man.

24: Therefore shall a man leave his father and his mother, and shall cleave unto his wife: and they shall be one flesh.

Eve was framed

Gen 3:12: And the man said, The woman whom thou gavest to be with me, she gave me of the tree, and I did eat.

13: And the LORD God said unto the woman, What is this that thou hast done? And the woman said, The serpent beguiled me, and I did eat.

Women "cursed"

Gen. 3:16: Unto the woman he said, I will greatly multiply thy sorrow and thy conception; in sorrow thou shalt bring forth children; and thy desire shall be to thy husband, and he shall rule over thee.

First plural marriage

Gen. 4:19: And Lamech took unto him two wives: the name of the one was Adah, and the name of the other Zillah.

Men beget (women don't bear)

Gen. 5:1: This is the book of the generations of Adam. In the day that God created man, in the likeness of God made he him;

2: Male and female created he them; and blessed them, and called their name Adam, in the day when they were created.

3: And Adam lived an hundred and thirty years, and begat a son in his own likeness, after his image; and called his name Seth:

4: And the days of Adam after he had begotten Seth were eight hundred years: and he begat sons and daughters:

5: And all the days that Adam lived were nine hundred and thirty years: and he died.

6: And Seth lived an hundred and five years, and begat Enos:

7: And Seth lived after he begat Enos eight hundred and seven years, and begat sons and daughters:

8: And all the days of Seth were nine hundred and twelve years: and he died.

9: And Enos lived ninety years, and begat Cainan:

10: And Enos lived after he begat Cainan eight hundred and fifteen years, and begat sons and daughters:

11: And all the days of Enos were nine hundred and five years: and he died.

12: And Cainan lived seventy years, and begat Mahalaleel:

13: And Cainan lived after he begat Mahalaleel eight hundred and forty years, and begat sons and daughters:

14: And all the days of Cainan were nine hundred and ten years: and he died.

15: And Mahalaleel lived sixty and five years, and begat Jared:

16: And Mahalaleel lived after he begat Jared eight hundred and thirty years, and begat sons and daughters:

17: And all the days of Mahalaleel were eight hundred ninety and five years: and he died.

18: And Jared lived an hundred sixty and two years, and he begat Enoch:

19: And Jared lived after he begat Enoch eight hundred years, and begat sons and daughters:

20: And all the days of Jared were nine hundred sixty and two years: and he died.

21: And Enoch lived sixty and five years, and begat Methuselah:

22: And Enoch walked with God after he begat Methuselah three hundred years, and begat sons and daughters:

23: And all the days of Enoch were three hundred sixty and five years:

24: And Enoch walked with God: and he was not; for God took him.

25: And Methuselah lived an hundred eighty and seven years, and begat Lamech:

26: And Methuselah lived after he begat Lamech seven hundred eighty and two years, and begat sons and daughters:

27: And all the days of Methuselah were nine hundred sixty and nine years: and he died.

28: And Lamech lived an hundred eighty and two years, and begat a son:

29: And he called his name Noah, saying, This name shall comfort us concerning our work and toil of our hands, because of the ground which the LORD hath cursed.

30: And Lamech lived after he begat Noah five hundred ninety and five years, and begat sons and daughters:

31: And all the days of Lamech were seven hundred seventy and seven years: and he died.

32: And Noah was five hundred years old: and Noah begat Shem, Ham, and Japheth.

Men are "sons of God" — women merely "daughters of men" (no female angels)

Gen. 6:2: That the sons of God saw the daughters of men that they were fair; and they took them wives of all which they chose.

Male ark animals own their female peers

Gen. 7:2: Of every clean beast thou shalt take to thee by sevens, the male and his female: and of beasts that are not clean by two, the male and his female.

Abram prostitutes wife

Gen. 12:11: And it came to pass, when he was come near to enter into Egypt, that he said unto Sarai his wife, Behold now, I know that thou art a fair woman to look upon:

12: Therefore it shall come to pass, when the Egyptians shall see thee, that they shall say, This is his wife: and they will kill me, but they will save thee alive.

13: Say, I pray thee, thou art my sister: that it may be well with me for thy sake; and my soul shall live because of thee.

14: And it came to pass, that, when Abram was come into Egypt, the Egyptians beheld the woman that she was very fair.

15: The princes also of Pharaoh saw her, and commended her before Pharaoh: and the woman was taken into Pharaoh's house.

16: And he entreated Abram well for her sake: and he had sheep, and oxen, and he asses, and menservants, and maidservants, and she asses, and camels.

17: And the LORD plagued Pharaoh and his house with great plagues because of Sarai Abram's wife.

18: And Pharaoh called Abram, and said, What is this that thou hast done unto me? why didst thou not tell me that she was thy wife?

19: Why saidst thou, She is my sister? so I might have taken her to me to wife: now therefore behold thy wife, take her, and go thy way.

Wife gives husband maid as surrogate

Gen. 16:2: And Sarai said unto Abram, Behold now, the LORD hath restrained me from bearing: I pray thee, go in unto my maid; it may be that I may obtain children by her. And Abram hearkened to the voice of Sarai.

Circumcision "elevates" men as God's chosen

Gen. 17:1: And when Abram was ninety years old and nine, the LORD appeared to Abram, and said unto him, I am the Almighty God; walk before me, and be thou perfect.

2: And I will make my covenant between me and thee, and will multiply thee exceedingly. . . . [His name changes to "Abraham."]

9: And God said unto Abraham, Thou shalt keep my covenant therefore, thou, and thy seed after thee in their generations.

10: This is my covenant, which ye shall keep, between me and you and thy seed after thee; Every man child among you shall be circumcised.

11: And ye shall circumcise the flesh of your foreskin; and it shall be a token of the covenant betwixt me and you.

12: And he that is eight days old shall be circumcised among you, every man child in your generations, he that is born in the house, or bought with money of any stranger, which is not of thy seed.

13: He that is born in thy house, and he that is bought with thy money, must needs be circumcised: and my covenant shall be in your flesh for an everlasting covenant.

14: And the uncircumcised man child whose flesh of his foreskin is not circumcised, that soul shall be cut off from his people; he hath broken my covenant.

Sarah pregnant at age 90!

Gen. 17:15: And God said unto Abraham, As for Sarai thy wife, thou shalt not call her name Sarai, but Sarah shall her name be.

16: And I will bless her, and give thee a son also of her: yea, I will bless her, and she shall be a mother of nations; kings of people shall be of her.

17: Then Abraham fell upon his face, and laughed, and said in his heart, Shall a child be born unto him that is an hundred years old? and shall Sarah, that is ninety years old, bear?

18: And Abraham said unto God, O that Ishmael might live before thee!

19: And God said, Sarah thy wife shall bear thee a son indeed; and thou shalt call his name Isaac: and I will establish my covenant with him for an everlasting covenant, and with his seed after him. . . .

Circumcision is "mark" . . .

Gen. 17:9: And God said unto Abraham, Thou shalt keep my covenant therefore, thou, and thy seed after thee in their generations.

10: This is my covenant, which ye shall keep, between me and you and thy seed after thee; Every man child among you shall be circumcised.

11: And ye shall circumcise the flesh of your foreskin; and it shall be a token of the covenant betwixt me and you.

12: And he that is eight days old shall be circumcised among you, every man child in your generations, he that is born in the house, or bought with money of any stranger, which is not of thy seed.

13: He that is born in thy house, and he that is bought with thy money, must needs be circumcised: and my covenant shall be in your flesh for an everlasting covenant.

14: And the uncircumcised man child whose flesh of his foreskin is not circumcised, that soul shall be cut off from his people; he hath broken my covenant.

"Do unto virgins as is good"

Gen. 19:1: And there came two angels to Sodom at even; and Lot sat in the gate of Sodom: and Lot seeing them rose up to meet them; and he bowed himself with his face toward the ground;

2: And he said, Behold now, my lords, turn in, I pray you, into your servant's house, and tarry all night, and wash your feet, and ye shall rise up early, and go on your ways. And they said, Nay; but we will abide in the street all night.

3: And he pressed upon them greatly; and they turned in unto him, and entered into his house; and he made them a feast, and did bake unleavened bread, and they did eat.

4: But before they lay down, the men of the city, even the men of Sodom, compassed the house round, both old and young, all the people from every quarter:

5: And they called unto Lot, and said unto him, Where are the men which came in to thee this night? bring them out unto us, that we may know them.

6: And Lot went out at the door unto them, and shut the door after him,

7: And said, I pray you, brethren, do not so wickedly.

8: Behold now, I have two daughters which have not known man; let me, I pray you, bring them out unto you, and do ye to them as is good in your eyes: only unto these men do nothing; for therefore came they under the shadow of my roof.

9: And they said, Stand back. And they said again, This one fellow came in to sojourn, and he will needs be a judge: now will we deal worse with thee, than with them. And they pressed sore upon the man, even Lot, and came near to break the door.

10: But the men put forth their hand, and pulled Lot into the house to them, and shut to the door.

11: And they smote the men that were at the door of the house with blindness, both small and great: so that they wearied themselves to find the door.

Sordid tale of Lot and daughters

Gen. 19:30: And Lot went up out of Zoar, and dwelt in the mountain, and his two daughters with him; for he feared to dwell in Zoar: and he dwelt in a cave, he and his two daughters.

31: And the firstborn said unto the younger, Our father is old, and there is not a man in the earth to come in unto us after the manner of all the earth:

32: Come, let us make our father drink wine, and we will lie with him, that we may preserve seed of our father.

33: And they made their father drink wine that night: and the firstborn went in, and lay with her father; and he perceived not when she lay down, nor when she arose.

34: And it came to pass on the morrow, that the firstborn said unto the younger, Behold, I lay yesternight with my father: let us make him drink wine this night also; and go thou in, and lie with him, that we may preserve seed of our Father.

35: And they made their father drink wine that night also: and the younger arose, and lay with him; and he perceived not when she lay down, nor when she arose.

36: Thus were both the daughters of Lot with child by their father.

37: And the firstborn bare a son, and called his name Moab: the same is the father of the Moabites unto this day.

38: And the younger, she also bare a son, and called his name Benammi: the same is the father of the children of Ammon unto this day.

Abraham tries to prostitute his wife again

Gen. 20:1: And Abraham journeyed from thence toward the south country, and dwelled between Kadesh and Shur, and sojourned in Gerar.

2: And Abraham said of Sarah his wife, She is my sister: and Abimelech king of Gerar sent, and took Sarah.

3: But God came to Abimelech in a dream by night, and said to him, Behold, thou art but a dead man, for the woman which thou hast taken; for she is a man's wife.

4: But Abimelech had not come near her: and he said, Lord, wilt thou slay also a righteous nation?

5: Said he not unto me, She is my sister? and she, even she herself said, He is my brother: in the integrity of my heart and innocency of my hands have I done this.

6: And God said unto him in a dream, Yea, I know that thou didst this in the integrity of thy heart; for I also withheld thee from sinning against me: therefore suffered I thee not to touch her.

7: Now therefore restore the man his wife; for he is a prophet, and he shall pray for thee, and thou shalt live: and if thou restore her not, know thou that thou shalt surely die, thou, and all that are thine.

8: Therefore Abimelech rose early in the morning, and called all his servants, and told all these things in their ears: and the men were sore afraid.

9: Then Abimelech called Abraham, and said unto him, What hast thou done unto us? and what have I offended thee, that thou hast brought on me and on my kingdom a great sin? thou hast done deeds unto me that ought not to be done.

10: And Abimelech said unto Abraham, What sawest thou, that thou hast done this thing?

11: And Abraham said, Because I thought, Surely the fear of God is not in this place; and they will slay me for my wife's sake.

12: And yet indeed she is my sister; she is the daughter of my father, but not the daughter of my mother; and she became my wife.

13: And it came to pass, when God caused me to wander from my father's house, that I said unto her, This is thy kindness which thou shalt shew unto me; at every place whither we shall come, say of me, He is my brother.

Tabloid headline: God knocks up Sarah, age 90

Gen. 21:1: And the LORD visited Sarah as he had said, and the LORD did unto Sarah as he had spoken.

2: For Sarah conceived, and bare Abraham a son in his old age, at the set time of which God had spoken to him.

Rebekah's divine insemination

Gen. 25:21: And Isaac intreated the LORD for his wife, because she was barren: and the LORD was intreated of him, and Rebekah his wife conceived.

22: And the children struggled together within her; and she said, If it be so, why am I thus? And she went to inquire of the LORD.

23: And the LORD said unto her, Two nations are in thy womb, and two manner of people shall be separated from thy bowels; and the one people shall be stronger than the other people; and the elder shall serve the younger.

24: And when her days to be delivered were fulfilled, behold, there were twins in her womb.

Isaac fobs off wife as his sister

Gen. 26:7: And the men of the place asked him of his wife; and he said, She is my sister: for he feared to say, She is my wife; lest, said he, the men of the place should kill me for Rebekah; because she was fair to look upon.

8: And it came to pass, when he had been there a long time, that Abimelech king of the Philistines looked out at a window, and saw, and, behold, Isaac was sporting with Rebekah his wife.

9: And Abimelech called Isaac, and said, Behold, of a surety she is thy wife: and how saidst thou, She is my sister? And Isaac said unto him, Because I said, Lest I die for her.

Esau marries two women

Gen. 26:34: And Esau was forty years old when he took to wife Judith the daughter of Beeri the Hittite, and Bashemath the daughter of Elon the Hittite:

Esau adds to his harem

Gen. 28:9: Then went Esau unto Ishmael, and took unto the wives which he had Mahalath the daughter of Ishmael Abraham's son, the sister of Nebajoth, to be his wife.

Village massacred to avenge rape

Gen. 34:1: And Dinah the daughter of Leah, which she bare unto Jacob, went out to see the daughters of the land.

2: And when Shechem the son of Hamor the Hivite, prince of the country, saw her, he took her, and lay with her, and defiled her.

3: And his soul clave unto Dinah the daughter of Jacob, and he loved the damsel, and spake kindly unto the damsel.

4: And Shechem spake unto his father Hamor, saying, Get me this damsel to wife.

5: And Jacob heard that he had defiled Dinah his daughter: now his sons were with his cattle in the field: and Jacob held his peace until they were come.

6: And Hamor the father of Shechem went out unto Jacob to commune with him.

7: And the sons of Jacob came out of the field when they heard it: and the men were grieved, and they were very wroth, because he had wrought folly in Israel in lying with Jacob's daughter; which thing ought not to be done.

8: And Hamor communed with them, saying, The soul of my son Shechem longeth for your daughter: I pray you give her him to wife.

9: And make ye marriages with us, and give your daughters unto us, and take our daughters unto you.

10: And ye shall dwell with us: and the land shall be before you; dwell and trade ye therein, and get you possessions therein.

11: And Shechem said unto her father and unto her brethren, Let me find grace in your eyes, and what ye shall say unto me I will give.

12: Ask me never so much dowry and gift, and I will give according as ye shall say unto me: but give me the damsel to wife.

13: And the sons of Jacob answered Shechem and Hamor his father deceitfully, and said, because he had defiled Dinah their sister:

14: And they said unto them, We cannot do this thing, to give our sister to one that is uncircumcised; for that were a reproach unto us:

15: But in this will we consent unto you: If ye will be as we be, that every male of you be circumcised;

16: Then will we give our daughters unto you, and we will take your daughters to us, and we will dwell with you, and we will become one people.

17: But if ye will not hearken unto us, to be circumcised; then will we take our daughter, and we will be gone.

18: And their words pleased Hamor, and Shechem Hamor's son.

19: And the young man deferred not to do the thing, because he had delight in Jacob's daughter: and he was more honourable than all the house of his father.

20: And Hamor and Shechem his son came unto the gate of their city, and communed with the men of their city, saying,

21: These men are peaceable with us; therefore let them dwell in the land, and trade therein; for the land, behold, it is large enough for them; let us take their daughters to us for wives, and let us give them our daughters.

22: Only herein will the men consent unto us for to dwell with us, to be one people, if every male among us be circumcised, as they are circumcised.

23: Shall not their cattle and their substance and every beast of theirs be ours? only let us consent unto them, and they will dwell with us.

24: And unto Hamor and unto Shechem his son hearkened all that went out of the gate of his city; and every male was circumcised, all that went out of the gate of his city.

25: And it came to pass on the third day, when they were sore, that two of the sons of Jacob, Simeon and Levi, Dinah's brethren, took each man his sword, and came upon the city boldly, and slew all the males.

26: And they slew Hamor and Shechem his son with the edge of the sword, and took Dinah out of Shechem's house, and went out.

27: The sons of Jacob came upon the slain, and spoiled the city, because they had defiled their sister.

28: They took their sheep, and their oxen, and their asses, and that which was in the city, and that which was in the field,

29: And all their wealth, and all their little ones, and their wives took they captive, and spoiled even all that was in the house.

30: And Jacob said to Simeon and Levi, Ye have troubled me to make me to stink among the inhabitants of the land, among the Canaanites and the Perizzites: and I being few in number, they shall gather themselves together against me, and slay me; and I shall be destroyed, I and my house.

31: And they said, Should he deal with our sister as with an harlot?

Rachel, dying in childbirth, told to "fear not; thou shalt have this son"

Gen. 35:17: And it came to pass, when she was in hard labour, that the midwife said unto her, Fear not; thou shalt have this son also.

18: And it came to pass, as her soul was in departing, (for she died) that she called his name Ben-oni: but his father called him Benjamin.

"He took her and went in unto her"

Gen. 38:2: And Judah saw there a daughter of a certain Canaanite, whose name was Shuah; and he took her, and went in unto her.

Law of Onan

Gen. 38:7: And Er, Judah's firstborn, was wicked in the sight of the LORD; and the LORD slew him.

8: And Judah said unto Onan, Go in unto thy brother's wife, and marry her, and raise up seed to thy brother.

9: And Onan knew that the seed should not be his; and it came to pass, when he went in unto his brother's wife, that he spilled it on the ground, lest that he should give seed to his brother.

10: And the thing which he did displeased the LORD: wherefore he slew him also.

Woman falsely accuses Joseph of rape

Gen. 39:7: And it came to pass after these things, that his master's wife cast her eyes upon Joseph; and she said, Lie with me.

8: But he refused, and said unto his master's wife, Behold, my master wotteth not what is with me in the house, and he hath committed all that he hath to my hand;

9: There is none greater in this house than I; neither hath he kept back any thing from me but thee, because thou art his wife: how then can I do this great wickedness, and sin against God?

10: And it came to pass, as she spake to Joseph day by day, that he hearkened not unto her, to lie by her, or to be with her.

11: And it came to pass about this time, that Joseph went into the house to do his business; and there was none of the men of the house there within.

12: And she caught him by his garment, saying, Lie with me: and he left his garment in her hand, and fled, and got him out.

13: And it came to pass, when she saw that he had left his garment in her hand, and was fled forth,

14: That she called unto the men of her house, and spake unto them, saying, See, he hath brought in an Hebrew unto us to mock us; he came in unto me to lie with me, and I cried with a loud voice:

15: And it came to pass, when he heard that I lifted up my voice and cried, that he left his garment with me, and fled, and got him out.

16: And she laid up his garment by her, until his lord came home.

17: And she spake unto him according to these words, saying, The Hebrew servant, which thou hast brought unto us, came in unto me to mock me:

18: And it came to pass, as I lifted up my voice and cried, that he left his garment with me, and fled out.

19: And it came to pass, when his master heard the words of his wife, which she spake unto him, saying, After this manner did thy servant to me; that his wrath was kindled.

20: And Joseph's master took him, and put him into the prison, a place where the king's prisoners were bound: and he was there in the prison.

EXODUS

Circumcision, Zipporah-style

4:24: And it came to pass by the way in the inn, that the LORD met him, and sought to kill him.

25: Then Zipporah took a sharp stone, and cut off the foreskin of her son, and cast it at his feet, and said, Surely a bloody husband art thou to me.

26: So he let him go: then she said, A bloody husband thou art, because of the circumcision.

"Come not at your wives"

Ex. 19:15: And he said unto the people, Be ready against the third day: come not at your wives.

Wife second in "coveting" proscription

Ex. 20:17: Thou shalt not covet thy neighbour's house, thou shalt not covet thy neighbour's wife, nor his manservant, nor his maidservant, nor his ox, nor his ass, nor any thing that is thy neighbour's.

Sexist, barbaric slavery rules

Ex. 21:2: If thou buy an Hebrew servant, six years he shall serve: and in the seventh he shall go out free for nothing.

3: If he came in by himself, he shall go out by himself: if he were married, then his wife shall go out with him.

4: If his master have given him a wife, and she have born him sons or daughters; the wife and her children shall be her master's, and he shall go out by himself.

5: And if the servant shall plainly say, I love my master, my wife, and my children; I will not go out free:

6: Then his master shall bring him unto the judges; he shall also bring him to the door, or unto the door post; and his master shall bore his ear through with an aul; and he shall serve him for ever.

Female slaves may be used sexually

Ex. 21:7: And if a man sell his daughter to be a maidservant, she shall not go out as the menservants do.

8: If she please not her master, who hath betrothed her to himself, then shall he let her be redeemed: to sell her unto a strange nation he shall have no power, seeing he hath dealt deceitfully with her.

9: And if he have betrothed her unto his son, he shall deal with her after the manner of daughters.

Polygyny rules

Ex. 21:10: If he take him another wife; her food, her raiment, and her duty of marriage, shall he not diminish.

11: And if he do not these three unto her, then shall she go out free without money.

May kill servants slowly

Ex. 21:20: And if a man smite his servant, or his maid, with a rod, and he die under his hand; he shall be surely punished.

21: Notwithstanding, if he continue a day or two, he shall not be punished: for he is his money.

Forced miscarriage not equivalent of manslaughter

Ex. 21:22: If men strive, and hurt a woman with child, so that her fruit depart from her, and yet no mischief follow: he shall be surely punished, according as the woman's husband will lay upon him; and he shall pay as the judges determine.

23: And if any mischief follow, then thou shalt give life for life,

24: Eye for eye, tooth for tooth, hand for hand, foot for foot,

25: Burning for burning, wound for wound, stripe for stripe.

Enticement rules

Ex. 22:16: And if a man entice a maid that is not betrothed, and lie with her, he shall surely endow her to be his wife.

17: If her father utterly refuse to give her unto him, he shall pay money according to the dowry of virgins.

Kill witches

Ex. 22:18: Thou shalt not suffer a witch to live.

Sacrifice firstborn?

Ex. 22:29: Thou shalt not delay to offer the first of thy ripe fruits, and of thy liquors: the firstborn of thy sons shalt thou give unto me.

Lord plays X-rated peek-a-boo

Ex. 33:23: And I will take away mine hand, and thou shalt see my back parts: but my face shall not be seen.

"Daughters go a-whoring"

Ex. 34:14: For thou shalt worship no other god: for the LORD, whose name is Jealous, is a jealous God:

15: Lest thou make a covenant with the inhabitants of the land, and they go a whoring after their gods , and do sacrifice unto their gods, and one call thee, and thou eat of his sacrifice;

16: And thou take of their daughters unto thy sons, and their daughters go a whoring after their gods, and make thy sons go a whoring after their gods.

Males report to Lord 3 times a year to ward off a-whoring women

Ex. 34:23: Thrice in the year shall all your men children appear before the Lord GOD, the God of Israel.

Women can't enter tabernacle they decorate. Only male Levites and priests could enter the tabernacle (Numbers 3:10, etc.)

Ex. 38:8: And he made the laver of brass, and the foot of it of brass, of the looking-glasses of the women assembling, which assembled at the door of the tabernacle of the congregation.

LEVITICUS

Rulers sacrifice *male* kids

4:22: When a ruler hath sinned, and done somewhat through ignorance against any of the commandments of the LORD his God concerning things which should not be done, and is guilty;

23: Or if his sin, wherein he hath sinned, come to his knowledge; he shall bring his offering, a kid of the goats, a male without blemish:

Commoners sacrifice *female* kids

Lev. 4:27: And if any one of the common people sin through ignorance, while he doeth somewhat against any of the commandments of the LORD concerning things which ought not to be done, and be guilty;

28: Or if his sin, which he hath sinned, come to his knowledge: then he shall bring his offering, a kid of the goats, a female without blemish, for his sin which he hath sinned.

Male children only offered meat

Lev. 6:14: And this is the law of the meat offering: the sons of Aaron shall offer it before the LORD, before the altar.

15: And he shall take of it his handful, of the flour of the meat offering, and of the oil thereof, and all the frankincense which is upon the meat offering, and shall burn it upon the altar for a sweet savour, even the memorial of it, unto the LORD.

16: And the remainder thereof shall Aaron and his sons eat: with unleavened bread shall it be eaten in the holy place; in the court of the tabernacle of the congregation they shall eat it.

17: It shall not be baken with leaven. I have given it unto them for their portion of my offerings made by fire; it is most holy, as is the sin offering, and as the trespass offering.

18: All the males among the children of Aaron shall eat of it. It shall be a statute for ever in your generations concerning the offerings of the LORD made by fire: every one that toucheth them shall be holy.

Mothers "unclean" 7 days for bearing sons

Lev. 12:1: And the LORD spake unto Moses, saying,

2: Speak unto the children of Israel, saying, If a woman have conceived seed, and born a man child: then she shall be unclean seven days; according to the days of the separation for her infirmity shall she be unclean.

3: And in the eighth day the flesh of his foreskin shall be circumcised.

4: And she shall then continue in the blood of her purifying three and thirty days; she shall touch no hallowed thing, nor come into the sanctuary, until the days of her purifying be fulfilled.

Mothers "unclean" 14 days for bearing daughters

Lev. 12:5: But if she bear a maid child, then she shall be unclean two weeks, as in her separation: and she shall continue in the blood of her purifying threescore and six days.

Sperm unclean

Lev. 15:16: And if any man's seed of copulation go out from him, then he shall wash all his flesh in water, and be unclean until the even.

Intercourse unclean

Lev. 15:18: The woman also with whom man shall lie with seed of copulation, they shall both bathe themselves in water, and be unclean until the even.

Menstruating women unclean, must be set apart

Lev. 15:19: And if a woman have an issue, and her issue in her flesh be blood, she shall be put apart seven days: and whosoever toucheth her shall be unclean until the even.

20: And every thing that she lieth upon in her separation shall be unclean: every thing also that she sitteth upon shall be unclean.

21: And whosoever toucheth her bed shall wash his clothes, and bathe himself in water, and be unclean until the even.

22: And whosoever toucheth any thing that she sat upon shall wash his clothes, and bathe himself in water, and be unclean until the even.

23: And if it be on her bed, or on any thing whereon she sitteth, when he toucheth it, he shall be unclean until the even.

24: And if any man lie with her at all, and her flowers be upon him, he shall be unclean seven days; and all the bed whereon he lieth shall be unclean.

25: And if a woman have an issue of her blood many days out of the time of her separation, or if it run beyond the time of her separation; all the days of the issue of her uncleanness shall be as the days of her separation: she shall be unclean.

26: Every bed whereon she lieth all the days of her issue shall be unto her as the bed of her separation: and whatsoever she sitteth upon shall be unclean, as the uncleanness of her separation.

27: And whosoever toucheth those things shall be unclean, and shall wash his clothes, and bathe himself in water, and be unclean until the even.

28: But if she be cleansed of her issue, then she shall number to herself seven days, and after that she shall be clean.

29: And on the eighth day she shall take unto her two turtles, or two young pigeons, and bring them unto the priest, to the door of the tabernacle of the congregation.

30: And the priest shall offer the one for a sin offering, and the other for a burnt offering; and the priest shall make an atonement for her before the LORD for the issue of her uncleanness.

31: Thus shall ye separate the children of Israel from their uncleanness; that they die not in their uncleanness, when they defile my tabernacle that is among them.

32: This is the law of him that hath an issue, and of him whose seed goeth from him, and is defiled therewith;

33: And of her that is sick of her flowers, and of him that hath an issue, of the man, and of the woman, and of him that lieth with her that is unclean.

Menstrual sex unclean

Lev. 15:24: And if any man lie with her at all, and her flowers be upon him, he shall be unclean seven days; and all the bed whereon he lieth shall be unclean.

Homosexuality an "abomination"

Lev. 18:22: Thou shalt not lie with mankind, as with womankind: it is abomination.

25: And the land is defiled: therefore I do visit the iniquity thereof upon it, and the land itself vomiteth out her inhabitants.

Woman slave used sexually "shall be scourged"; he shall be forgiven

Lev. 19:20: And whosoever lieth carnally with a woman, that is a bondmaid, betrothed to an husband, and not at all redeemed, nor freedom given her; she shall be scourged; they shall not be put to death, because she was not free.

21: And he shall bring his trespass offering unto the LORD, unto the door of the tabernacle of the congregation, even a ram for a trespass offering.

22: And the priest shall make an atonement for him with the ram of the trespass offering before the LORD for his sin which he hath done: and the sin which he hath done shall be forgiven him.

Kill homosexuals

Lev. 20:13: If a man also lie with mankind, as he lieth with a woman, both of them have committed an abomination: they shall surely be put to death; their blood shall be upon them.

Couple "cut off" for menstrual sex

Lev. 20:18: And if a man shall lie with a woman having her sickness, and shall uncover her nakedness; he hath discovered her fountain, and she hath uncovered the fountain of her blood: and both of them shall be cut off from among their people.

If priest's daughter a "whore," burn her

Lev. 21:9: And the daughter of any priest, if she profane herself by playing the whore, she profaneth her father: she shall be burnt with fire.

No "unblemished" priests; discrimination against the handicapped

Lev. 21:17: Speak unto Aaron, saying, Whosoever he be of thy seed in their generations that hath any blemish, let him not approach to offer the bread of his God.

18: For whatsoever man he be that hath a blemish, he shall not approach: a blind man, or a lame, or he that hath a flat nose, or any thing superfluous,

19: Or a man that is brokenfooted, or brokenhanded,

20: Or crookbackt, or a dwarf, or that hath a blemish in his eye, or be scurvy, or scabbed, or hath his stones broken;

21: No man that hath a blemish of the seed of Aaron the priest shall come nigh to offer the offerings of the LORD made by fire: he hath a blemish; he shall not come nigh to offer the bread of his God.

Absolute equality

Lev. 26:29: And ye shall eat the flesh of your sons, and the flesh of your daughters shall ye eat.

Women literally devalued

Lev. 27:3: And thy estimation shall be of the male from twenty years old even unto sixty years old, even thy estimation shall be fifty shekels of silver, after the shekel of the sanctuary.

4: And if it be a female, then thy estimation shall be thirty shekels.

5: And if it be from five years old even unto twenty years old, then thy estimation shall be of the male twenty shekels, and for the female ten shekels.

6: And if it be from a month old even unto five years old, then thy estimation shall be of the male five shekels of silver, and for the female thy estimation shall be three shekels of silver.

7: And if it be from sixty years old and above; if it be a male, then thy estimation shall be fifteen shekels, and for the female ten shekels.

NUMBERS

National poll only includes men

1:2: Take ye the sum of all the congregation of the children of Israel, after their families, by the house of their fathers, with the number of their names, every male by their polls;

Cruel adulteress test

Num. 5:11: And the LORD spake onto Moses, saying,

12: Speak unto the children of Israel, and say unto them, If any man's wife go aside, and commit a trespass against him

13: And [if] a man lie with her carnally, and it be hid from the eyes of her husband, and be kept close, and she be defiled, and there be no witness against her, neither she be taken with the manner;

14: And the spirit of jealousy come upon him, and he be jealous of his wife, and she be defiled: or if the spirit of jealousy come upon him, and he be jealous of his wife, and she be not defiled:

15: Then shall the man bring his wife unto the priest, and he shall bring her offering for her, the tenth part of an ephah of barley meal; he shall pour no oil upon it, nor put frankincense thereon; for it is an offering of jealousy, an offering of memorial, bringing iniquity to remembrance.

16: And the priest shall bring her near, and set her before the LORD:

17: And the priest shall take holy water in an earthen vessel; and of the dust that is in the floor of the tabernacle the priest shall take, and put it into the water:

18: And the priest shall set the woman before the LORD, and uncover the woman's head, and put the offering of memorial in her hands, which is the jealousy offering: and the priest shall have in his hand the bitter water that causeth the curse:

19: And the priest shall charge her by an oath, and say unto the woman, If no man have lain with thee, and if thou hast not gone aside to uncleanness with another instead of thy husband, be thou free from this bitter water that causeth the curse:

20: But if thou hast gone aside to another instead of thy husband, and if thou be defiled, and some man have lain with thee beside thine husband:

21: Then the priest shall charge the woman with an oath of cursing, and the priest shall say unto the woman, The LORD make thee a curse and an oath among thy people, when the LORD doth make thy thigh to rot, and thy belly to swell;

22: And this water that causeth the curse shall go into thy bowels, to make thy belly to swell, and thy thigh to rot: And the woman shall say, Amen, amen.

23: And the priest shall write these curses in a book, and he shall blot them out with the bitter water:

24: And he shall cause the woman to drink the bitter water that causeth the curse: and the water that causeth the curse shall enter into her, and become bitter.

25: Then the priest shall take the jealousy offering out of the woman's hand, and shall wave the offering before the LORD, and offer it upon the altar:

26: And the priest shall take an handful of the offering, even the memorial thereof, and burn it upon the altar, and afterward shall cause the woman to drink the water.

27: And when he hath made her to drink the water, then it shall come to pass, that, if she be defiled, and have done trespass against her husband, that the water that causeth the curse shall enter into her, and become bitter, and her belly shall swell, and her thigh shall rot: and the woman shall be a curse among her people.

28: And if the woman be not defiled, but be clean; then she shall be free, and shall conceive seed.

29: This is the law of jealousies, when a wife goeth aside to another instead of her husband, and is defiled;

30: Or when the spirit of jealousy cometh upon him, and he be jealous over his wife, and shall set the woman before the LORD, and the priest shall execute upon her all this law.

31: Then shall the man be guiltless from iniquity, and this woman shall bear her iniquity.

"Whoredoms" inspire massacre, impaling of foreign princess

Num. 25:1: And Israel abode in Shittim, and the people began to commit whoredom with the daughters of Moab.

2: And they called the people unto the sacrifices of their gods: and the people did eat, and bowed down to their gods.

3: And Israel joined himself unto Baal-peor: and the anger of the LORD was kindled against Israel.

4: And the LORD said unto Moses, Take all the heads of the people, and hang them up before the LORD against the sun, that the fierce anger of the LORD may be turned away from Israel.

5: And Moses said unto the judges of Israel, Slay ye every one his men that were joined unto Baal-peor.

6: And, behold, one of the children of Israel came and brought unto his brethren a Midianitish woman in the sight of Moses, and in the sight of all the congregation of the children of Israel, who were weeping before the door of the tabernacle of the congregation.

7: And when Phinehas, the son of Eleazar, the son of Aaron the priest, saw it, he rose up from among the congregation, and took a javelin in his hand;

8: And he went after the man of Israel into the tent, and thrust both of them through, the man of Israel, and the woman through her belly. So the plague was stayed from the children of Israel.

9: And those that died in the plague were twenty and four thousand.

Daughters successfully protest inheritance rules

Num. 27:1: Then came the daughters of Zelophehad, the son of Hepher, the son of Gilead, the son of Machir, the son of Manasseh, of the families of Manasseh the son of Joseph: and these are the names of his daughters; Mahlah, Noah, and Hoglah, and Milcah, and Tirzah.

2: And they stood before Moses, and before Eleazar the priest, and before the princes and all the congregation, by the door of the tabernacle of the congregation, saying,

3: Our father died in the wilderness, and he was not in the company of them that gathered themselves together against the LORD in the company of Korah; but died in his own sin, and had no sons.

4: Why should the name of our father be done away from among his family, because he hath no son? Give unto us therefore a possession among the brethren of our father.

5: And Moses brought their cause before the LORD.

6: And the LORD spake unto Moses, saying,

7: The daughters of Zelophehad speak right: thou shalt surely give them a possession of an inheritance among their father's brethren; and thou shalt cause the inheritance of their father to pass unto them.

8: And thou shalt speak unto the children of Israel, saying, If a man die, and have no son, then ye shall cause his inheritance to pass unto his daughter.

9: And if he have no daughter, then ye shall give his inheritance unto his brethren.

10: And if he have no brethren, then ye shall give his inheritance unto his father's brethren.

11: And if his father have no brethren, then ye shall give his inheritance unto his kinsman that is next to him of his family, and he shall possess it: and it shall be unto the children of Israel a statute of judgment, as the LORD commanded Moses.

Most women cannot make vows; only widows and divorced women have spiritual rights

Num. 30:1: And Moses spake unto the heads of the tribes concerning the children of Israel, saying, This is the thing which the LORD hath commanded.

2: If a man vow a vow unto the LORD, or swear an oath to bind his soul with a bond; he shall not break his word, he shall do according to all that proceedeth out of his mouth.

3: If a woman also vow a vow unto the LORD, and bind herself by a bond, being in her father's house in her youth;

4: And her father hear her vow, and her bond wherewith she hath bound her soul, and her father shall hold his peace at her: then all her vows shall stand, and every bond wherewith she hath bound her soul shall stand.

5: But if her father disallow her in the day that he heareth; not any of her vows, or of her bonds wherewith she hath bound her soul, shall stand: and the LORD shall forgive her, because her father disallowed her.

6: And if she had at all an husband, when she vowed, or uttered ought out of her lips, wherewith she bound her soul;

7: And her husband heard it, and held his peace at her in the day that he heard it: then her vows shall stand, and her bonds wherewith she bound her soul shall stand.

8: But if her husband disallowed her on the day that he heard it; then he shall make her vow which she vowed, and that which she uttered with her lips, wherewith she bound her soul, of none effect: and the LORD shall forgive her.

9: But every vow of a widow, and of her that is divorced, wherewith they have bound their souls, shall stand against her.

10: And if she vowed in her husband's house, or bound her soul by a bond with an oath;

11: And her husband heard it, and held his peace at her, and disallowed her not: then all her vows shall stand, and every bond wherewith she bound her soul shall stand.

12: But if her husband hath utterly made them void on the day he heard them; then whatsoever proceeded out of her lips concerning her vows, or concerning the bond of her soul, shall not stand: her husband hath made them void; and the LORD shall forgive her.

13: Every vow, and every binding oath to afflict the soul, her husband may establish it, or her husband may make it void.

14: But if her husband altogether hold his peace at her from day to day; then he establisheth all her vows, or all her bonds, which are upon her: he confirmeth them, because he held his peace at her in the day that he heard them.

15: But if he shall any ways make them void after that he hath heard them; then he shall bear her iniquity.

16: These are the statutes, which the LORD commanded Moses, between a man and his wife, between the father and his daughter, being yet in her youth in her father's house.

"Virgins" last item in list of war booty

Num. 31:17: Now therefore kill every male among the little ones, and kill every woman that hath known man by lying with him.

18: But all the women children, that have not known a man by lying with him, keep alive for yourselves.

19: And do ye abide without the camp seven days: whosoever hath killed any person, and whosoever hath touched any slain, purify both yourselves and your captives on the third day, and on the seventh day.

20: And purify all your raiment, and all that is made of skins, and all work of goats' hair, and all things made of wood.

21: And Eleazar the priest said unto the men of war which went to the battle, This is the ordinance of the law which the LORD commanded Moses;

22: Only the gold, and the silver, the brass, the iron, the tin, and the lead,

23: Every thing that may abide the fire, ye shall make it go through the fire, and it shall be clean: nevertheless it shall be purified with the water of separation: and all that abideth not the fire ye shall make go through the water.

24: And ye shall wash your clothes on the seventh day, and ye shall be clean, and afterward ye shall come into the camp.

25: And the LORD spake unto Moses, saying,

26: Take the sum of the prey that was taken, both of man and of beast, thou, and Eleazar the priest, and the chief fathers of the congregation:

27: And divide the prey into two parts; between them that took the war upon them, who went out to battle, and between all the congregation:

28: And levy a tribute unto the LORD of the men of war which went out to battle: one soul of five hundred, both of the persons, and of the beeves, and of the asses, and of the sheep:

29: Take it of their half, and give it unto Eleazar the priest, for an heave offering of the LORD.

30: And of the children of Israel's half, thou shalt take one portion of fifty, of the persons, of the beeves, of the asses, and of the flocks, of all manner of beasts, and give them unto the Levites, which keep the charge of the tabernacle of the LORD.

31: And Moses and Eleazar the priest did as the LORD commanded Moses.

32: And the booty, being the rest of the prey which the men of war had caught, was six hundred thousand and seventy thousand and five thousand sheep,

33: And threescore and twelve thousand beeves,

34: And threescore and one thousand asses,

35: And thirty and two thousand persons in all, of women that had not known man by lying with him.

Daughters only inherit to pass on to male relatives

Num. 36:1: And the chief fathers of the families of the children of Gilead, the son of Machir, the son of Manasseh, of the families of the sons of Joseph, came near, and spake before Moses, and before the princes, the chief fathers of the children of Israel:

2: And they said, The LORD commanded my lord to give the land for an inheritance by lot to the children of Israel: and my lord was commanded by the LORD to give the inheritance of Zelophehad our brother unto his daughters.

3: And if they be married to any of the sons of the other tribes of the children of Israel, then shall their inheritance be taken from the inheritance of our fathers, and shall be put to the inheritance of the tribe whereunto they are received: so shall it be taken from the lot of our inheritance.

4: And when the jubile of the children of Israel shall be, then shall their inheritance be put unto the inheritance of the tribe whereunto they are received: so shall their inheritance be taken away from the inheritance of the tribe of our fathers.

5: And Moses commanded the children of Israel according to the word of the LORD, saying, The tribe of the sons of Joseph hath said well.

6: This is the thing which the LORD doth command concerning the daughters of Zelophehad, saying, Let them marry to whom they think best; only to the family of the tribe of their father shall they marry.

7: So shall not the inheritance of the children of Israel remove from tribe to tribe: for every one of the children of Israel shall keep himself to the inheritance of the tribe of his fathers.

8: And every daughter, that possesseth an inheritance in any tribe of the children of Israel, shall be wife unto one of the family of the tribe of her father, that the children of Israel may enjoy every man the inheritance of his fathers.

9: Neither shall the inheritance remove from one tribe to another tribe; but every one of the tribes of the children of Israel shall keep himself to his own inheritance.

10: Even as the LORD commanded Moses, so did the daughters of

Zelophehad:

11: For Mahlal, Tirzah, and Hoglah, and Milcah, and Noah, the daughters of Zelophehad, were married unto their father's brothers' sons:

12: And they were married into the families of the sons of Manasseh the son of Joseph, and their inheritance remained in the tribe of the family of their father.

13: These are the commandments and the judgments, which the LORD commanded by the hand of Moses unto the children of Israel in the plains of Moab by Jordan near Jericho.

DEUTERONOMY

Destroy little ones

2:34: And we took all his cities at that time, and utterly destroyed the men, and the women, and the little ones, of every city, we left none to remain:

Don't desire neighbor's wife or ass

Deut. 5:21: Neither shalt thou desire thy neighbour's wife, neither shalt thou covet thy neighbour's house, his field, or his manservant, or his maidservant, his ox, or his ass, or any thing that is thy neighbour's.

Scorched earth policy

Deut. 7:1: When the LORD thy God shall bring thee into the land whither thou goest to possess it, and hath cast out many nations before thee, the Hittites, and the Girgashites, and the Amorites, and the Canaanites, and the Perizzites, and the Hivites, and the Jebusites, seven nations greater and mightier than thou;

2: And when the LORD thy God shall deliver them before thee; thou shalt smite them, and utterly destroy them; thou shalt make no covenant with them, nor shew mercy unto them:

3: Neither shalt thou make marriages with them; thy daughter thou shalt not give unto his son, nor his daughter shalt thou take unto thy son.

4: For they will turn away thy son from following me, that they may serve other gods: so will the anger of the LORD be kindled against you, and destroy thee suddenly.

5: But thus shall ye deal with them; ye shall destroy their altars, and break down their images, and cut down their groves, and burn their graven images with fire.

6: For thou art an holy people unto the LORD thy God: the LORD thy God hath chosen thee to be a special people unto himself, above all people that are upon the face of the earth.

7: The LORD did not set his love upon you, nor choose you, because ye were more in number than any people; for ye were the fewest of all people:

8: But because the LORD loved you, and because he would keep the oath which he had sworn unto your fathers, hath the LORD brought you out with a mighty hand, and redeemed you out of the house of bondmen, from the hand of Pharaoh king of Egypt.

Unisex rules for indentured servants

Deut. 15:12: And if thy brother, an Hebrew man, or an Hebrew woman, be sold unto thee, and serve thee six years; then in the seventh year thou shalt let him go free from thee.

13: And when thou sendest him out free from thee, thou shalt not let him go away empty:

14: Thou shalt furnish him liberally out of thy flock, and out of thy floor, and out of thy winepress: of that wherewith the LORD thy God hath blessed thee thou shalt give unto him.

15: And thou shalt remember that thou wast a bondman in the land of Egypt, and the LORD thy God redeemed thee: therefore I command thee this thing to day.

Instructions for sexual use of captive female war booty

Deut. 21:11: And seest among the captives a beautiful woman, and hast a desire unto her, that thou wouldest have her to thy wife;

12: Then thou shalt bring her home to thine house; and she shall shave her head, and pare her nails;

13: And she shall put the raiment of her captivity from off her, and shall remain in thine house, and bewail her father and her mother a full month: and after that thou shalt go in unto her, and be her husband, and she shall be thy wife.

14: And it shall be, if thou have no delight in her, then thou shalt let her go whither she will; but thou shalt not sell her at all for money, thou shalt not make merchandise of her, because thou hast humbled her.

Polygyny inheritance rules

Deut. 21:15: If a man have two wives, one beloved, and another hated, and they have born him children, both the beloved and the hated; and if the firstborn son be hers that was hated:

16: Then it shall be, when he maketh his sons to inherit that which he hath, that he may not make the son of the beloved firstborn before the son of the hated, which is indeed the firstborn:

17: But he shall acknowledge the son of the hated for the firstborn, by giving him a double portion of all that he hath: for he is the beginning of his strength; the right of the firstborn is his.

Draconian dress code

Deut. 22:5: The woman shall not wear that which pertaineth unto a man, neither shall a man put on a woman's garment: for all that do so are abomination unto the LORD thy God.

Barbaric test for virginity

Deut. 22:13: If any man take a wife, and go in unto her, and hate her,

14: And give occasions of speech against her, and bring up an evil name upon her, and say, I took this woman, and when I came to her, I found her not a maid:

15: Then shall the father of the damsel, and her mother, take and bring forth the tokens of the damsel's virginity unto the elders of the city in the gate:

16: And the damsel's father shall say unto the elders, I gave my daughter unto this man to wife, and he hateth her;

17: And, lo, he hath given occasions of speech against her, saying, I found not thy daughter a maid; and yet these are the tokens of my daughter's virginity. And they shall spread the cloth before the elders of the city.

18: And the elders of that city shall take that man and chastise him;

19: And they shall amerce him in an hundred shekels of silver, and give them unto the father of the damsel, because he hath brought up an evil name upon a virgin of Israel: and she shall be his wife; he may not put her away all his days.

20: But if this thing be true, and the tokens of virginity be not found for the damsel:

21: Then they shall bring out the damsel to the door of her father's house, and the men of her city shall stone her with stones that she die: because she hath wrought folly in Israel, to play the whore in her father's house: so shalt thou put evil away from among you.

Betrothed damsel in city and her apparent rapist both stoned to death

Deut. 22:23: If a damsel that is a virgin be betrothed unto an husband, and a man find her in the city, and lie with her;

24: Then ye shall bring them both out unto the gate of that city, and ye shall stone them with stones that they die; the damsel, because she cried not, being in the city; and the man, because he hath humbled his neighbour's wife: so thou shalt put away evil from among you.

Betrothed rural rape victim spared

Deut. 22:25: But if a man find a betrothed damsel in the field, and the man force her, and lie with her: then the man only that lay with her shall die:

26: But unto the damsel thou shalt do nothing; there is in the damsel no sin worthy of death: for as when a man riseth against his neighbour, and slayeth him, even so is this matter:

27: For he found her in the field, and the betrothed damsel cried, and there was none to save her.

Unbetrothed apparent rape victim must marry her attacker

Deut. 22:28: If a man find a damsel that is a virgin, which is not betrothed, and lay hold on her, and lie with her, and they be found;

29: Then the man that lay with her shall give unto the damsel's father fifty shekels of silver, and she shall be his wife; because he hath humbled her, he may not put her away all his days.

Sexually wounded males shunned

Deut. 23:1: He that is wounded in the stones, or hath his privy member cut off, shall not enter into the congregation of the LORD.

"Bastard" shunned to tenth generation

Deut. 23:2: A bastard shall not enter into the congregation of the LORD; even to his tenth generation shall he not enter into the congregation of the LORD.

Instant full-fault divorce of wife permitted

Deut. 24:1: When a man hath taken a wife, and married her, and it come to pass that she find no favour in his eyes, because he hath found some uncleanness in her: then let him write her a bill of divorcement, and give it in her hand, and send her out of his house.

Divorced woman who remarries first husband an "abomination"

Deut. 24:4: Her former husband, which sent her away, may not take her again to be his wife, after that she is defiled; for that is abomination before the LORD: and thou shalt not cause the land to sin, which the LORD thy God giveth thee for an inheritance.

Men rewarded for divorcing, remarrying (follows Deut. 24:4)

Deut. 24:5: When a man hath taken a new wife, he shall not go out to war, neither shall he be charged with any business: but he shall be free at home one year, and shall cheer up his wife which he hath taken.

Brother must marry dead brother's wife

Deut. 25:5: If brethren dwell together, and one of them die, and have no child, the wife of the dead shall not marry without unto a stranger: her husband's brother shall go in unto her, and take her to him to wife, and perform the duty of an husband's brother unto her.

6: And it shall be, that the firstborn which she beareth shall succeed in the name of his brother which is dead, that his name be not put out of Israel.

7: And if the man like not to take his brother's wife, then let his brother's wife go up to the gate unto the elders, and say, My husband's brother refuseth to raise up unto his brother a name in Israel, he will not perform the duty of my husband's brother.

8: Then the elders of his city shall call him, and speak unto him: and if he stand to it, and say, I like not to take her;

9: Then shall his brother's wife come unto him in the presence of the elders, and loose his shoe from off his foot, and spit in his face, and shall answer and say, So shall it be done unto that man that will not build up his brother's house.

10: And his name shall be called in Israel, The house of him that hath his shoe loosed.

Amputate hand of wife who touches genitalia of husband's foe to defend him

Deut. 25:11: When men strive together one with another, and the wife of the one draweth near for to deliver her husband out of the hand of him that smiteth him, and putteth forth her hand, and taketh him by the secrets:

12: Then thou shalt cut off her hand, thine eye shall not pity her.

"Delicate" women shall eat their children

Deut. 28:53: And thou shalt eat the fruit of thine own body, the flesh of thy sons and of thy daughters, which the LORD thy God hath given thee, in the siege, and in the straitness, wherewith thine enemies shall distress thee: . . .

56: The tender and delicate woman among you, which would not adventure to set the sole of her foot upon the ground for delicateness and tenderness, her eye shall be evil toward the husband of her bosom, and toward her son, and toward her daughter,

57: And toward her young one that cometh out from between her feet, and toward her children which she shall bear: for she shall eat them for want of all things secretly in the siege and straitness, wherewith thine enemy shall distress thee in thy gates.

JUDGES

Daughter "reward" for murder

1:12: And Caleb said, He that smiteth Kirjath-sepher, and taketh it, to him will I give Achsah my daughter to wife.

13: And Othniel the son of Kenaz, Caleb's younger brother, took it: and he gave him Achsah his daughter to wife.

Jael "blessed above women" for hammering nail through Sisera's temples

Judges 5:24: Blessed above women shall Jael the wife of Heber the Kenite be, blessed shall she be above women in the tent.

25: He asked water, and she gave him milk; she brought forth butter in a lordly dish.

26: She put her hand to the nail, and her right hand to the workmen's hammer; and with the hammer she smote Sisera, she smote off his head, when she had pierced and stricken through his temples.

"To every man a damsel or two"

Judges 5:30: Have they not sped? have they not divided the prey; to every man a damsel or two; . . .

Gideon's many wives, concubine

Judges 8:30: And Gideon had threescore and ten sons of his body begotten: for he had many wives.

31: And his concubine that was in Shechem, she also bare him a son, whose name he called Abimelech.

Dishonor of being slain by a woman

Judges 9:53: And a certain woman cast a piece of a millstone upon Abimelech's head, and all to brake his skull.

54: Then he called hastily unto the young man his armourbearer, and said unto him, Draw thy sword, and slay me, that men say not of me, A woman slew him. And his young man thrust him through, and he died.

Sacrifice of Jephthah's nameless daughter

Judges 11:30: And Jephthah vowed a vow unto the LORD, and said, If thou shalt without fail deliver the children of Ammon into mine hands,

31: Then it shall be, that whatsoever cometh forth of the doors of my house to meet me, when I return in peace from the children of Ammon, shall surely be the LORD's, and I will offer it up for a burnt offering.

32: So Jephthah passed over unto the children of Ammon to fight against them; and the LORD delivered them into his hands.

33: And he smote them from Aroer, even till thou come to Minnith, even twenty cities, and unto the plain of the vineyards, with a very great slaughter. Thus the children of Ammon were subdued before the children of Israel.

34: And Jephthah came to Mizpeh unto his house, and, behold, his daughter came out to meet him with timbrels and with dances: and she was his only child; beside her he had neither son nor daughter.

35: And it came to pass, when he saw her, that he rent his clothes, and said, Alas, my daughter! thou hast brought me very low, and thou art one of them that trouble me: for I have opened my mouth unto the LORD, and I cannot go back.

36: And she said unto him, My father, if thou hast opened thy mouth unto the LORD, do to me according to that which hath proceeded out of thy mouth; forasmuch as the LORD hath taken vengeance for thee of thine enemies, even of the children of Ammon.

37: And she said unto her father, Let this thing be done for me: let me alone two months, that I may go up and down upon the mountains, and bewail my virginity, I and my fellows.

38: And he said, Go. And he sent her away for two months: and she went with her companions, and bewailed her virginity upon the mountains.

39: And it came to pass at the end of two months, that she returned unto her father, who did with her according to his vow which he had vowed: and she knew no man. And it was a custom in Israel,

40: That the daughters of Israel went yearly to lament the daughter of Jephthah the Gileadite four days in a year.

Angel impregnates nameless wife

Judges 13:3: And the angel of the LORD appeared unto the woman, and said unto her, Behold now, thou art barren, and bearest not: but thou shalt conceive, and bear a son.

"Strange" wife betrays Samson

Judges 14:1: And Samson went down to Timnath, and saw a woman in Timnath of the daughters of the Philistines.

2: And he came up, and told his father and his mother, and said, I have seen a woman in Timnath of the daughters of the Philistines: now therefore get her for me to wife.

3: Then his father and his mother said unto him, Is there never a woman among the daughters of thy brethren, or among all my people, that thou goest to take a wife of the uncircumcised Philistines? And Samson said unto his father, Get her for me; for she pleaseth me well.

4: But his father and his mother knew not that it was of the LORD, that he sought an occasion against the Philistines: for at that time the Philistines had dominion over Israel.

5: Then went Samson down, and his father and his mother, to Timnath, and came to the vineyards of Timnath: and, behold, a young lion roared against him.

6: And the Spirit of the LORD came mightily upon him, and he rent him as he would have rent a kid, and he had nothing in his hand: but he told not his father or his mother what he had done.

7: And he went down, and talked with the woman; and she pleased Samson well.

8: And after a time he returned to take her, and he turned aside to see the carcase of the lion: and, behold, there was a swarm of bees and honey in the carcase of the lion.

9: And he took thereof in his hands, and went on eating, and came to his father and mother, and he gave them, and they did eat: but he told not them that he had taken the honey out of the carcase of the lion.

10: So his father went down unto the woman: and Samson made

there a feast; for so used the young men to do.

11: And it came to pass, when they saw him, that they brought thirty companions to be with him.

12: And Samson said unto them, I will now put forth a riddle unto you: if ye can certainly declare it me within the seven days of the feast, and find it out, then I will give you thirty sheets and thirty change of garments:

13: But if ye cannot declare it me, then shall ye give me thirty sheets and thirty change of garments. And they said unto him, Put forth thy riddle, that we may hear it.

14: And he said unto them, Out of the eater came forth meat, and out of the strong came forth sweetness. And they could not in three days expound the riddle.

15: And it came to pass on the seventh day, that they said unto Samson's wife, Entice thy husband, that he may declare unto us the riddle, lest we burn thee and thy father's house with fire: have ye called us to take that we have? is it not so?

16: And Samson's wife wept before him, and said, Thou dost but hate me, and lovest me not: thou hast put forth a riddle unto the children of my people, and hast not told it me. And he said unto her, Behold, I have not told it my father nor my mother, and shall I tell it thee?

17: And she wept before him the seven days, while their feast lasted: and it came to pass on the seventh day, that he told her, because she lay sore upon him: and she told the riddle to the children of her people.

18: And the men of the city said unto him on the seventh day before the sun went down, What is sweeter than honey? and what is stronger than a lion? And he said unto them, If ye had not plowed with my heifer, ye had not found out my riddle.

19: And the Spirit of the LORD came upon him, and he went down to Ashkelon, and slew thirty men of them, and took their spoil, and gave change of garments unto them which expounded the riddle. And his anger was kindled, and he went up to his father's house.

20: But Samson's wife was given to his companion, whom he had used as his friend.

Delilah betrays Samson, too

Judges 16:4: And it came to pass afterward, that he loved a woman in the valley of Sorek, whose name was Delilah.

5: And the lords of the Philistines came up unto her, and said unto her, Entice him, and see wherein his great strength lieth, and by what means we may prevail against him, that we may bind him to afflict him: and we will give thee every one of us eleven hundred pieces of silver.

6: And Delilah said to Samson, Tell me, I pray thee, wherein thy great strength lieth, and wherewith thou mightest be bound to afflict thee.

7: And Samson said unto her, If they bind me with seven green withs that were never dried, then shall I be weak, and be as another man.

8: Then the lords of the Philistines brought up to her seven green withs which had not been dried, and she bound him with them.

9: Now there were men lying in wait, abiding with her in the chamber. And she said unto him, The Philistines be upon thee, Samson. And he brake the withs, as a thread of tow is broken when it toucheth the fire. So his strength was not known.

10: And Delilah said unto Samson, Behold, thou hast mocked me, and told me lies: now tell me, I pray thee, wherewith thou mightest be bound.

11: And he said unto her, If they bind me fast with new ropes that never were occupied, then shall I be weak, and be as another man.

12: Delilah therefore took new ropes, and bound him therewith, and said unto him, The Philistines be upon thee, Samson. And there were liers in wait abiding in the chamber. And he brake them from off his arms like a thread.

13: And Delilah said unto Samson, Hitherto thou hast mocked me, and told me lies: tell me wherewith thou mightest be bound. And he said unto her, If thou weavest the seven locks of my head with the web.

14: And she fastened it with the pin, and said unto him, The Philistines be upon thee, Samson. And he awaked out of his sleep, and went away with the pin of the beam, and with the web.

15: And she said unto him, How canst thou say, I love thee, when thine heart is not with me? thou hast mocked me these three times, and hast not told me wherein thy great strength lieth.

16: And it came to pass, when she pressed him daily with her words, and urged him, so that his soul was vexed unto death;

17: That he told her all his heart, and said unto her. There hath not come a rasor upon mine head; for I have been a Nazarite unto God from my mother's womb: if I be shaven, then my strength will go from me, and I shall become weak, and be like any other man.

18: And when Delilah saw that he had told her all his heart, she sent and called for the lords of the Philistines, saying, Come up this once, for he hath shewed me all his heart. Then the lords of the Philistines came up unto her, and brought money in their hand.

19: And she made him sleep upon her knees; and she called for a man, and she caused him to shave off the seven locks of his head; and she began to afflict him, and his strength went from him.

20: And she said, The Philistines be upon thee, Samson. And he awoke out of his sleep, and said, I will go out as at other times before, and shake myself. And he wist not that the LORD was departed from him.

21: But the Philistines took him, and put out his eyes, and brought him down to Gaza, and bound him with fetters of brass; and he did grind in the prison house.

Grisly, cruel sacrifice of concubine

Judges 19:22: Now as they were making their hearts merry, behold, the men of the city, certain sons of Belial, beset the house round about, and beat at the door, and spake to the master of the house, the old man, saying, Bring forth the man that came into thine house, that we may know him.

23: And the man, the master of the house, went out unto them, Nay, my brethren, nay, I pray you, do not so wickedly; seeing that this man is come into mine house, do not this folly.

24: Behold, here is my daughter a maiden, and his concubine; them I will bring out now, and humble ye them, and do with them what seemeth good unto you: but unto this man do not so vile a thing.

25: But the men would not hearken to him: so the man took his concubine, and brought her forth unto them; and they knew her, and abused her all the night until the morning: and when the day began to spring, they let her go.

26: Then came the woman in the dawning of the day, and fell down at the door of the man's house where her lord was, till it was light.

27: And her lord rose up in the morning, and opened the doors of the house, and went out to go his way: and, behold, the woman his concubine was fallen down at the door of the house, and her hands were upon the threshold.

28: And he said unto her, Up, and let us be going. But none answered. Then the man took her up upon an ass, and the man rose up, and gat him unto his place.

29: And when he was come into his house, he took a knife, and laid hold on his concubine, and divided her, together with her bones, into twelve pieces, and sent her into all the coasts of Israel.

Destroy everyone except 400 virgin captives

Judges 21:11: And this is the thing that ye shall do, Ye shall utterly destroy every male, and every woman that hath lain by man.

12: And they found among the inhabitants of Jabesh-gilead four hundred young virgins, that had known no man by lying with any male: and they brought them unto the camp to Shiloh, which is in the land of Canaan.

". . . catch you every man his wife . . ."

Judges 21:19: Then they said, Behold, there is a feast of the LORD in Shiloh yearly in a place which is on the north side of Bethel, on the east side of the highway that goeth up from Bethel to Shechem, and on the south of Lebonah.

20: Therefore they commanded the children of Benjamin, saying, Go and lie in wait in the vineyards;

21: And see, and, behold, if the daughters of Shiloh come out to dance in dances, then come ye out of the vineyards, and catch you every man his wife of the daughters of Shiloh, and go to the land of Benjamin.

22: And it shall be, when their fathers or their brethren come unto us to complain, that we will say unto them, Be favourable unto them for our sakes: because we reserved not to each man his wife in the war: for ye did not give unto them at this time, that ye should be guilty.

23: And the children of Benjamin did so, and took them wives, according to their number, of them that danced, whom they caught: and they went and returned unto their inheritance, and repaired the cities, and dwelt in them.

RUTH

Boaz buys Ruth

4:10: Moreover Ruth the Moabitess, the wife of Mahlon, have I purchased to be my wife, to raise up the name of the dead upon his inheritance, that the name of the dead be not cut off from among his brethren, and from the gate of his place: ye are witnesses this day.

1 SAMUEL

Divine sperm bank

2:21: And the LORD visited Hannah, so that she conceived, and bare three sons and two daughters. And the child Samuel grew before the LORD.

Slay suckling

1 Sam. 15:3: Now go and smite Amalek, and utterly destroy all that they have, and spare them not; but slay both man and woman, infant and suckling, ox and sheep, camel and ass.

Women cheerlead for male warriors

1 Sam. 18:6: And it came to pass as they came, when David was returned from the slaughter of the Philistine, that the women came out of all cities of Israel, singing and dancing, to meet king Saul, with tabrets, with joy, and with instruments of musick.

7: And the women answered one another as they played, and said, Saul hath slain his thousands, and David his ten thousands.

David buys Michal with 200 foreskins

1 Sam. 18:27: Wherefore David arose and went, he and his men, and slew of the Philistines two hundred men; and David brought their foreskins, and they gave them in full tale to the king, that he might be the king's son in law. And Saul gave him Michal his daughter to wife.

Men are holy if they stay away from women

1 Sam. 21:4: And the priest answered David, and said, There is no common bread under mine hand, but there is hallowed bread; if the young men have kept themselves at least from women.

5: And David answered the priest, and said unto him, Of a truth women have been kept from us about these three days, since I came out, and the vessels of the young men are holy, and the bread is in a manner common, yea, though it were sanctified this day in the vessel.

David increases his harem

1 Sam. 25:39: And when David heard that Nabal was dead, he said, Blessed be the LORD, that hath pleaded the cause of my reproach from the hand of Nabal, and hath kept his servant from evil: for the LORD hath returned the wickedness of Nabal upon his own head, And David sent and communed with Abigail, to take her to him to wife.

40: And when the servants of David were come to Abigail to Carmel, they spake unto her, saying, David sent us unto thee to take thee to him to wife.

41: And she arose, and bowed herself on her face to the earth, and said, Behold, let thine handmaid be a servant to wash the feet of the servants of my lord.

42: And Abigail hasted, and arose, and rode upon an ass, with five damsels of hers that went after her; and she went after the messengers of David, and became his wife.

43: David also took Ahinoam of Jezreel; and they were also both of them his wives.

"Neither man nor woman (left) alive"

1 Sam. 27:9: And David smote the land, and left neither man nor woman alive, and took away the sheep, and the oxen, and the asses, and the camels, and the apparel, and returned, and came to Achish.

2 SAMUEL

David took more concubines and wives

5:13: And David took him more concubines and wives out of Jerusalem, after he was come from Hebron: and there were yet sons and daughters born to David.

Michal barren for reproving David's exhibitionism

2 Sam. 6:20: Then David returned to bless his household. And Michal the daughter of Saul came out to meet David, and said, How glorious was the king of Israel to day, who uncovered himself to day in the eyes of the handmaids of his servants, as one of the vain fellows shamelessly uncovereth himself!

21: And David said unto Michal, It was before the LORD, which chose me before thy father, and before all his house, to appoint me ruler over the people of the LORD, over Israel: therefore will I play before the LORD.

22: And I will yet be more vile than thus, and will be base in mine own sight: and of the maidservants which thou hast spoken of, of them shall I be had in honour.

23: Therefore Michal the daughter of Saul had no child unto the day of her death.

David a Peeping Tom

2 Sam. 11:2: And it came to pass in an eveningtide, that David arose from off his bed, and walked upon the roof of the king's house: and from the roof he saw a woman washing herself; and the woman was very beautiful to look upon.

3: And David sent and inquired after the woman. And one said, Is not this Bath-sheba, the daughter of Eliam, the wife of Uriah the Hittite?

4: And David sent messengers, and took her; and she came in unto him, and he lay with her; for she was purified from her uncleanness: and she returned unto her house.

God orders rape of David's *wives* to punish David

2 Sam. 12:11: Thus saith the LORD, Behold, I will raise up evil against thee out of thine own house, and I will take thy wives before thine eyes, and give them unto thy neighbour, and he shall lie with thy wives in the sight of this sun.

12: For thou didst it secretly: but I will do this thing before all Israel, and before the sun.

Incest-rape avenged through male honor code

2 Sam. 13:1: And it came to pass after this, that Absalom the son of David had a fair sister, whose name was Tamar; and Amnon the son of David loved her.

2: And Amnon was so vexed, that he fell sick for his sister Tamar; for she was a virgin; and Amnon thought it hard for him to do any thing to her.

3: But Amnon had a friend, whose name was Jonadab, the son of Shimeah David's brother: and Jonadab was a very subtil man.

4: And he said unto him, Why art thou, being the king's son, lean from day to day? wilt thou not tell me? And Amnon said unto him, I love Tamar, my brother Absalom's sister.

5: And Jonadab said unto him, Lay thee down on thy bed, and make thyself sick: and when thy father cometh to see thee, say unto him, I pray thee, let my sister Tamar come, and give me meat, and dress the meat in my sight, that I may see it, and eat it at her hand.

6: So Amnon lay down, and made himself sick: and when the king was come to see him, Amnon said unto the king, I pray thee, let Tamar my sister come, and make me a couple of cakes in my sight, that I may eat at her hand.

7: Then David sent home to Tamar, saying, Go now to thy brother

Amnon's house, and dress him meat.

8: So Tamar went to her brother Amnon's house; and he was laid down. And she took flour, and kneaded it, and made cakes in his sight, and did bake the cakes.

9: And she took a pan, and poured them out before him; but he refused to eat. And Amnon said, Have out all men from me. And they went out every man from him.

10: And Amnon said unto Tamar, Bring the meat into the chamber, that I may eat of thine hand. And Tamar took the cakes which she had made, and brought them into the chamber to Amnon her brother.

11: And when she had brought them unto him to eat, he took hold of her, and said unto her, Come lie with me, my sister.

12: And she answered him, Nay, my brother, do not force me; for no such thing ought to be done in Israel: do not thou this folly.

13: And I, whither shall I cause my shame to go? and as for thee, thou shalt be as one of the fools in Israel. Now therefore, I pray thee, speak unto the king; for he will not withhold me from thee.

14: Howbeit he would not hearken unto her voice: but, being stronger than she, forced her, and lay with her.

15: Then Amnon hated her exceedingly; so that the hatred wherewith he hated her was greater than the love wherewith he had loved her. And Amnon said unto her, Arise, be gone.

16: And she said unto him, There is no cause: this evil in sending me away is greater than the other that thou didst unto me. But he would not hearken unto her.

17: Then he called his servant that ministered unto him, and said, Put now this woman out from me, and bolt the door after her.

18: And she had a garment of divers colours upon her: for with such robes were the king's daughters that were virgins apparelled. Then his servant brought her out, and bolted the door after her.

19: And Tamar put ashes on her head, and rent her garment of divers colours that was on her, and laid her hand on her head, and went on crying.

20: And Absalom her brother said unto her, Hath Amnon thy brother been with thee? but hold now thy peace, my sister: he is thy brother; regard not this thing. So Tamar remained desolate in her brother Absalom's house.

21: But when king David heard of all these things, he was very wroth.

22: And Absalom spake unto his brother Amnon neither good nor bad: for Absalom hated Amnon, because he had forced his sister Tamar.

23: And it came to pass after two full years, that Absalom had sheepshearers in Baal-hazor, which is beside Ephraim: and Absalom invited all the king's sons.

24: And Absalom came to the king, and said, Behold now, thy servant hath sheepshearers; let the king, I beseech thee, and his servants go with thy servant.

25: And the king said to Absalom, Nay, my son, let us not all now go, lest we be chargeable unto thee. And he pressed him: howbeit he would not go, but blessed him.

26: Then said Absalom, If not, I pray thee, let my brother Amnon go with us. And the king said unto him, Why should he go with thee?

27: But Absalom pressed him, that he let Amnon and all the king's sons go with him.

28: Now Absalom had commanded his servants, saying, Mark ye now when Amnon's heart is merry with wine, and when I say unto you, Smite Amnon; then kill him, fear not: have not I commanded you? be courageous and be valiant.

29: And the servants of Absalom did unto Amnon as Absalom had commanded. Then all the king's sons arose, and every man gat him up upon his mule, and fled.

Absalom rapes dad's concubines in public

2 Sam. 16:22: So they spread Absalom a tent upon the top of the house; and Absalom went in unto his father's concubines in the sight of all Israel.

David's concubines imprisoned because they were raped [see 16:22 above]

2 Sam. 20:3: And David came to his house at Jerusalem; and the king took the ten women his concubines, whom he had left to keep the house, and put them in ward, and fed them, but went not in unto them. So they were shut up unto the day of their death, living in widowhood.

1 KINGS

Virgin offered to "warm up" dying David

1:1 Now king David was old and stricken in years; and they covered him with clothes, but he gat no heat.

2: Wherefore his servants said unto him, Let there be sought for my lord the king a young virgin: and let her stand before the king, and let her cherish him, and let her lie in thy bosom, that my lord the king may get heat.

3: So they sought for a fair damsel throughout all the coasts of Israel, and found Abishag a Shunammite, and brought her to the king.

4: And the damsel was very fair, and cherished the king, and ministered to him: but the king knew her not.

Demeaning story about "two harlots"

1 Kings 3:16: Then came there two women, that were harlots, unto the king, and stood before him.

17: And the one woman said, O my lord, I and this woman dwell in one house; and I was delivered of a child with her in the house.

18: And it came to pass the third day after that I was delivered, that this woman was delivered also: and we were together; there was no stranger with us in the house, save we two in the house.

19: And this woman's child died in the night; because she overlaid it.

20: And she arose at midnight, and took my son from beside me, while thine handmaid slept, and laid it in her bosom, and laid her dead child in my bosom.

21: And when I rose in the morning to give my child suck, behold, it was dead: but when I had considered it in the morning, behold, it was not my son, which I did bear.

22: And the other woman said, Nay; but the living is my son, and the dead is thy son. And this said, No; but the dead is thy son, and the living is my son. Thus they spake before the king.

23: Then said the king, The one saith, This is my son that liveth, and thy son is the dead: and the other saith, Nay; but thy son is the dead, and my son is the living.

24: And the king said, Bring me a sword. And they brought a sword before the king.

25: And the king said, Divide the living child in two, and give half to the one, and half to the other.

26: Then spake the woman whose the living child was unto the king, for her bowels yearned upon her son, and she said, O my lord, give her the living child, and in no wise slay it. But the other said, Let it be neither mine nor thine, but divide it.

27: Then the king answered and said, Give her the living child, and in no wise slay it: she is the mother thereof.

28: And all Israel heard of the judgment which the king had judged; and they feared the king: for they saw that the wisdom of God was in him, to do judgment.

Solomon had 700 wives and 300 concubines who "turned away his heart"

1 Kings 11:1: But king Solomon loved many strange women, together with the daughter of Pharaoh, women of the Moabites, Ammonites, Edomites, Zidonians, and Hittites;

2: Of the nations concerning which the LORD said unto the children of Israel, Ye shall not go in to them, neither shall they come in unto you: for surely they will turn away your heart after their gods: Solomon clave unto these in love.

3: And he had seven hundred wives, princesses, and three hundred concubines: and his wives turned away his heart.

4: For it came to pass, when Solomon was old, that his wives turned away his heart after other gods: and his heart was not perfect with the LORD his God, as was the heart of David his father.

Jezebel "stirs up" husband's wickedness

1 Kings 21:1: And it came to pass after these things, that Naboth the Jezreelite had a vineyard, which was in Jezreel, hard by the palace of Ahab king of Samaria.

2: And Ahab spake unto Naboth, saying, Give me thy vineyard, that I may have it for a garden of herbs, because it is near unto my house: and I will give thee for it a better vineyard than it; or, if it seem good to thee, I will give thee the worth of it in money.

3: And Naboth said to Ahab, The LORD forbid it me, that I should give the inheritance of my fathers unto thee.

4: And Ahab came into his house heavy and displeased because of the word which Naboth the Jezreelite had spoken to him: for he had said, I will not give thee the inheritance of my fathers. And he laid him down upon his bed, and turned away his face, and would eat no bread.

5: But Jezebel his wife came to him, and said unto him, Why is thy spirit so sad, that thou eatest no bread?

6: And he said unto her, Because I spake unto Naboth the Jezreelite, and said unto him, Give me thy vineyard for money; or else, if it please thee, I will give thee another vineyard for it: and he answered, I will not give thee my vineyard.

7: And Jezebel his wife said unto him, Dost thou now govern the kingdom of Israel? arise, and eat bread, and let thine heart be merry: I will give thee the vineyard of Naboth the Jezreelite.

8: So she wrote letters in Ahab's name, and sealed them with his seal, and sent the letters unto the elders and to the nobles that were in his city, dwelling with Naboth.

9: And she wrote in the letters, saying, Proclaim a fast, and set Naboth on high among the people:

10: And set two men, sons of Belial, before him, to bear witness against him, saying, Thou didst blaspheme God and the king. And then carry him out, and stone him, that he may die.

11: And the men of his city, even the elders and the nobles who were the inhabitants in his city, did as Jezebel had sent unto them, and as it was written in the letters which she had sent unto them.

12: They proclaimed a fast, and set Naboth on high among the people.

13: And there came in two men, children of Belial, and sat before him: and the men of Belial witnessed against him, even against Naboth, in the presence of the people, saying, Naboth did blaspheme God and the king. Then they carried him forth out of the city, and stoned him with stones, that he died.

14: Then they sent to Jezebel, saying, Naboth is stoned, and is dead.

15: And it came to pass, when Jezebel heard that Naboth was stoned, and was dead, that Jezebel said to Ahab, Arise, take possession of the vineyard of Naboth the Jezreelite, which he refused to give thee for money: for Naboth is not alive, but dead.

16: And it came to pass, when Ahab heard that Naboth was dead, that Ahab rose up to go down to the vineyard of Naboth the Jezreelite, to take possession of it.

17: And the word of the LORD came to Elijah the Tishbite, saying,

18: Arise, go down to meet Ahab king of Israel, which is in Samaria: behold, he is in the vineyard of Naboth, whither he is gone down to possess it.

19: And thou shalt speak unto him, saying, Thus saith the LORD, Hast thou killed, and also taken possession? And thou shalt speak unto him, saying, Thus saith the LORD, In the place where dogs licked the blood of Naboth shall dogs lick thy blood, even thine.

20: And Ahab said to Elijah, Hast thou found me, O mine enemy? And he answered, I have found thee: because thou hast sold thyself to work evil in the sight of the LORD.

21: Behold, I will bring evil upon thee, and will take away thy posterity, and will cut off from Ahab him that pisseth against the wall, and him that is shut up and left in Israel,

22: And will make thine house like the house of Jeroboam the son of Nebat, and like the house of Baasha the son of Ahijah, for the provocation wherewith thou hast provoked me to anger, and made

Israel to sin.

23: And of Jezebel also spake the LORD, saying, The dogs shall eat Jezebel by the wall of Jezreel.

24: Him that dieth of Ahab in the city the dogs shall eat; and him that dieth in the field shall the fowls of the air eat.

25: But there was none like unto Ahab, which did sell himself to work wickedness in the sight of the LORD, whom Jezebel his wife stirred up.

26: And he did very abominably in following idols, according to all things as did the Amorites, whom the LORD cast out before the children of Israel.

27: And it came to pass, when Ahab heard those words, that he rent his clothes, and put sackcloth upon his flesh, and fasted, and lay in sackcloth, and went softly.

28: And the word of the LORD came to Elijah the Tishbite, saying,

29: Seest thou how Ahab humbleth himself before me? because he humbleth himself before me, I will not bring the evil in his days: but in his son's days will I bring the evil upon his house.

2 KINGS

Jezebel is brutally killed as her murderer dines and drinks

2 Kings 9:32: And he lifted up his face to the window, and said, Who is on my side? who? And there looked out to him two or three eunuchs.

33: And he said, Throw her down. So they threw her down: and some of her blood was sprinkled on the wall, and on the horses: and he trode her under foot.

34: And when he was come in, he did eat and drink, and said, Go, see now this cursed woman, and bury her: for she is a king's daughter.

35: And they went to bury her: but they found no more of her than the skull, and the feet, and the palms of her hands.

36: Wherefore they came again, and told him. And he said, This is the word of the LORD, which he spake by his servant Elijah the Tishbite, saying, In the portion of Jezreel shall dogs eat the flesh of Jezebel:

37: And the carcase of Jezebel shall be as dung upon the face of the field in the portion of Jezreel; so that they shall not say, This is Jezebel.

More carnage

2 Kings 15:16: Then Menahem smote Tiphsah, and all that were therein, and the coasts thereof from Tirzah: because they opened not to him, therefore he smote it; and all the women therein that were with child he ripped up.

2 CHRONICLES

King Rehoboam had 18 wives and 60 concubines

11:21: And Rehoboam loved Maachah the daughter of Absalom above all his wives and his concubines: (for he took eighteen wives, and threescore concubines; and begat twenty and eight sons, and threescore daughters.)

Abijah has 14 wives

2 Chron. 13:21: But Abijah waxed mighty, and married fourteen wives, and begat twenty and two sons, and sixteen daughters.

ESTHER

Vashti, bible's only feminist dethroned; sordid tale of Esther

1:7: And they gave them drink in vessels of gold, (the vessels being diverse one from another,) and royal wine in abundance, according to the state of the king.

8: And the drinking was according to the law; none did compel: for so the king had appointed to all the officers of his house, that they should do according to every man's pleasure.

9: Also Vashti the queen made a feast for the women in the royal house which belonged to king Ahasuerus.

10: On the seventh day, when the heart of the king was merry with wine, he commanded Mehuman, Biztha, Harbona, Bigtha, and Abagtha, Zethar, and Carcas, the seven chamberlains that served in the presence of Ahasuerus the king,

11: To bring Vashti the queen before the king with the crown royal, to shew the people and the princes her beauty: for she was fair to look on.

12: But the queen Vashti refused to come at the king's commandment by his chamberlains: therefore was the king very wroth, and his anger burned in him.

13: Then the king said to the wise men, which knew the times, (for so was the king's manner toward all that knew law and judgment:

14: And the next unto him was Carshena, Shethar, Admatha, Tarshish, Meres, Marsena, and Memucan, the seven princes of Persia and Media, which saw the king's face, and which sat the first in the kingdom;)

15: What shall we do unto the queen Vashti according to law, because she hath not performed the commandment of the king Ahasuerus by the chamberlains?

16: And Memucan answered before the king and the princes, Vashti the queen hath not done wrong to the king only, but also to all the princes, and to all the people that are in all the provinces of the king Ahasuerus.

17: For this deed of the queen shall come abroad unto all women, so that they shall despise their husbands in their eyes, when it shall be reported, The king Ahasuerus commanded Vashti the queen to be brought in before him, but she came not.

18: Likewise shall the ladies of Persia and Media say this day unto all the king's princes, which have heard of the deed of the queen. Thus shall there arise too much contempt and wrath.

19: If it please the king, let there go a royal commandment from him, and let it be written among the laws of the Persians and the Medes, that it be not altered, That Vashti come no more before king Ahasuerus; and let the king give her royal estate unto another that is better than she.

20: And when the king's decree which he shall make shall be published throughout all his empire, (for it is great,) all the wives shall give to their husbands honour, both to great and small.

21: And the saying pleased the king and the princes; and the king did according to the word of Memucan:

22: For he sent letters into all the king's provinces, into every province according to the writing thereof, and to every people after their language, that every man should bear rule in his own house, and that it should be published according to the language of every people.

Esther is purified for a full year before "delighting" the king as Vashti's replacement

Esther 2:1: After these things, when the wrath of king Ahasuerus was appeased, he remembered Vashti, and what she had done, and what was decreed against her.

2: Then said the king's servants that ministered unto him, Let there be fair young virgins sought for the king:

3: And let the king appoint officers in all the provinces of his kingdom, that they may gather together all the fair young virgins unto Shushan the palace, to the house of the women unto the custody of Hege the king's chamberlain, keeper of the women; and let their things for purification be given them:

4: And let the maiden which pleaseth the king be queen instead of Vashti. And the thing pleased the king; and he did so.

5: Now in Shushan the palace there was a certain Jew, whose name was Mordecai, the son of Jair, the son of Shimei, the son of Kish, a Benjamite;

6: Who had been carried away from Jerusalem with the captivity which had been carried away with Jeconiah king of Judah, whom Nebuchadnezzar the king of Babylon had carried away.

7: And he brought up Hadassah, that is, Esther, his uncle's daughter: for she had neither father nor mother, and the maid was fair and beautiful; whom Mordecai, when her father and mother were dead, took for his own daughter.

8: So it came to pass, when the king's commandment and his decree was heard, and when many maidens were gathered together unto Shushan the palace, to the custody of Hegai, that Esther was brought also unto the king's house, to the custody of Hegai, keeper of the women.

9: And the maiden pleased him, and she obtained kindness of him; and he speedily gave her her things for purification, with such things as belonged to her, and seven maidens, which were meet to be given her, out of the king's house: and he preferred her and her maids unto the best place of the house of the women.

10: Esther had not shewed her people nor her kindred: for Mordecai had charged her that she should not shew it.

11: And Mordecai walked every day before the court of the women's house, to know how Esther did, and what should become of her.

12: Now when every maid's turn was come to go in to king Ahasuerus, after that she had been twelve months, according to the manner of the women, (for so were the days of their purifications accomplished, to wit, six months with oil of myrrh, and six months with sweet odours, and with other things for the purifying of the women;)

13: Then thus came every maiden unto the king; whatsoever she desired was given her to go with her out of the house of the women unto the king's house.

14: In the evening she went, and on the morrow she returned into the second house of the women, to the custody of Shaashgaz, the king's chamberlain, which kept the concubines: she came in unto the king no more, except the king delighted in her, and that she were called by name.

15: Now when the turn of Esther, the daughter of Abihail the uncle of Mordecai, who had taken her for his daughter, was come to go in unto the king, she required nothing but what Hegai the king's chamberlain, the keeper of the women, appointed. And Esther obtained favour in the sight of all them that looked upon her.

16: So Esther was taken unto king Ahasuerus into his house royal in the tenth month, which is the month Tebeth, in the seventh year of his reign.

17: And the king loved Esther above all the women, and she obtained grace and favour in his sight more than all the virgins; so that he set the royal crown upon her head, and made her queen instead of Vashti.

JOB

Job's wife "foolish" for cursing God for persecuting Job

2:9: Then said his wife unto him, Dost thou still retain thine integrity? curse God, and die.

10: But he said unto her, Thou speakest as one of the foolish women speaketh. What? shall we receive good at the hand of God, and shall we not receive evil? In all this did not Job sin with his lips.

"Who can bring a clean thing out of an unclean? not one . . ."

Job 14:1: Man that is born of a woman is of few days, and full of trouble.

2: He cometh forth like a flower, and is cut down: he fleeth also as a shadow, and continueth not.

3: And dost thou open thine eyes upon such an one, and bringest me into judgment with thee?

4: Who can bring a clean thing out of an unclean? not one.

More insults to mothers
Job 15:14: What is man, that he should be clean? and he which is born of a woman, that he should be righteous?

Women unclean
Job 25:4: How then can man be justified with God? or how can he be clean that is born of a woman?

PSALMS
"Blessed is the man . . ."
1:1: Blessed is the man that walketh not in the counsel of the ungodly, nor standeth in the way of sinners, nor sitteth in the seat of the scornful.

Man is "a little lower than the angels"
Psalms 8:5: For thou hast made him a little lower than the angels, and hast crowned him with glory and honour.

"In sin did my mother conceive me"
Psalms 51:5: Behold, I was shapen in iniquity; and in sin did my mother conceive me.

Dash the little ones against the stones
Psalms 137:9: Happy shall he be, that taketh and dasheth thy little ones against the stones.

PROVERBS
"Deliver thee from the strange woman . . ."
2:16: To deliver thee from the strange woman, even from the stranger which flattereth with her words;

17: Which forsaketh the guide of her youth, and forgetteth the covenant of her God.

18: For her house inclineth unto death, and her paths unto the dead.

"Keep thee from the evil woman"
Proverbs 6:24: To keep thee from the evil woman, from the flattery of the tongue of a strange woman.

25: Lust not after her beauty in thine heart; neither let her take thee with her eyelids.

26: For by means of a whorish woman a man is brought to a piece of bread: and the adulteress will hunt for the precious life.

27: Can a man take fire in his bosom, and his clothes not be burned?

28: Can one go upon hot coals, and his feet not be burned?

29: So he that goeth in to his neighbour's wife; whosoever toucheth her shall not be innocent.

"Strange" women seduce men, who are like an ox going to slaughter, in this pathological warning

Proverbs 7:9: In the twilight, in the evening, in the black and dark night:

10: And, behold, there met him a woman with the attire of an harlot, and subtil of heart.

11: (She is loud and stubborn; her feet abide not in her house:

12: Now is she without, now in the streets, and lieth in wait at every corner.)

13: So she caught him, and kissed him, and with an impudent face said unto him,

14: I have peace offerings with me; this day have I payed my vows.

15: Therefore came I forth to meet thee, diligently to seek thy face, and I have found thee.

16: I have decked my bed with coverings of tapestry, with carved works, with fine linen of Egypt.

17: I have perfumed my bed with myrrh, aloes, and cinnamon.

18: Come, let us take our fill of love until the morning: let us solace ourselves with loves.

19: For the goodman is not at home, he is gone a long journey:

20: He hath taken a bag of money with him, and will come home at the day appointed.

21: With her much fair speech she caused him to yield, with the flattering of her lips she forced him.

22: He goeth after her straightway, as an ox goeth to the slaughter, or as a fool to the correction of the stocks;

23: Till a dart strike through his liver; as a bird hasteth to the snare, and knoweth not that it is for his life.

24: Hearken unto me now therefore, O ye children, and attend to the words of my mouth.

25: Let not thine heart decline to her ways, go not astray in her paths.

26: For she hath cast down many wounded: yea, many strong men have been slain by her.

27: Her house is the way to hell, going down to the chambers of death.

"A foolish woman is clamorous"

Proverbs 9:13: A foolish woman is clamorous: she is simple, and knoweth nothing.

14: For she sitteth at the door of her house, on a seat in the high places of the city,

15: To call passengers who go right on their ways:

16: Whoso is simple, let him turn in hither: and as for him that wanteth understanding, she saith to him,

17: Stolen waters are sweet, and bread eaten in secret is pleasant.

18: But he knoweth not that the dead are there; and that her guests are in the depths of hell.

Father gets the credit, mother gets the blame

Proverbs 10:1: The proverbs of Solomon. A wise son maketh a glad father: but a foolish son is the heaviness of his mother.

Indiscreet women like jewel in swine's snout

Proverbs 11:22: As a jewel of gold in a swine's snout, so is a fair woman which is without discretion.

Don't spare for son's crying

Proverbs 19:18: Chasten thy son while there is hope, and let not thy soul spare for his crying.

"Mouth of strange women is a deep pit"

Proverbs 22:14: The mouth of strange women is a deep pit: he that is abhorred of the LORD shall fall therein.

"Beat your son — he won't die"

Proverbs 23:13: Withhold not correction from the child: for if thou beatest him with the rod, he shall not die.

14: Thou shalt beat him with the rod, and shalt deliver his soul from hell.

"Whores" and "strange women" increase men's sins

Proverbs 23:27: For a whore is a deep ditch; and a strange woman is a narrow pit.

28: She also lieth in wait as for a prey, and increaseth the transgressors among men.

"Brawling women" dissed

Proverbs 25:24: It is better to dwell in the corner of the housetop, than with a brawling woman and in a wide house.

Woman compared to nasty weather

Proverbs 27:15: A continual dropping in a very rainy day and a contentious woman are alike.

"She eateth and wipeth her mouth"

Proverbs 30:20: Such is the way of an adulterous woman; she eateth, and wipeth her mouth, and saith, I have done no wickedness.

"Odious woman" disquiets the earth

Proverbs 30:21: For three things the earth is disquieted, and for four which it cannot bear: . . .

23: For an odious woman when she is married; and an handmaid that is heir to her mistress.

"Give not thy strength unto women"

Proverbs 31:3: Give not thy strength unto women, nor thy ways to that which destroyeth kings.

"Who can find a virtuous woman?" and "a goodly woman" is a drudge

Proverbs 31:10: Who can find a virtuous woman? for her price is far above rubies.

11: The heart of her husband doth safely trust in her, so that he shall have no need of spoil.

12: She will do him good and not evil all the days of her life.

13: She seeketh wool, and flax, and worketh willingly with her hands.

14: She is like the merchants' ships; she bringeth her food from afar.

15: She riseth also while it is yet night, and giveth meat to her household, and a portion to her maidens.

16: She considereth a field, and buyeth it: with the fruit of her hands she planteth a vineyard.

17: She girdeth her loins with strength, and strengtheneth her arms.

18: She perceiveth that her merchandise is good: her candle goeth not out by night.

19: She layeth her hands to the spindle, and her hands hold the distaff.

20: She stretcheth out her hand to the poor; yea, she reacheth forth her hands to the needy.

21: She is not afraid of the snow for her household: for all her household are clothed with scarlet.

22: She maketh herself coverings of tapestry; her clothing is silk and purple.

23: Her husband is known in the gates, when he sitteth among the elders of the land.

24: She maketh fine linen, and selleth it; and delivereth girdles unto the merchant.

25: Strength and honour are her clothing; and she shall rejoice in time to come.

26: She openeth her mouth with wisdom; and in her tongue is the law of kindness.

27: She looketh well to the ways of her household, and eateth not the bread of idleness.

28: Her children arise up, and call her blessed; her husband also, and he praiseth her.

29: Many daughters have done virtuously, but thou excellest them all.

30: Favour is deceitful, and beauty is vain: but a woman that feareth the LORD, she shall be praised.

31: Give her of the fruit of her hands; and let her own works praise her in the gates.

ECCLESIASTES

". . . more bitter than death the woman . . ."

7:26: And I find more bitter than death the woman, whose heart is snares and nets, and her hands as bands: whoso pleaseth God shall escape from her; but the sinner shall be taken by her.

SONG OF SOLOMON

Not a romantic passage

5:4: My beloved put in his hand by the hole of the door, and my bowels were moved for him.

"Little sister hath no breasts"

Song of Solomon 8:8: We have a little sister, and she hath no breasts: what shall we do for our sister in the day when she shall be spoken for?

ISAIAH

"Women shall rule over Israel" — a threat

3:12: As for my people, children are their oppressors, and women rule over them. O my people, they which lead thee cause thee to err, and destroy the way of thy paths.

". . . and the Lord will discover their secret parts"

Isaiah 3:16: Moreover the LORD saith, Because the daughters of Zion are haughty, and walk with stretched forth necks and wanton eyes, walking and mincing as they go, and making a tinkling with their feet:

17: Therefore the LORD will smite with a scab the crown of the head of the daughters of Zion, and the LORD will discover their secret parts.

Aggressive women cited as threat

Isaiah 4:1: And in that day seven women shall take hold of one man, saying, We will eat our own bread, and wear our own apparel: only let us be called by thy name, to take away our reproach.

Grisly verse

Isaiah 9:20: And he shall snatch on the right hand, and be hungry; and he shall eat on the left hand, and they shall not be satisfied: they shall eat every man the flesh of his own arm.

Wives ravished

Isaiah 13:16: Their children also shall be dashed to pieces before their eyes; their houses shall be spoiled, and their wives ravished.

"No pity on the fruit of the womb"

Isaiah 13:18: Their bows also shall dash the young men to pieces; and they shall have no pity on the fruit of the womb; their eye shall not spare children.

Egypt shall be like a woman and shake with fear

Isaiah 19:16: In that day shall Egypt be like unto women: and it shall be afraid and fear because of the shaking of the hand of the LORD of hosts, which he shaketh over it.

"Tremble, ye women that are at ease"

Isaiah 32:11: Tremble, ye women that are at ease; be troubled, ye careless ones: strip you, and make you bare, and gird sackcloth upon your loins.

12: They shall lament for the teats, for the pleasant fields, for the fruitful vine.

Barren women rejoice

Isaiah 54:1: Sing, O barren, thou that didst not bear; break forth into singing, and cry aloud, thou that didst not travail with child: for more are the children of the desolate than the children of the married wife, saith the LORD.

JEREMIAH

Women stereotyped

2:32: Can a maid forget her ornaments, or a bride her attire? yet my people have forgotten me days without number.

Compares straying people to harlot (again)

Jer. 3:1: They say, If a man put away his wife, and she go from him, and become another man's, shall he return unto her again? shall not that land be greatly polluted? but thou hast played the harlot with many lovers; yet return again to me, saith the LORD.

Treacherous wife/nation metaphor

Jer. 3:20: Surely as a wife treacherously departeth from her husband, so have ye dealt treacherously with me, O house of Israel, saith the LORD.

"... send for cunning women ..."

Jer. 9:17: Thus saith the LORD of hosts, Consider ye, and call for the mourning women, that they may come; and send for cunning women, that they may come:

18: And let them make haste, and take up a wailing for us, that our eyes may run down with tears, and our eyelids gush out with waters.

19: For a voice of wailing is heard out of Zion, How are we spoiled! we are greatly confounded, because we have forsaken the land, because our dwellings have cast us out.

20: Yet hear the word of the LORD, O ye women, and let your ear receive the word of his mouth, and teach your daughters wailing, and every one her neighbour lamentation.

LAMENTATIONS

"Her filthiness is in her skirts ... Jerusalem is as a menstruous woman"

1:8: Jerusalem hath grievously sinned; therefore she is removed: all that honoured her despise her, because they have seen her nakedness: yea, she sigheth, and turneth backward.

9: Her filthiness is in her skirts; she remembereth not her last end; therefore she came down wonderfully: she had no comforter. O LORD, behold my affliction: for the enemy hath magnified himself.

10: The adversary hath spread out his hand upon all her pleasant things: for she hath seen that the heathen entered into her sanctuary, whom thou didst command that they should not enter into thy congregation.

11: All her people sigh, they seek bread; they have given their pleasant things for meat to relieve the soul: see, O LORD, and consider; for I am become vile.

12: Is it nothing to you, all ye that pass by? behold, and see if there be any sorrow like unto my sorrow, which is done unto me, wherewith the LORD hath afflicted me in the day of his fierce anger.

13: From above hath he sent fire into my bones, and it prevaileth against them: he hath spread a net for my feet, he hath turned me back: he hath made me desolate and faint all the day.

14: The yoke of my transgressions is bound by his hand: they are wreathed, and come up upon my neck: he hath made my strength to fall, the Lord hath delivered me into their hands, from whom I am not able to rise up.

15: The Lord hath trodden under foot all my mighty men in the midst of me: he hath called an assembly against me to crush my young men: the Lord hath trodden the virgin, the daughter of Judah, as in a winepress.

16: For these things I weep; mine eye, mine eye runneth down with water, because the comforter that should relieve my soul is far from me: my children are desolate, because the enemy prevailed.

17: Zion spreadeth forth her hands, and there is none to comfort her: the LORD hath commanded concerning Jacob, that his adversaries should be round about him: Jerusalem is as a menstruous woman among them.

Women to eat fetuses and children

Lam. 2:20: Behold, O LORD, and consider to whom thou hast done this. Shall the women eat their fruit, and children of a span long? shall the priest and the prophet be slain in the sanctuary of the Lord?

EZEKIEL

Familial cannibalism

5:10: Therefore the fathers shall eat the sons in the midst of thee, and the sons shall eat their fathers; and I will execute judgments in thee, and the whole remnant of thee will I scatter into all the winds.

Lord's loins appear

Ezekiel 8:2: Then I beheld, and lo a likeness as the appearance of fire: from the appearance of his loins even downward, fire; and from his loins even upward, as the appearance of brightness, as the colour of amber.

"Slay utterly" all but circumcised men

Ezekiel 9:6: Slay utterly old and young, both maids, and little children, and women: but come not near any man upon whom is the mark; and begin at my sanctuary. Then they began at the ancient men which were before the house.

"Woe to the women . . ."

Ezekiel 13:18: And say, Thus saith the Lord GOD; Woe to the women that sew pillows to all armholes, and make kerchiefs upon the head of every stature to hunt souls! Will ye hunt the souls of my people, and will ye save the souls alive that come unto you?

19: And will ye pollute me among my people for handfuls of barley and for pieces of bread, to slay the souls that should not die, and to save the souls alive that should not live, by your lying to my people that hear your lies?

20: Wherefore thus saith the Lord GOD; Behold, I am against your pillows, wherewith ye there hunt the souls to make them fly, and I will tear them from your arms, and will let the souls go, even the souls that ye hunt to make them fly.

Lord as vengeful pimp

Ezekiel 16:1: Again the word of the LORD came unto me, saying,

2: Son of man, cause Jerusalem to know her abominations,

3: And say, Thus saith the Lord GOD unto Jerusalem; Thy birth and thy nativity is of the land of Canaan; thy father was an Amorite, and thy mother an Hittite.

4: And as for thy nativity, in the day thou wast born thy navel was not cut, neither wast thou washed in water to supple thee; thou wast not salted at all, nor swaddled at all.

5: None eye pitied thee, to do any of these unto thee, to have compassion upon thee; but thou wast cast out in the open field, to the lothing of thy person, in the day that thou wast born.

6: And when I passed by thee, and saw thee polluted in thine own blood, I said unto thee when thou wast in thy blood, Live; yea, I said unto thee when thou wast in thy blood, Live.

7: I have caused thee to multiply as the bud of the field, and thou hast increased and waxen great, and thou art come to excellent ornaments: thy breasts are fashioned, and thine hair is grown, whereas thou wast naked and bare.

8: Now when I passed by thee, and looked upon thee, behold, thy time was the time of love; and I spread my skirt over thee, and covered thy nakedness: yea, I sware unto thee, and entered into a covenant with thee, saith the Lord GOD, and thou becamest mine.

9: Then washed I thee with water; yea, I throughly washed away thy blood from thee, and I anointed thee with oil.

10: I clothed thee also with broidered work, and shod thee with badgers' skin, and I girded thee about with fine linen, and I covered thee with silk.

11: I decked thee also with ornaments, and I put bracelets upon thy hands, and a chain on thy neck.

12: And I put a jewel on thy forehead, and earrings in thine ears, and a beautiful crown upon thine head.

13: Thus wast thou decked with gold and silver; and thy raiment was of fine linen, and silk, and broidered work; thou didst eat fine flour, and honey, and oil: and thou wast exceeding beautiful, and thou didst prosper into a kingdom.

14: And thy renown went forth among the heathen for thy beauty: for it was perfect through my comeliness, which I had put upon thee, saith the Lord GOD.

15: But thou didst trust in thine own beauty, and playedst the harlot because of thy renown, and pouredst out thy fornications on every one that passed by; his it was.

16: And of thy garments thou didst take, and deckedst thy high places with divers colours, and playedst the harlot thereupon: the like things shall not come, neither shall it be so.

17: Thou hast also taken thy fair jewels of my gold and of my silver, which I had given thee, and madest to thyself images of men, and didst commit whoredom with them,

18: And tookest thy broidered garments, and coveredst them: and thou hast set mine oil and mine incense before them.

19: My meat also which I gave thee, fine flour, and oil, and honey, wherewith I fed thee, thou hast even set it before them for a sweet savour: and thus it was, saith the Lord GOD.

20: Moreover thou hast taken thy sons and thy daughters, whom thou hast borne unto me, and these hast thou sacrificed unto them to be devoured. Is this of thy whoredoms a small matter,

21: That thou hast slain my children, and delivered them to cause them to pass through the fire for them?

22: And in all thine abominations and thy whoredoms thou hast not remembered the days of thy youth, when thou wast naked and bare, and wast polluted in thy blood.

23: And it came to pass after all thy wickedness, (woe, woe unto thee! saith the Lord GOD;)

24: That thou hast also built unto thee an eminent place, and hast made thee an high place in every street.

25: Thou hast built thy high place at every head of the way, and hast made thy beauty to be abhorred, and hast opened thy feet to every one that passed by, and multiplied thy whoredoms.

26: Thou hast also committed fornication with the Egyptians thy neighbours, great of flesh; and hast increased thy whoredoms, to provoke me to anger.

27: Behold, therefore I have stretched out my hand over thee, and have diminished thine ordinary food, and delivered thee unto the will of them that hate thee, the daughters of the Philistines, which are ashamed of thy lewd way.

28: Thou hast played the whore also with the Assyrians, because thou wast unsatiable; yea, thou hast played the harlot with them, and yet couldest not be satisfied.

29: Thou hast moreover multiplied thy fornication in the land of Canaan unto Chaldea; and yet thou wast not satisfied herewith.

30: How weak is thine heart, saith the Lord GOD, seeing thou doest all these things, the work of an imperious whorish woman;

31: In that thou buildest thine eminent place in the head of every way, and makest thine high place in every street; and hast not been as an harlot, in that thou scornest hire;

32: But as a wife that committeth adultery, which taketh strangers instead of her husband!

33: They give gifts to all whores: but thou givest thy gifts to all thy lovers, and hirest them, that they may come unto thee on every side for thy whoredom.

34: And the contrary is in thee from other women in thy whoredoms, whereas none followeth thee to commit whoredoms: and in that thou givest a reward, and no reward is given unto thee, therefore thou art contrary.

35: Wherefore, O harlot, hear the word of the LORD:

36: Thus saith the Lord GOD; Because thy filthiness was poured out, and thy nakedness discovered through thy whoredoms with thy lovers, and with all the idols of thy abominations, and by the blood of thy children, which thou didst give unto them;

37: Behold, therefore I will gather all thy lovers, with whom thou hast taken pleasure, and all them that thou hast loved, with all them that thou hast hated; I will even gather them round about against thee, and will discover thy nakedness unto them, that they may see all thy nakedness.

38: And I will judge thee, as women that break wedlock and shed blood are judged; and I will give thee blood in fury and jealousy.

39: And I will also give thee into their hand, and they shall throw down thine eminent place, and shall break down thy high places: they shall strip thee also of thy clothes, and shall take thy fair jewels, and leave thee naked and bare.

40: They shall also bring up a company against thee, and they shall stone thee with stones, and thrust thee through with their swords.

41: And they shall burn thine houses with fire, and execute judgments upon thee in the sight of many women: and I will cause thee to cease from playing the harlot, and thou also shalt give no hire any more.

42: So will I make my fury toward thee to rest, and my jealousy shall depart from thee, and I will be quiet, and will be no more angry.

43: Because thou hast not remembered the days of thy youth, but hast fretted me in all these things; behold, therefore I also will recompense thy way upon thine head, saith the Lord GOD: and thou shalt not commit this lewdness above all thine abominations.

44: Behold, every one that useth proverbs shall use this proverb against thee, saying, As is the mother, so is her daughter.

45: Thou art thy mother's daughter, that lotheth her husband and her children; and thou art the sister of thy sisters, which lothed their husbands and their children: your mother was an Hittite, and your father an Amorite.

46: And thine elder sister is Samaria, she and her daughters that dwell at thy left hand: and thy younger sister, that dwelleth at thy right hand, is Sodom and her daughters.

47: Yet hast thou not walked after their ways, nor done after their abominations: but, as if that were a very little thing, thou wast corrupted more than they in all thy ways.

48: As I live, saith the Lord GOD, Sodom thy sister hath not done, she nor her daughters, as thou hast done, thou and thy daughters.

49: Behold, this was the iniquity of thy sister Sodom, pride, fullness of bread, and abundance of idleness was in her and in her daughters, neither did she strengthen the hand of the poor and needy.

50: And they were haughty, and committed abomination before me: therefore I took them away as I saw good.

51: Neither hath Samaria committed half of thy sins; but thou hast multiplied thine abominations more than they, and hast justified thy sisters in all thine abominations which thou hast done.

52: Thou also, which hast judged thy sisters, bear thine own shame for thy sins that thou hast committed more abominable than they: they are more righteous than thou: yea, be thou confounded also, and bear thy shame, in that thou hast justified thy sisters.

53: When I shall bring again their captivity, the captivity of Sodom and her daughters, and the captivity of Samaria and her daughters, then will I bring again the captivity of thy captives in the midst of them:

54: That thou mayest bear thine own shame, and mayest be confounded in all that thou hast done, in that thou art a comfort unto them.

55: When thy sisters, Sodom and her daughters, shall return to their former estate, and Samaria and her daughters shall return to their former estate, then thou and thy daughters shall return to your former estate.

56: For thy sister Sodom was not mentioned by thy mouth in the day of thy pride,

57: Before thy wickedness was discovered, as at the time of thy reproach of the daughters of Syria, and all that are round about her, the daughters of the Philistines, which despise thee round about.

58: Thou hast borne thy lewdness and thine abominations, saith the LORD.

59: For thus saith the Lord GOD; I will even deal with thee as thou hast done, which hast despised the oath in breaking the covenant.

60: Nevertheless I will remember my covenant with thee in the days of thy youth, and I will establish unto thee an everlasting covenant.

61: Then thou shalt remember thy ways, and be ashamed, when thou shalt receive thy sisters, thine elder and thy younger: and I will give them unto thee for daughters, but not by thy covenant.

62: And I will establish my covenant with thee; and thou shalt know that I am the LORD:

63: That thou mayest remember, and be confounded, and never open thy mouth any more because of thy shame, when I am pacified toward thee for all that thou hast done, saith the Lord GOD.

Coming near menstruous woman is like abandoning God

Ezekiel 18:5: But if a man be just, and do that which is lawful and right,

6: And hath not eaten upon the mountains, neither hath lifted up his eyes to the idols of the house of Israel, neither hath defiled his neighbour's wife, neither hath come near to a menstruous woman, . . .

A change of pace — a respectful motherhood metaphor

Ezekiel 19:1: Moreover take thou up a lamentation for the princes of Israel,

2: And say, What is thy mother? A lioness: she lay down among lions, she nourished her whelps among young lions.

3: And she brought up one of her whelps: it became a young lion, and it learned to catch the prey; it devoured men.

4: The nations also heard of him; he was taken in their pit, and they brought him with chains unto the land of Egypt.

5: Now when she saw that she had waited, and her hope was lost, then she took another of her whelps, and made him a young lion.

6: And he went up and down among the lions, he became a young lion, and learned to catch the prey, and devoured men.

7: And he knew their desolate palaces, and he laid waste their cities; and the land was desolate, and the fullness thereof, by the noise of his roaring.

8: Then the nations set against him on every side from the provinces, and spread their net over him: he was taken in their pit.

9: And they put him in ward in chains, and brought him to the king of Babylon: they brought him into holds, that his voice should no more be heard upon the mountains of Israel.

10: Thy mother is like a vine in thy blood, planted by the waters: she was fruitful and full of branches by reason of many waters.

11: And she had strong rods for the sceptres of them that bare rule, and her stature was exalted among the thick branches, and she appeared in her height with the multitude of her branches.

12: But she was plucked up in fury, she was cast down to the ground, and the east wind dried up her fruit: her strong rods were broken and withered; the fire consumed them.

13: And now she is planted in the wilderness, in a dry and thirsty ground.

14: And fire is gone out of a rod of her branches, which hath devoured her fruit, so that she hath no strong rod to be a sceptre to rule. This is a lamentation, and shall be for a lamentation.

"Bloody" city defiles itself

Ezekiel 22:2: Now, thou son of man, wilt thou judge, wilt thou judge the bloody city? yea, thou shalt shew her all her abominations.

3: Then say thou, Thus saith the Lord GOD, The city sheddeth blood in the midst of it, that her time may come, and maketh idols against herself to defile herself.

4: Thou art become guilty in thy blood that thou hast shed; and hast defiled thyself in thine idols which thou hast made; and thou hast caused thy days to draw near, and art come even unto thy years: therefore have I made thee a reproach unto the heathen, and a mocking to all countries.

5: Those that be near, and those that be far from thee, shall mock thee, which art infamous and much vexed.

6: Behold, the princes of Israel, every one were in thee to their power to shed blood.

God orders Aholah, a whore, slain

Ezekiel 23:1: The word of the LORD came again unto me, saying,

2: Son of man, there were two women, the daughters of one mother:

3: And they committed whoredoms in Egypt; they committed whoredoms in their youth: there were their breasts pressed, and there they bruised the teats of their virginity.

4: And the names of them were Aholah the elder, and Aholibah her sister: and they were mine, and they bare sons and daughters. Thus were their names; Samaria is Aholah, and Jerusalem Aholibah.

5: And Aholah played the harlot when she was mine; and she doted on her lovers, on the Assyrians her neighbours,

6: Which were clothed with blue, captains and rulers, all of them desirable young men, horsemen riding upon horses.

7: Thus she committed her whoredoms with them, with all them that were the chosen men of Assyria, and with all on whom she doted: with all their idols she defiled herself.

8: Neither left she her whoredoms brought from Egypt: for in her youth they lay with her, and they bruised the breasts of her virginity, and poured their whoredom upon her.

9: Wherefore I have delivered her into the hand of her lovers, into the hand of the Assyrians, upon whom she doted.

10: These discovered her nakedness: they took her sons and her daughters, and slew her with the sword: and she became famous among women; for they had executed judgment upon her.

Sister Aholibah likewise slain and sexually mutilated

Ezekiel 23:11: And when her sister Aholibah saw this, she was more corrupt in her inordinate love than she, and in her whoredoms more than her sister in her whoredoms.

12: She doted upon the Assyrians her neighbours, captains and rulers clothed most gorgeously, horsemen riding upon horses, all of them desirable young men.

13: Then I saw that she was defiled, that they took both one way,

14: And that she increased her whoredoms: for when she saw men pourtrayed upon the wall, the images of the Chaldeans pourtrayed with vermilion,

15: Girded with girdles upon their loins, exceeding in dyed attire upon their heads, all of them princes to look to, after the manner of the Babylonians of Chaldea, the land of their nativity:

16: And as soon as she saw them with her eyes, she doted upon them, and sent messengers unto them into Chaldea.

17: And the Babylonians came to her into the bed of love, and they defiled her with their whoredom, and she was polluted with them, and her mind was alienated from them.

18: So she discovered her whoredoms, and discovered her nakedness: then my mind was alienated from her, like as my mind was alienated from her sister.

19: Yet she multiplied her whoredoms, in calling to remembrance the days of her youth, wherein she had played the harlot in the land of Egypt.

20: For she doted upon their paramours, whose flesh is as the flesh of asses, and whose issue is like the issue of horses.

21: Thus thou calledst to remembrance the lewdness of thy youth, in bruising thy teats by the Egyptians for the paps of thy youth.

22: There, O Aholibah, thus saith the Lord GOD; Behold, I will raise up thy lovers against thee, from whom thy mind is alienated, and I will bring them against thee on every side;

23: The Babylonians, and all the Chaldeans, Pekod, and Shoa, and Koa, and all the Assyrians with them: all of them desirable young men, captains and rulers, great lords and renowned, all of them riding upon horses.

24: And they shall come against thee with chariots, wagons, and wheels, and with an assembly of people, which shall set against thee buckler and shield and helmet round about: and I will set judgment before them, and they shall judge thee according to their judgments.

25: And I will set my jealousy against thee, and they shall deal furiously with thee: they shall take away thy nose and thine ears; and thy remnant shall fall by the sword: they shall take thy sons and thy daughters; and thy residue shall be devoured by the fire.

26: They shall also strip thee out of thy clothes, and take away thy fair jewels.

27: Thus will I make thy lewdness to cease from thee, and thy whoredom brought from the land of Egypt: so that thou shalt not lift up thine eyes unto them, nor remember Egypt any more.

28: For thus saith the Lord GOD; Behold, I will deliver thee into the hand of them whom thou hatest, into the hand of them from whom thy mind is alienated:

29: And they shall deal with thee hatefully, and shall take away all thy labour, and shall leave thee naked and bare: and the nakedness of thy whoredoms shall be discovered, both thy lewdness and thy whoredoms.

30: I will do these things unto thee, because thou hast gone a whoring after the heathen, and because thou art polluted with their idols.

31: Thou hast walked in the way of thy sister; therefore will I give her cup into thine hand.

32: Thus saith the Lord GOD; Thou shalt drink of thy sister's cup deep and large: thou shalt be laughed to scorn and had in derision; it containeth much.

33: Thou shalt be filled with drunkenness and sorrow, with the cup of astonishment and desolation, with the cup of thy sister Samaria.

34: Thou shalt even drink it and suck it out, and thou shalt break the sherds thereof, and pluck off thine own breasts: for I have spoken it, saith the Lord GOD.

35: Therefore thus saith the Lord GOD; Because thou hast forgotten me, and cast me behind thy back, therefore bear thou also thy lewdness and thy whoredoms.

36: The LORD said moreover unto me; Son of man, wilt thou judge Aholah and Aholibah? yea, declare unto them their abominations;

37: That they have committed adultery, and blood is in their hands, and with their idols have they committed adultery, and have also caused their sons, whom they bare unto me, to pass for them through the fire, to devour them.

38: Moreover this they have done unto me: they have defiled my sanctuary in the same day, and have profaned my sabbaths.

39: For when they had slain their children to their idols, then they came the same day into my sanctuary to profane it; and, lo, thus have they done in the midst of mine house.

40: And furthermore, that ye have sent for men to come from far, unto whom a messenger was sent; and, lo, they came: for whom thou didst wash thyself, paintedst thy eyes, and deckedst thyself with ornaments,

41: And satest upon a stately bed, and a table prepared before it, whereupon thou hast set mine incense and mine oil.

42: And a voice of a multitude being at ease was with her: and with the men of the common sort were brought Sabeans from the wilderness, which put bracelets upon their hands, and beautiful crowns upon their heads.

43: Then said I unto her that was old in adulteries, Will they now commit whoredoms with her, and she with them?

44: Yet they went in unto her, as they go in unto a woman that playeth the harlot: so went they in unto Aholah and unto Aholibah, the lewd women.

45: And the righteous men, they shall judge them after the manner of adulteresses, and after the manner of women that shed blood; because they are adulteresses, and blood is in their hands.

46: For thus saith the Lord GOD; I will bring up a company upon them, and will give them to be removed and spoiled.

47: And the company shall stone them with stones, and dispatch them with their swords; they shall slay their sons and their daughters, and burn up their houses with fire.

48: Thus will I cause lewdness to cease out of the land, that all women may be taught not to do after your lewdness.

49: And they shall recompense your lewdness upon you, and ye shall bear the sins of your idols: and ye shall know that I am the Lord GOD.

"Whores" had to be killed to teach women not to be "lewd"

Ezekiel 23:48: Thus will I cause lewdness to cease out of the land, that all women may be taught not to do after your lewdness.

Slay daughters in the field metaphor

Ezekiel 26:6: And her daughters which are in the field shall be slain by the sword; and they shall know that I am the LORD.

7: For thus saith the Lord GOD; Behold, I will bring upon Tyrus Nebuchadrezzar king of Babylon, a king of kings, from the north, with horses, and with chariots, and with horsemen, and companies, and much people.

8: He shall slay with the sword thy daughters in the field: and he shall make a fort against thee, and cast a mount against thee, and lift up the buckler against thee.

God performs bloody castration with a sword

Ezekiel 29:7: When they took hold of thee by thy hand, thou didst break, and rend all their shoulder: and when they leaned upon thee, thou brakest, and madest all their loins to be at a stand.

8: Therefore thus saith the Lord GOD; Behold, I will bring a sword upon thee, and cut off man and beast out of thee.

"The uncleanness of a removed woman"

Ezekiel 36:17: Son of man, when the house of Israel dwelt in their own land, they defiled it by their own way and by their doings: their way was before me as the uncleanness of a removed woman.

HOSEA

"Land commiteth great whoredom"

1:2: The beginning of the word of the LORD by Hosea. And the LORD said to Hosea, Go, take unto thee a wife of whoredoms and children of whoredoms: for the land hath committed great whoredom, departing from the LORD.

". . . discover her lewdness in the sight of her lovers"

Hosea 2:10: And now will I discover her lewdness in the sight of her lovers, and none shall deliver her out of mine hand.

A woman is purchased with silver and barley

Hosea 3:2: So I bought her to me for fifteen pieces of silver, and for an homer of barley, and an half homer of barley:

Miscarrying womb and dry breasts

Hosea 9:14: Give them, O LORD: what wilt thou give? give them a miscarrying womb and dry breasts.

Women with child "ripped up"

Hosea 13:16: Samaria shall become desolate; for she hath rebelled against her God: they shall fall by the sword: their infants shall be dashed in pieces, and their women with child shall be ripped up.

NAHUM

"I will discover thy skirts upon thy face"

3:4: Because of the multitude of the whoredoms of the wellfavoured harlot, the mistress of witchcrafts, that selleth nations through her whoredoms, and families through her witchcrafts.

5: Behold, I am against thee, saith the LORD of hosts; and I will discover thy skirts upon thy face, and I will shew the nations thy nakedness, and the kingdoms thy shame.

"Thy people in the midst of thee are women"

Nahum 3:6: And I will cast abominable filth upon thee, and make thee vile, and will set thee as a gazingstock. . . .

13: Behold, thy people in the midst of thee are women: the gates of thy land shall be set wide open unto thine enemies: the fire shall devour thy bars.

ZECHARIAH

The city shall be taken and the women ravished

14:2: For I will gather all nations against Jerusalem to battle; and the city shall be taken, and the houses rifled, and the women ravished; and half of the city shall go forth into captivity, and the residue of the people shall not be cut off from the city.

New Testament

MATTHEW

52 generations of Jesus cited from *Joseph's* side

1:16: And Jacob begat Joseph the husband of Mary, of whom was born Jesus, who is called Christ.

17: So all the generations from Abraham to David are fourteen generations; and from David until the carrying away into Babylon are fourteen generations; and from the carrying away into Babylon unto Christ are fourteen generations.

Holy Ghost knocks up Virgin Mary

1:18: Now the birth of Jesus Christ was on this wise: When as his mother Mary was espoused to Joseph, before they came together, she was found with child of the Holy Ghost.

Jesus came to uphold, not reform, the law

Matt. 5:17: Think not that I am come to destroy the law, or the prophets: I am not come to destroy, but to fulfill.

18: For verily I say unto you, Till heaven and earth pass, one jot or one tittle shall in no wise pass from the law, till all be fulfilled.

Mutilate yourself if you "lust in your heart"

Matt. 5:28: But I say unto you, That whosoever looketh on a woman to lust after her hath committed adultery with her already in his heart.

29: And if thy right eye offend thee, pluck it out, and cast it from thee: for it is profitable for thee that one of thy members should perish, and not that thy whole body should be cast into hell.

Divorce double standard

Matt. 5:32: But I say unto you, That whosoever shall put away his wife, saving for the cause of fornication, causeth her to commit adultery: and whosoever shall marry her that is divorced committeth adultery.

"Who is my mother?"

Matt. 12:48: But he answered and said unto him that told him, Who is my mother? and who are my brethren?

Gentile woman and daughter called "dogs" by Jesus

Matt. 15:22: And, behold, a woman of Canaan came out of the same coasts, and cried unto him, saying, Have mercy on me, O Lord, thou Son of David; my daughter is grievously vexed with a devil.

23: But he answered her not a word. And his disciples came and besought him, saying, Send her away; for she crieth after us.

24: But he answered and said, I am not sent but unto the lost sheep of the house of Israel.

25: Then came she and worshipped him, saying, Lord, help me.

26: But he answered and said, It is not meet to take the children's bread, and to cast it to dogs.

"One flesh" marriage — no divorce

Matt. 19:6: Wherefore they are no more twain, but one flesh. What therefore God hath joined together, let not man put asunder.

Eunuchs praised

Matt. 19:12: For there are some eunuchs, which were so born from their mother's womb: and there are some eunuchs, which were made eunuchs of men: and there be eunuchs, which have made themselves eunuchs for the kingdom of heaven's sake. He that is able to receive it, let him receive it.

"Woe unto them that are with child"

Matt. 24:19: And woe unto them that are with child, and to them that give suck in those days!

Jesus tells polygyny parable without censure

Matt. 25:1: Then shall the kingdom of heaven be likened unto ten virgins, which took their lamps, and went forth to meet the bridegroom.

2: And five of them were wise, and five were foolish.

3: They that were foolish took their lamps, and took no oil with them:

4: But the wise took oil in their vessels with their lamps.

5: While the bridegroom tarried, they all slumbered and slept.

6: And at midnight there was a cry made, Behold, the bridegroom cometh; go ye out to meet him.

7: Then all those virgins arose, and trimmed their lamps.

8: And the foolish said unto the wise, Give us of your oil; for our lamps are gone out.

9: But the wise answered, saying, Not so; lest there be not enough for us and you: but go ye rather to them that sell, and buy for yourselves.

10: And while they went to buy, the bridegroom came; and they that were ready went in with him to the marriage: and the door was shut.

11: Afterward came also the other virgins, saying, Lord, Lord, open to us.

12: But he answered and said, Verily I say unto you, I know you not.

13: Watch therefore, for ye know neither the day nor the hour wherein the Son of man cometh.

MARK

Jesus asks, "Who is my mother?"

3:33: And he answered them, saying, Who is my mother, or my brethren?

"Virtue" goes out of Jesus when menstruating woman touches him

Mark 5:25: And a certain woman, which had an issue of blood twelve years,

26: And had suffered many things of many physicians, and had spent all that she had, and was nothing bettered, but rather grew worse,

27: When she had heard of Jesus, came in the press behind, and touched his garment.

28: For she said, If I may touch but his clothes, I shall be whole.

29: And straightway the fountain of her blood was dried up; and she felt in her body that she was healed of that plague.

30: And Jesus, immediately knowing in himself that virtue had gone out of him, turned him about in the press, and said, Who touched my clothes?

Repeat of J.C.'s "dog" remarks

Mark 7:25: For a certain woman, whose young daughter had an unclean spirit, heard of him, and came and fell at his feet:

26: The woman was a Greek, a Syrophenician by nation; and she besought him that he would cast forth the devil out of her daughter.

27: But Jesus said unto her, Let the children first be filled: for it is not meet to take the children's bread, and to cast it unto the dogs.

28: And she answered and said unto him, Yes, Lord: yet the dogs under the table eat of the children's crumbs.

29: And he said unto her, For this saying go thy way; the devil is gone out of thy daughter.

30: And when she was come to her house, she found the devil gone out, and her daughter laid upon the bed.

Jesus forbids all divorce here

Mark 10:2: And the Pharisees came to him, and asked him, Is it lawful for a man to put away his wife? tempting him.

3: And he answered and said unto them, What did Moses command you?

4: And they said, Moses suffered to write a bill of divorcement, and to put her away.

5: And Jesus answered and said unto them, For the hardness of your heart he wrote you this precept.

6: But from the beginning of the creation God made them male and female.

7: For this cause shall a man leave his father and mother, and cleave to his wife;

8: And they twain shall be one flesh: so then they are no more twain, but one flesh.

9: What therefore God hath joined together, let not man put asunder.

Jesus calls both male and female divorcees who remarry adulterers

Mark 10:11: And he saith unto them, Whosoever shall put away his wife, and marry another, committeth adultery against her.

12: And if a woman shall put away her husband, and be married to another, she committeth adultery.

Jesus casts out seven devils from Mary Magdalene

Mark 16:9: Now when Jesus was risen early the first day of the week, he appeared first to Mary Magdalene, out of whom he had cast seven devils.

LUKE

Mary unclean after birth of Jesus

2:22: And when the days of her purification according to the law of Moses were accomplished, they brought him to Jerusalem, to present him to the Lord;

"Every male that openeth the womb shall be called holy to the Lord"

Luke 2:23: (As it is written in the law of the Lord, Every male that openeth the womb shall be called holy to the Lord;)

Woman "sinner" bathes J.C.'s feet with tears and dries them with her hair — he "forgives" her sins

Luke 7:37: And, behold, a woman in the city, which was a sinner, when she knew that Jesus sat at meat in the Pharisee's house, brought an alabaster box of ointment,

38: And stood at his feet behind him weeping, and began to wash his feet with tears, and did wipe them with the hairs of her head, and kissed his feet, and anointed them with the ointment.

39: Now when the Pharisee which had bidden him saw it, he spake within himself, saying, This man, if he were a prophet, would have known who and what manner of woman this is that toucheth him: for she is a sinner.

40: And Jesus answering said unto him, Simon, I have somewhat to say unto thee. And he saith, Master, say on.

41: There was a certain creditor which had two debtors: the one owed five hundred pence, and the other fifty.

42: And when they had nothing to pay, he frankly forgave them both. Tell me therefore, which of them will love him most?

43: Simon answered and said, I suppose that he, to whom he forgave most. And he said unto him, Thou hast rightly judged.

44: And he turned to the woman, and said unto Simon, Seest thou this woman? I entered into thine house, thou gavest me no water for my feet: but she hath washed my feet with tears, and wiped them with the hairs of her head.

45: Thou gavest me no kiss: but this woman since the time I came in hath not ceased to kiss my feet.

46: My head with oil thou didst not anoint: but this woman hath anointed my feet with ointment.

47: Wherefore I say unto thee, Her sins, which are many, are forgiven; for she loved much: but to whom little is forgiven, the same loveth little.

48: And he said unto her, Thy sins are forgiven.

Mary Magdalene has devil infestation

Luke 8:2: And certain women, which had been healed of evil spirits and infirmities, Mary called Magdalene, out of whom went seven devils, . . .

Jesus refuses to bless his mother. Happy Non-Mother's Day!

Luke 11:27: And it came to pass, as he spake these things, a certain woman of the company lifted up her voice, and said unto him, Blessed is the womb that bare thee, and the paps which thou hast sucked.

28: But he said, Yea rather, blessed are they that hear the word of God, and keep it.

Cannot be disciple unless you hate your mother, etc.

Luke 14:26: If any man come to me, and hate not his father, and mother, and wife, and children, and brethren, and sisters, yea, and his own life also, he cannot be my disciple.

Heaven more likely for unmarried

Luke 20:34: And Jesus answering said unto them, The children of this world marry, and are given in marriage:

35: But they which shall be accounted worthy to obtain that world, and the resurrection from the dead, neither marry, nor are given in marriage

"Blessed are the barren"

Luke 23:29: For, behold, the days are coming, in the which they shall say, Blessed are the barren, and the wombs that never bare, and the paps which never gave suck.

JOHN
"Woman, what have I to do with thee?"

2:1: And the third day there was a marriage in Cana of Galilee; and the mother of Jesus was there:

2: And both Jesus was called, and his disciples, to the marriage.

3: And when they wanted wine, the mother of Jesus saith unto him, They have no wine.

4: Jesus saith unto her, Woman, what have I to do with thee? mine hour is not yet come.

Jesus risks adulteress' life

John 8:3: And the scribes and Pharisees brought unto him a woman taken in adultery; and when they had set her in the midst,

4: They say unto him, Master, this woman was taken in adultery, in the very act.

5: Now Moses in the law commanded us, that such should be stoned: but what sayest thou?

6: This they said, tempting him, that they might have to accuse him. But Jesus stooped down, and with his finger wrote on the ground, as though he heard them not.

7: So when they continued asking him, he lifted up himself, and said unto them, He that is without sin among you, let him first cast a stone at her.

8: And again he stooped down, and wrote on the ground.

9: And they which heard it, being convicted by their own conscience, went out one by one, beginning at the eldest, even unto the last: and Jesus was left alone, and the woman standing in the midst.

10: When Jesus had lifted up himself, and saw none but the woman, he said unto her, Woman, where are those thine accusers? hath no man condemned thee?

11: She said, No man, Lord. And Jesus said unto her, Neither do I condemn thee: go, and sin no more.

Woman will forget childbirth pain as soon as "a man is born into the world" — hallelujah!

John 16:21: A woman when she is in travail hath sorrow, because her hour is come: but as soon as she is delivered of the child, she remembereth no more the anguish, for joy that a man is born into the world.

"Touch me not" — Jesus to Mary Magdalene. But he let Thomas touch him, 20:27

John 20:17: Jesus saith unto her, Touch me not; for I am not yet ascended to my Father: but go to my brethren, and say unto them, I ascend unto my Father, and your Father; and to my God, and your God.

ROMANS

Reiterates death penalty for homosexuals

1:26: For this cause God gave them up unto vile affections: for even their women did change the natural use into that which is against nature:

27: And likewise also the men, leaving the natural use of the woman, burned in their lust one toward another; men with men working that which is unseemly, and receiving in themselves that recompence of their error which was meet.

28: And even as they did not like to retain God in their knowledge, God gave them over to a reprobate mind, to do those things which are not convenient;

29: Being filled with all unrighteousness, fornication, wickedness, covetousness, maliciousness; full of envy, murder, debate, deceit, malignity; whisperers,

30: Backbiters, haters of God, despiteful, proud, boasters, inventors of evil things, disobedient to parents,

31: Without understanding, covenantbreakers, without natural affection, implacable, unmerciful:

32: Who knowing the judgment of God, that they which commit such things are worthy of death, not only do the same, but have pleasure in them that do them.

Unfair adultery rule

Romans 7:1: Know ye not, brethren, (for I speak to them that know the law,) how that the law hath dominion over a man as long as he liveth?

2: For the woman which hath an husband is bound by the law to her husband so long as he liveth; but if the husband be dead, she is loosed from the law of her husband.

3: So then if, while her husband liveth, she be married to another man, she shall be called an adulteress: but if her husband be dead, she is free from that law; so that she is no adulteress, though she be married to another man.

1 CORINTHIANS

"Deliver to Satan . . ."

5:1: It is reported commonly that there is fornication among you, and such fornication as is not so much as named among the Gentiles, that one should have his father's wife. . . .

2: And ye are puffed up, and have not rather mourned, that he that hath done this deed might be taken away from among you. . . .

5: To deliver such an one unto Satan for the destruction of the flesh, that the spirit may be saved in the day of the Lord Jesus.

Effeminate or homosexual men barred from heaven

1 Cor. 6:9: Know ye not that the unrighteous shall not inherit the kingdom of God? Be not deceived: neither fornicators, nor idolaters, nor adulterers, nor effeminate, nor abusers of themselves with mankind,

"It is good for a man not to touch a woman"

1 Cor. 7:1: Now concerning the things whereof ye wrote unto me: It is good for a man not to touch a woman.

"It is better to marry than to burn"

1 Cor. 7:2: Nevertheless, to avoid fornication, let every man have his own wife, and let every woman have her own husband.

3: Let the husband render unto the wife due benevolence: and likewise also the wife unto the husband.

4: The wife hath not power of her own body, but the husband: and likewise also the husband hath not power of his own body, but the wife.

5: Defraud ye not one the other, except it be with consent for a time, that ye may give yourselves to fasting and prayer; and come together again, that Satan tempt you not for your incontinency.

6: But I speak this by permission, and not of commandment.

7: For I would that all men were even as I myself. But every man hath his proper gift of God, one after this manner, and another after that.

8: I say therefore to the unmarried and widows, It is good for them if they abide even as I.

9: But if they cannot contain, let them marry: for it is better to marry than to burn.

10: And unto the married I command, yet not I, but the Lord, Let not the wife depart from her husband:

11: But and if she depart, let her remain unmarried, or be reconciled to her husband: and let not the husband put away his wife.

12: But to the rest speak I, not the Lord: If any brother hath a wife that believeth not, and she be pleased to dwell with him, let him not put her away.

13: And the woman which hath an husband that believeth not, and if he be pleased to dwell with her, let her not leave him.

14: For the unbelieving husband is sanctified by the wife, and the unbelieving wife is sanctified by the husband: else were your children unclean; but now are they holy.

15: But if the unbelieving depart, let him depart. A brother or a sister is not under bondage in such cases: but God hath called us to peace.

16: For what knowest thou, O wife, whether thou shalt save thy husband? or how knowest thou, O man, whether thou shalt save thy wife?

17: But as God hath distributed to every man, as the Lord hath called every one, so let him walk. And so ordain I in all churches.

18: Is any man called being circumcised? let him not become uncircumcised. Is any called in uncircumcision? let him not be circumcised.

19: Circumcision is nothing, and uncircumcision is nothing, but the keeping of the commandments of God.

20: Let every man abide in the same calling wherein he was called.

21: Art thou called being a servant? care not for it: but if thou mayest be made free, use it rather.

22: For he that is called in the Lord, being a servant, is the Lord's freeman: likewise also he that is called, being free, is Christ's servant.

23: Ye are bought with a price; be not ye the servants of men.

24: Brethren, let every man, wherein he is called, therein abide with God.

Marriage belittled

1 Cor. 7:25: Now concerning virgins I have no commandment of the Lord: yet I give my judgment, as one that hath obtained mercy of the Lord to be faithful.

26: I suppose therefore that this is good for the present distress, I say, that it is good for a man so to be.

27: Art thou bound unto a wife? seek not to be loosed. Art thou loosed from a wife? seek not a wife.

28: But and if thou marry, thou hast not sinned; and if a virgin marry, she hath not sinned. Nevertheless such shall have trouble in the flesh: but I spare you.

29: But this I say, brethren, the time is short: it remaineth, that both they that have wives be as though they had none;

30: And they that weep, as though they wept not; and they that rejoice, as though they rejoiced not; and they that buy, as though they possessed not;

31: And they that use this world, as not abusing it: for the fashion of this world passeth away.

32: But I would have you without carefulness. He that is unmarried careth for the things that belong to the Lord, how he may please the Lord:

33: But he that is married careth for the things that are of the world, how he may please his wife.

34: There is difference also between a wife and a virgin. The unmarried woman careth for the things of the Lord, that she may be holy both in body and in spirit: but she that is married careth for the things of the world, how she may please her husband.

35: And this I speak for your own profit; not that I may cast a snare upon you, but for that which is comely, and that ye may attend upon the Lord without distraction.

36: But if any man think that he behaveth himself uncomely toward his virgin, if she pass the flower of her age, and need so require, let him do what he will, he sinneth not: let them marry.

37: Nevertheless he that standeth stedfast in his heart, having no necessity, but hath power over his own will, and hath so decreed in his heart that he will keep his virgin, doeth well.

38: So then he that giveth her in marriage doeth well; but he that giveth her not in marriage doeth better.

39: The wife is bound by the law as long as her husband liveth; but if her husband be dead, she is at liberty to be married to whom she will; only in the Lord.

40: But she is happier if she so abide, after my judgment: and I think also that I have the Spirit of God.

The "head of every woman is the man," long hair is "shame" for men, women must cover heads when praying

1 Cor. 11:3: But I would have you know, that the head of every man is Christ; and the head of the woman is the man; and the head of Christ is God.

4: Every man praying or prophesying, having his head covered, dishonoureth his head.

5: But every woman that prayeth or prophesieth with her head uncovered dishonoureth her head: for that is even all one as if she were shaven.

6: For if the woman be not covered, let her also be shorn: but if it be a shame for a woman to be shorn or shaven, let her be covered.

7: For a man indeed ought not to cover his head, forasmuch as he is the image and glory of God: but the woman is the glory of the man.

8: For the man is not of the woman; but the woman of the man.

9: Neither was the man created for the woman; but the woman for the man.

10: For this cause ought the woman to have power on her head because of the angels.

11: Nevertheless neither is the man without the woman, neither the woman without the man, in the Lord.

12: For as the woman is of the man, even so is the man also by the woman; but all things of god.

13: Judge in yourselves: is it comely that a woman pray unto God uncovered?

14: Doth not even nature itself teach you, that, if a man have long hair, it is a shame unto him?

15: But if a woman have long hair, it is a glory to her: for her hair is given her for a covering.

Women: Shut up!

1 Cor. 14:34: Let your women keep silence in the churches: for it is not permitted unto them to speak; but they are commanded to be under obedience, as also saith the law.

35: And if they will learn any thing, let them ask their husbands at home: for it is a shame for women to speak in the church.

GALATIANS

"There is neither male nor female"

3:27: For as many of you as have been baptized into Christ have put on Christ.

28: There is neither Jew nor Greek, there is neither bond nor free, there is neither male nor female: for ye are all one in Christ Jesus.

29: And if ye be Christ's, then are ye Abraham's seed, and heirs according to the promise.

"Rejoice, thou barren"

Gal. 4:27: For it is written, [in Isaiah 54:1] Rejoice, thou barren that bearest not; break forth and cry, thou that travailest not: for the desolate hath many more children than she which hath an husband.

EPHESIANS

Wives, submit . . .

5:22: Wives, submit yourselves unto your own husbands, as unto the Lord.

23: For the husband is the head of the wife, even as Christ is the head of the church: and he is the saviour of the body.

24: Therefore as the church is subject unto Christ, so let the wives be to their own husbands in every thing.

25: Husbands, love your wives, even as Christ also loved the church, and gave himself for it;

26: That he might sanctify and cleanse it with the washing of water by the word,

27: That he might present it to himself a glorious church, not having spot, or wrinkle, or any such thing; but that it should be holy and without blemish.

28: So ought men to love their wives as their own bodies. He that loveth his wife loveth himself.

29: For no man ever yet hated his own flesh; but nourisheth and cherisheth it, even as the Lord the church:

30: For we are members of his body, of his flesh, and of his bones.

31: For this cause shall a man leave his father and mother, and shall be joined unto his wife, and they two shall be one flesh.

32: This is a great mystery: but I speak concerning Christ and the church.

33: Nevertheless let every one of you in particular so love his wife even as himself; and the wife see that she reverence her husband.

Servants, obey your masters

Ephesians 6:5: Servants, be obedient to them that are your masters according to the flesh, with fear and trembling, in singleness of your heart, as unto Christ;

COLOSSIANS

More wives, submit yourselves

3:18: Wives, submit yourselves unto your own husbands, as it is fit in the Lord.

1 THESSALONIANS

Women described as possessed "vessel"

4:4: That every one of you should know how to possess his vessel in sanctification and honour;

1 TIMOTHY

Women adorn selves in shamefacedness and godliness

2:9: In like manner also, that women adorn themselves in modest apparel, with shamefacedness and sobriety; not with broided hair, or gold, or pearls, or costly array;

10: But (which becometh women professing godliness) with good works.

Women should learn in all subjection, Eve sinful, Adam blameless

1 Tim. 2:11: Let the woman learn in silence with all subjection.

12: But I suffer not a woman to teach, nor to usurp authority over the man, but to be in silence.

13: For Adam was first formed, then Eve.

14: And Adam was not deceived, but the woman being deceived was in the transgression.

Faithful women won't die in childbirth

1 Tim. 2:15: Notwithstanding she shall be saved in childbearing, if they continue in faith and charity and holiness with sobriety.

Bishops should have only one wife (Pope should know about this verse)

1 Tim. 3:2: A bishop then must be blameless, the husband of one wife, vigilant, sober, of good behaviour, given to hospitality, apt to teach;

3: Not given to wine, no striker, not greedy of filthy lucre; but patient, not a brawler, not covetous;

4: One that ruleth well his own house, having his children in subjection with all gravity;

5: (For if a man know not how to rule his own house, how shall he take care of the church of God?)

Sexist warning of "old wives' tales"

1 Tim. 4:7: But refuse profane and old wives' fables, and exercise thyself rather unto godliness.

Widows should wash saints' feet, not "wax wanton"

1 Tim. 5:5: Now she that is a widow indeed, and desolate, trusteth in God, and continueth in supplications and prayers night and day.

6: But she that liveth in pleasure is dead while she liveth.

7: And these things give in charge, that they may be blameless.

8: But if any provide not for his own, and specially for those of his own house, he hath denied the faith, and is worse than an infidel.

9: Let not a widow be taken into the number under threescore years old, having been the wife of one man,

10: Well reported of for good works; if she have brought up children, if she have lodged strangers, if she have washed the saints' feet, if she have relieved the afflicted, if she have diligently followed every good work.

11: But the younger widows refuse: for when they have begun to wax wanton against Christ, they will marry;

12: Having damnation, because they have cast off their first faith.

13: And withal they learn to be idle, wandering about from house to house; and not only idle, but tattlers also and busybodies, speaking things which they ought not.

Instructions for housewives to avoid Satan

1 Tim. 5:14: I will therefore that the younger women marry, bear children, guide the house, give none occasion to the adversary to speak reproachfully.

15: For some are already turned aside after Satan.

TITUS

Instructions for behavior of elderly women

2:2: That the aged men be sober, grave, temperate, sound in faith, in charity, in patience.

3: The aged women likewise, that they be in behaviour as becometh holiness, not false accusers, not given to much wine, teachers of good things;

4: That they may teach the young women to be sober, to love their husbands, to love their children,

5: To be discreet, chaste, keepers at home, good, obedient to their own husbands, that the word of God be not blasphemed.

HEBREWS

Hebrews faithfulness rewarded by son

11:11: Through faith also Sara herself received strength to conceive seed, and was delivered of a child when she was past age, because she judged him faithful who had promised.

1 PETER

Women should talk to husbands in fear, not wear braids, gold or fine apparel, and be obedient

3:1: Likewise, ye wives, be in subjection to your own husbands; that, if any obey not the word, they also may without the word be won by the conversation of the wives;

2: While they behold your chaste conversation coupled with fear.

3: Whose adorning let it not be that outward adorning of plaiting the hair, and of wearing of gold, or of putting on of apparel;

4: But let it be the hidden man of the heart, in that which is not corruptible, even the ornament of a meek and quiet spirit, which is in the sight of God of great price.

5: For after this manner in the old time the holy women also, who trusted in God, adorned themselves, being in subjection unto their own husbands:

6: Even as Sara obeyed Abraham, calling him lord: whose daughters ye are, as long as ye do well, and are not afraid with any amazement.

7: Likewise, ye husbands, dwell with them according to knowledge, giving honour unto the wife, as unto the weaker vessel, and as being heirs together of the grace of life; that your prayers be not hindered

2 PETER

Incestuous Lot called "righteous"

2:4: For if God spared not the angels that sinned, but cast them down to hell, and delivered them into chains of darkness, to be reserved unto judgment;

5: And spared not the old world, but saved Noah the eighth person, a preacher of righteousness, bringing in the flood upon the world of the ungodly;

6: And turning the cities of Sodom and Gomorrha into ashes condemned them with an overthrow, making them an ensample unto those that after should live ungodly;

7: And delivered just Lot, vexed with the filthy conversation of the wicked:

8: (For that righteous man dwelling among them, in seeing and hearing, vexed his righteous soul from day to day with their unlawful deeds;) . . .

REVELATION

Jezebel's "crime" changed from religious treason to "fornication"

2:20: Notwithstanding I have a few things against thee, because thou sufferest that woman Jezebel, which calleth herself a prophetess, to teach and to seduce my servants to commit fornication, and to eat things sacrificed unto idols.

21: And I gave her space to repent of her fornication; and she repented not.

22: Behold, I will cast her into a bed, and them that commit adultery with her into great tribulation, except they repent of their deeds.

23: And I will kill her children with death; and all the churches shall know that I am he which searcheth the reins and hearts: and I will give unto every one of you according to your works.

Virgin males are "not defiled by women"

Rev. 14:4: These are they which were not defiled with women; for they are virgins. These are they which follow the Lamb whithersoever he goeth. These were redeemed from among men, being the firstfruits unto God and to the Lamb.

Whore is brutally stripped, eaten, and burned

Rev. 17:1: And there came one of the seven angels which had the seven vials, and talked with me, saying unto me, Come hither; I will shew unto thee the judgment of the great whore that sitteth upon many waters:

2: With whom the kings of the earth have committed fornication, and the inhabitants of the earth have been made drunk with the wine of her fornication.

3: So he carried me away in the spirit into the wilderness: and I saw a woman sit upon a scarlet coloured beast, full of names of blasphemy, having seven heads and ten horns.

4: And the woman was arrayed in purple and scarlet colour, and decked with gold and precious stones and pearls, having a golden cup in her hand full of abominations and filthiness of her fornication:

5: And upon her forehead was a name written, MYSTERY, BABYLON THE GREAT, THE MOTHER OF HARLOTS AND ABOMINATIONS OF THE EARTH.

6: And I saw the woman drunken with the blood of the saints, and with the blood of the martyrs of Jesus: and when I saw her, I wondered with great admiration.

7: And the angel said unto me, Wherefore didst thou marvel? I will tell thee the mystery of the woman, and of the beast that carrieth her, which hath the seven heads and ten horns.

8: The beast that thou sawest was, and is not; and shall ascend out of the bottomless pit, and go into perdition: and they that dwell on the earth shall wonder, whose names were not written in the book of life from the foundation of the world, when they behold the beast that was, and is not, and yet is.

9: And here is the mind which hath wisdom. The seven heads are seven mountains, on which the woman sitteth.

10: And there are seven kings: five are fallen, and one is, and the other is not yet come; and when he cometh, he must continue a short space.

11: And the beast that was, and is not, even he is the eighth, and is of the seven, and goeth into perdition.

12: And the ten horns which thou sawest are ten kings, which have received no kingdom as yet; but receive power as kings one hour with the beast.

13: These have one mind, and shall give their power and strength unto the beast.

14: These shall make war with the Lamb, and the Lamb shall overcome them: for he is Lord of lords, and King of kings: and they that are with him are called, and chosen, and faithful.

15: And he saith unto me, The waters which thou sawest, where the whore sitteth, are peoples, and multitudes, and nations, and tongues.

16: And the ten horns which thou sawest upon the beast, these shall hate the whore, and shall make her desolate and naked, and shall eat her flesh, and burn her with fire.

INDEX

Y

Z

Also published by the Freedom From Religion Foundation

Women Without Superstition: "No Gods - No Masters"
Edited by Annie Laurie Gaylor. The collected writings of women
freethinkers of the 19th & 20th centuries. First anthology of
women freethinkers. 696-page hardback, 51 photographs. $25

One Woman's Fight
by Vashti McCollum. Legal battle to a historic Supreme Court
victory removing a religious instruction from public schools.
Warmly told from the family's perspective. 240-page paperback.
$15

The Born Again Skeptic's Guide to the Bible
by Ruth Hurmence Green. A Missouri grandmother debunks the
bible as no one has debunked it since Thomas Paine. Also includes
the popular "Book of Ruth" essays. 440-page paperback. $15

Losing Faith in Faith: From Preacher to Atheist
by Dan Barker. "An arsenal for skeptics. A challenge to believers."
342-page paperback. $20

American Infidel: Robert G. Ingersoll
by Orvin Larsen. Prof. Larsen writes with affection and respect of
this illustrious 19th century freethinker. 316-page paperback. $20

Just Pretend: A Freethought Book for Children
by Dan Barker, appealingly illustrated by Alma Cuebas. $12

World Famous Atheist Cookbook
edited by Anne Nicol Gaylor. Food for freethought. Tried-and-true
recipes for those who prefer to do their frying in the here and now.
165-page paperback. $15

Betrayal of Trust: Clergy Abuse of Children
by Annie Laurie Gaylor. Documents and analyzes the epidemic of
clergymen who sexually molest children. Originally published in
1988, and now out-of-print. Bound photocopy. $10

Why Abortion? The Myth of Choice for Women Who Are Poor
by Anne Nicol Gaylor. A booklet. $3

U.S. prices include shipping and handling. Wis. residents add 5.5%

FFRF, Inc.
PO Box 750
Madison WI 53701
(608) 256-8900 • www.ffrf.org